SHIP BUSTERS!

SHIP BUSTERS!

A CLASSIC ACCOUNT OF
RAF TORPEDO-BOMBERS IN WWII

RALPH BARKER

'I seek my prey in the waters…'
Squadron Motto

GRUB STREET · LONDON

Originally published in 1957 by
Chatto & Windus Ltd, London

The new edition first published 2009 by
Grub Street, 4 Rainham Close, London SW11 6SS

British Library Cataloguing in Publication Data
Barker, Ralph, 1917-
  Ship busters!: a classic account of RAF torpedo-bombers in WWII.
  1. Great Britain, Royal Air Force – History – World War,
  1939-1945. 2. World War, 1939-1945 – Aerial operations, British.
  I. Title
  940.5′44941-dc22

ISBN: 9781906502294

Printed and bound by MPG Ltd, Bodmin, Cornwall

Grub Street only uses Forest Stewardship Council (FSC)
paper for its books.

The author and publisher are hugely indebted to Roger Haywood for
supplying most of the images used in this publication. Also thanks
to Lawrie Evans for his assistance.

CONTENTS

ACKNOWLEDGMENTS

For most of the material used in the writing of this book I am indebted to the survivors of the anti-shipping squadrons, who have been most generous and enthusiastic in their help. I must also gratefully acknowledge the access I have been given by the Air Ministry to various operational records.

For background I have consulted the following books and publications:—*Not Peace but a Sword*, by Wing Commander R. P. M. Gibbs, D.S.O., D.F.C. (Cassell); *The Rommel Papers*, edited by B. H. Liddell Hart (Collins); *The First and the Last*, by Adolf Galland (Methuen); *The Second World War*, by Winston Churchill (Cassell); *Royal Air Force 1939-1945*, by Denis Richards and Hilary St.G. Saunders (H.M.S.O.). Permission to quote from Cmd. Paper 6775 (the Report of the Board of Enquiry into the escape of the *Scharnhorst*, *Gneisenau* and *Prinz Eugen* from Brest) is acknowledged to the Controller of H.M. Stationery Office.

I should perhaps add that the narrative treatment and the opinions expressed are entirely my own.

RALPH BARKER

PREAMBLE: THE BEAUFORTS

They met at Chivenor. Chivenor, near Barnstaple, in North Devon. The pilot was an Australian, Dick Marshall, a sergeant, wearing the dark-blue uniform of an Australian volunteer, magnificently built, with a jutting jaw. Beginning his training in Canada, that prognathous jaw, reminiscent of the hulking North American elk or moose, coupled with the Canadian town of Moose-Jaw, inevitably led to the nickname of 'Moose'. The name stuck. He was always 'Moose' Marshall from then on. His navigator, 'Tommy' Thompson, a New Zealander, built like an All-Blacks rugby three-quarter, was a gentle giant, if anything even bigger than Moose was. Even in the melee of expectant aircrew on view at Chivenor, pilots, navigators, radio-operators and air-gunners, they made an outstanding pair. They had been posted to fly Beauforts, a development of the Bristol Blenheim, but more modern and faster, armed with the 18-inch torpedo, ostensibly for sinking ships at sea. Bombing, mine-laying, and reconnaissance were accessory feats, but the principal weapon was the torpedo.

What did the powers-that-be expect of the aerial torpedo? Air Ministry compared it unfavourably with the wielder of any other wartime weapon: one man in six might survive.

They would need a crew of four – a wireless-operator and an air-gunner, one to find their way round, the other for protection. The tasks were to be filled by two WOP/AGs, one manning the twin-Brownings gun-turret, half-way along the fuselage, the other, going into action, manning the waist guns. But where were they? A block of trainees had arrived at Chivenor, fully-trained in radio, but the gunnery schools were full, and most had arrived minus a gunnery course. Once having taken it, they found themselves promoted and in the Sergeant's Mess. There, two southerners caught the eye of the friendly Thompson, who turned out to be a chum of Moose Marshall. Mostly it was the gunners, looking for someone who might not kill them, who chose the crew.

Thus 'Doggie' Doggett, a young apprentice with de Havillands, and 19-year-old Lawrie Evans, a Surrey man, working in Fleet Street, made up the requisite four. They had both left school at sixteen, and with the giant Marshall and Thompson, they provided the long and the short of it: they were both five-foot-six.

Doggie and Lawrie joined Marshall and Thompson and went right through the two-month course at Chivenor. They had their evenings off, when they visited Barnstaple, or Braunton Sands, or mingled with the holidaymakers at Ilfracombe, delighting when the shrill voices of the children, from high on a promontory, sang the popular air 'Johnny Pedlar'. Then it was on to Abbotsinch, near Paisley, where they learned to aim dummy torpedoes at naval targets. From there they graduated to a squadron – and were soon earmarked for overseas. At the Overseas Aircraft Despatch Unit at Honeybourne, in Worcestershire, they flew their final fuel consumption tests prior to the big trip – to staging posts via Portreath (Cornwall), Gibraltar, Malta (now under siege), and thence to the Middle East. Consumption tests, though, had their hazards.

They flew long hours over the Irish Sea to test their fuel consumption – but suddenly the weather clamped. It was a foggy day, the met-man shouldn't have sent them off, and somewhere in the Midlands they began to look for a pinpoint. England in 1941 wasn't like England in 1944, when you couldn't fly for five minutes without crossing an airfield. For hour after hour they peered through the thickening fog – while static silenced the radio. Getting short of petrol, Marshall looked for a field. It was just an ordinary farmer's field, with hedges that he hoped to circumvent, but in emergency it would have to do. He tried a low run over the field, decided it would be enough, and landed.

The nearest airfield proved to be quite close – R.A.F. Meir, in Staffordshire. Meir – and the farmer – were ready to help, and after a farmhouse tea, a guard was posted on the aircraft. Next day, 'scrambled egg' types came out from Group, H.Q., and as the Beaufort was undamaged, and Moose said, characteristically, "I'll give it a go", the whole crew, full of confidence in Moose, elected to go with him. His was not the only near-disaster due to the weather, strictly speaking they were at fault for getting lost, and the met-man, too, had to answer some questions. Back at Honeybourne, faced with the possibility of disciplinary action of some kind, and fearing a court of enquiry, the 'scrambled egg' at H.Q. decided to hush the whole thing up. Lawrie Evans remembers that the incident was expunged from their log books. Moose and crew took off soon afterwards for Portreath and the Middle East, arriving eventually on posting at No. 39 Squadron in the Western Desert, at Landing Ground 86.

In 1941 there had been a hiatus in the Desert war, relieved by Operation Crusader. Malta still lay under siege, but 39 Squadron, rearmed with the Bristol Beaufort, had recently moved into position, and were now 40 miles west of Alexandria. After digging out their own accommodation under tents, they refreshed themselves in Alexandria. Meanwhile the Afrika Korps, now under Rommel, were threatening a 'big push'. The Italian Fleet were alerted, and Rommel expected his push to take him to the Nile and beyond, at the same time occupying Malta.

Lawrie Evans, from LG 86, now takes up the story.

"On March 26th we were warned to stand by for a strike, and we loaded up. We assembled for a dawn take-off, but we crashed through engine failure. Our Beaufort was wrecked, but fortunately it didn't catch fire. Also we were lucky that the

4

torpedo didn't go off. We then had another long wait for more aircraft, while Rommel's forces advanced beyond Tobruk, forcing us to move back to Sidi Barrani. But we knew that the squadron was building up for something big. A strike was laid on to deter the Italian Battle Fleet's designs on the relief convoys. If we were to attack the fleet, the aircraft would now be out of range of base and would have to land at Malta."

The Allied plan was to run two convoys to Malta, one from the west via Gibraltar, one from the east from Alexandria, the latter to be covered by the Beauforts of 39 (see page 177). Another Beaufort squadron, No. 217, positioned at Malta, supposedly on its way to Ceylon, had already done splendid work, despite heavy losses (see pages 178-182).

After moving up to Sidi Barrani, twelve Beauforts of 39 took off at 06.15 on 15th June to intercept the Italian Fleet. Four vics of three Beauforts were led by Wing Commander A.J. Mason, C.O. of the squadron, Flight Lieutenant Pat Gibbs, posted in from Headquarters Middle East, Flight Lieutenant Alastair Taylor, and Flying Officer Tony Leaning. Near the coast at Derna they were jumped by Me109s. Most crews were completely unaware of their presence at first, until one Beaufort suddenly disappeared. "All pilots," says Lawrie, "thereupon slammed open their throttles and began violent evasive action. I personally found it ineffectual to attempt to score against the 109s, with my puny .303 Brownings. One aircraft crashed inshore." He also tells the story of Lionel Daffurn (see pages 184-185).

"With fuel consumption vastly increased during this pursuit, other pilots realised they had no hope of reaching Malta and returned to base. After the 109s finally departed, Mason found he only had 5 aircraft left. The remainder closed ranks and steadfastly continued.

"When we were sighted by the Italians, their battleships opened fire with their fifteen-inch armament, presuming that splashes from these giant shells would be enough to bring down the Beauforts. Flak of every kind was hurled at our five aircraft. Moose was throwing our plane all over the sky, side-slipping, climbing for short spells, then diving away in a new direction. Suddenly the leading battleship turned broadside on to the Beauforts, and all that was necessary was to aim steadily and drop the torpedo.

"At that point both Gibbs's and Moose's aircraft were hit, and we lost rudder control and hydraulics, and were forced to drop the torpedo too early. The sheer size of the battleships led us into wrongly estimating our distance. No target so large had ever been visualised by Beaufort crews during training.

"In the barrage of fire Tommy Thompson, exposed in the

5

nose of the Beaufort, was peppered with shrapnel, but he went on navigating, while Moose was forced to concentrate on keeping us flying. Despite wallowing alarmingly, we managed to set course for Malta."

All five Beauforts survived to fly on to Malta. But Gibbs was in trouble, belly-landing his Beaufort, and Moose, after using his emergency cartridges to lower his undercarriage, was hampered by poor rudder controls, with very little hydraulic pressure for his brakes, and he veered off the runway on landing and crashed into a 217 Squadron Beaufort which earlier in the day had run out of petrol. Both caught fire. Somehow they managed to get the wounded Thompson out.

Many Beauforts had been lost. None of the torpedoes had struck home. But they had left their mark, and the Italian Fleet never put to sea again.

In place of Tommy Thompson, who had been with Moose since Chivenor days, they substituted a navigator named Paterson. 'Slap-happy' Paterson was another Australian. He was a personal friend and Bridge partner of Moose, from those impatient days when they were waiting for aircraft at LG 86. They had suffered, too, together that night in Alexandria (see pages 212-213). He stayed on – he was a fine navigator.

It was now that Gibbs's proselytising of the Beaufort at Headquarters bore fruit. The A.O.C. Malta hi-jacked the remnants of 217 Squadron, and Gibbs's Beauforts, after losing half their task force on 15th June, were left to reform before returning to Malta. The island was then practically starving. It was in this period that Malta was awarded the George Cross.

Meanwhile, in Malta, N.C.O.s were billeted in what was known as the 'Poor House', a former Leper colony, on Machonachies. The N.C.O.s had no beds, just palliasses on the floor, and no furniture, just their original half-empty kit-bags, very little water, no coal for heating, or water for beer. The officers, in a hotel at Sliema, fared little better. But there, under Gibbs, they hit back with the N.C.O.s at the Axis forces, sinking much of their transport, which was on its way now from Italian bases to Bizerta or Tunis, threatened by Beauforts by day and Wellingtons by night, and, perhaps best of all, by Adrian Warburton and his reconnaissance Spitfire, acting on the Enigma secrets that were constantly emerging from the Code and Cypher School at Bletchley Park.

Losses continued to be tragic, but it was not all doom and gloom. A Beaufort crew, having ditched, were picked up by the Italians whom they were attacking, and were soon on their way into captivity, by air, in a Cant floatplane. But they over-powered their captors and flew back to Malta (see *Down in the Drink*, recently published). Most of the few who survived had to endure long years of captivity, as did one of the original Beaufort men from LG 86, Johnny Coles, who survived in a tit-for-tat gesture when his pilot, Jimmy Hewitson (Rhodesian) was drowned, only to be saved with his crew when the captain of an Italian torpedo boat, in dangerous waters, remembered that his own brother, a submarine commander, had been depth-charged but then saved by the Royal Navy. Coles afterwards compared his diet on Malta unfavourably with what he got later as a POW.

Amongst other survivors, Marshall and Paterson were still there. For the fanatical Gibbs his time was up, he was wanted back at Air Ministry, to be replaced by 'Larry' Gaine. Known as 'Do it by the book' Gaine, he was 31 years old and a veteran of torpedo instruction at Abbotsinch. His navigator John Cresswell still drove them forward, followed by the more circumspect Gaine.

It was the same throughout November 1942, followed by a rest for 39's aircrew at Shallufa (Canal Zone), then back to Malta in January 1943. The faithful Moose Marshall, now commissioned and awarded the DFC, was appointed squadron leader and flight commander. Relief, of a kind, came in February, when a friend of Moose's, the Australian P.J. Twomey, was short of a gunner, and Moose asked Lawrie Evans if he'd fill for the gunner. It was tempting fate, but to Moose, of all people, Lawrie couldn't say no. It was to be Twomey's last trip but one. On his next trip he and his crew didn't come back.

Moose and Slap and Lawrie, incredibly, with a new radio man named Jim Parker (Doggie had gone sick with trench feet), had completed a total of eleven torpedo strikes and many minelaying adventures in enemy waters. Gibbs had called Marshall "great-hearted", which was surely an understatement. On 21st February, after they blew up a 10,000-ton tanker before sinking it, they received congratulations from the A.O.C. Then on the night of 3rd March 1943 they took off again to strike at a convoy north of Palermo. It was to be their twelfth torpedo strike. Half an hour later, without warning, they crashed in to the Mediterranean. Lawrie, in his Mae West as usual, was flung out of the turret, concussed and bleeding, with a multiple head injury, his left fore-arm broken, and barely conscious, but still alive. Calling for survivors proved useless. Some distance away he glimpsed the aircraft dinghy, which had released itself. By the light of burning pieces of aircraft wreckage, he struggled towards it.

Lawrie remembered afterwards that their plane had been the subject of a fortnight's repair after an earlier strike. Air-testing had been negated because fuel had been short, but it had recently been resumed. What happened to two men of Moose and Slap's experience and calibre, was never established. Casualties in 39 had always been appalling. The squadron had lost in all 59 Beauforts, mostly from intense enemy fire, but also from crashes on take-off and landing. And Moose had survived a great deal of mine-laying and reconnaissance. 217 Squadron, hi-jacked at Malta by the A.O.C. the previous summer, as Lawrie himself remembered, had lost 29 of their N.C.O. aircrew in a few short weeks, with only seven of their originals left. Officers too had been decimated. Nevertheless, before the Beauforts finally gave way to Beaufighter TFXs carrying rocket-firing projectiles, they had achieved outstanding success. But Moose and Slap, and Jim Parker too, were gone.

THE NORTH SEA AND ENGLISH CHANNEL

PROLOGUE

NINE Beauforts of No. 42 Squadron attacked the *Scharnhorst* on 21st June 1940 as she steamed triumphantly down the Norwegian coast soon after sinking the aircraft carrier *Glorious*. This was the first strike to be carried out by Beauforts.

The Beaufort was a twin-engined, all-metal, mid-wing monoplane, successor to the Bristol Blenheim, intended primarily for use as a torpedo-bomber. But her high speed and modern construction compared with earlier torpedo-carrying aircraft had revolutionized the science of torpedo dropping; and partly because the crews were not fully trained in torpedo tactics in the new type of aircraft, and partly because torpedoes were not available at the base from which they were operating, the attack on the *Scharnhorst* was made with bombs.

The weakness of this form of attack was that, with the bombs in use at that time, not even a direct hit could cause serious damage to a ship with armour-plated decks. Only a hit below the water-line could cripple such a ship; hence the predilection for the torpedo.

On the morning of the 21st the *Scharnhorst* was reported to have left the harbour at Trondheim and to be steaming south at 25 knots. At 11.05 she was sighted by a Hudson some fifty miles north of Bergen. An hour later, nine Beauforts of 42 Squadron were ordered to bomb up with two 500-lb. bombs each and take off and attack the enemy battle-cruiser. The target was out of range of our fighters and no escort was to be provided. The nine Beauforts took off from their base at Wick in northern Scotland in three flights of three at 14.30 and set course for the Norwegian coast.

On the way out across the North Sea the 42 Squadron aircraft flew at 6000 feet in three sub-flights in line astern. A landfall was made off the Norwegian coast, fifteen miles north of Bergen, at 16.00 hours. On information radioed by a Sunderland on patrol the squadron turned south and flew down the coast twenty miles out to sea. Soon they saw what appeared to be black smoke in the distance, some thirty miles south of the estimated point of interception. This turned out to be the battle-cruiser, escorted by six destroyers and a motor torpedo-boat. Nine fighters could be seen in the distance, six circling low over the battle-cruiser and three seeking to remain hidden in a thin layer of cloud at 9000 feet, 3000 feet above the Beauforts. The weather was clear and the visibility was good.

The squadron approached the battle fleet from landward on the port quarter. At a distance of about ten miles the destroyer screen began to spread out round the battle-cruiser on a radius of about 1500 yards, evidently anticipating torpedo attack.

Five miles from the target, the leading aircraft began a preliminary dive down to 4500 feet. The rest of the formation followed. The battle fleet opened up a long-range barrage and the *Scharnhorst* began a turn to starboard, presenting her stern to the Beauforts. The after turrets of the battle-cruiser were firing continuously. When the aircraft reached 4500 feet they ran into an intense anti-aircraft and pom-pom barrage which continued throughout the action. The formation now went into a steep dive through 3000 feet, pilots and navigators staring straight down at the target. At the bottom of the dive, down to 1500 feet, each aircraft released its bombs, its nose still pointed straight down at the shining deck of the *Scharnhorst*. Then they turned away to starboard and flattened out gently, continuing to lose height down to 500 feet. This set them all on an approximate course for home.

As the aircraft released their bombs, the *Scharnhorst* stopped turning to starboard and began a sharp turn to port, which she maintained. The destroyer screen was still frantically getting into position to fend off torpedo attack.

The leader of the formation saw his bombs splash into the sea a few yards from the battle-cruiser, amidships on the port side. Two other pilots watched their bombs straddle the target and claimed direct hits.

As the leading sub-flight broke away, and before they could re-form, they were engaged by the three Me 109s they had seen circling at 9000 feet as they went into the attack. These three aircraft had followed the Beauforts down in the dive and quickly overtaken them. The first enemy fighter came in on the same level in a skidding turn and attacked the leading aircraft on the port beam. After delivering its attack it broke away astern and was shot down in flames by the leader's air gunner.[1]

Meanwhile, Nos. 2 and 3 of the leading sub-flight were trying to re-form with their leader. They were both suffering attacks from the other two enemy high-level fighters. The leader throttled back, and both pilots strove desperately to shake off pursuit and regain formation. Soon No. 2, under severe pressure, overshot the leader, followed closely by an Me 109. The German fighter passed directly over the leader's aircraft and flew on ahead, giving the pilot a point-blank shot. The engine of the Me 109 was seen to stop and pick up again. This fighter then broke away abruptly to port, out of the cone of fire. Meanwhile No. 2 had turned away to starboard, where it was followed by one of the low-level fighters, which had now caught up with the formation. Later the Me 109 was seen returning alone. The Beaufort was never seen again.

No. 3 of the leading sub-flight was now seen to be only 200 yards astern; but bullets were falling into the sea below the leader's aircraft, indicating that No. 3 was still under attack from above. Suddenly No. 3 lifted and turned away sharply to starboard, an enemy fighter in pursuit. This aircraft, too, was not seen again.

The second sub-flight was engaged by several fighters five minutes after the attack; there were only two aircraft left of this flight, as the third had lost formation during the attack and joined up with the third sub-flight. The two remaining aircraft of the second sub-flight were attacked continuously for the next eight minutes. The gunners were having trouble with stoppages due to empty cartridges fouling the shute, which had broken away from the gun through vibration. For most of the time they did not have a single gun in action. They succeeded in avoiding most of the attacks by keeping down to fifty feet above the water and turning and skidding violently as each attack was delivered.

[1] Air gunners at this time were ordinary ground maintenance crews, in receipt of special flying pay. The rate for the job was 1s. 6d. a day.

But eventually the second of these two aircraft burst into flames and crashed into the sea.

The third sub-flight, now consisting of four aircraft, escaped the attentions of the enemy fighters and returned safely.

Suppose the Beauforts had been carrying torpedoes? How would they have fared?

The manœuvring carried out by the destroyers would have made the dropping of torpedoes extremely difficult, and the opposition encountered during a torpedo attack would have been more intense from the destroyer screen and also from the low-level fighter escort. Casualties would inevitably have been higher. It might have been possible to obtain a beam shot with one or two torpedoes as the battle-cruiser turned to port, but the aircraft dropping these torpedoes would probably have been accounted for by the fighters. The slower speed necessary for the launching of torpedoes would have made the whole formation more vulnerable.

Other obvious shortcomings were the rear armament, which was both inadequate and inefficient, all gunners reporting stoppages; and the lack of a long-range fighter escort.

The Beaufort had had an inauspicious baptism. No hits had in fact been scored. They had suffered $33\frac{1}{3}$ per cent losses. There had been trouble with the guns. And worse was to come. Ten days before the action, following a number of unaccountable losses in training flights, a court of enquiry had assembled to make recommendations on the operational efficiency of the Beaufort and its engines. The crews had been aware of this and all had volunteered for the operation against the *Scharnhorst*. Soon after the attack, all Beauforts were grounded for modifications to the Taurus engine.

There was little indication yet that the Beaufort and its torpedoes were to play a vital part in the war against enemy shipping and in the Battle of the Atlantic in 1941, or that, in 1942-43, they were to dictate the course of land battles to no less a general than Rommel.

Chapter 1

THE CURTAIN RAISER

"BY the way," said the wing commander, "this is the ship that sank the *Rawalpindi*."

So they were going to get a crack at the 14,000-ton *Lutzow*[1], sister pocket-battleship to the *Admiral Scheer* and the *Graf Spee*.

Flight Sergeant Ray Loveitt, 22-year-old Coventry-born Beaufort pilot, went through in that moment all the nuances of excitement and trepidation. He remembered how, when the war started, Hitler had changed the name of this ship from *Deutschland* to *Lutzow*, because, it was said, he had feared that the loss of a ship so named might be disastrous for German morale. In his imagination Loveitt torpedoed the *Lutzow*, and missed it; was shot down, and got safely home.

Loveitt was no square-jawed, steely-eyed, ready-made hero. He was just a very young Englishman, little more than a boy, the down on his cheeks scarcely turned to stubble, the fair hair still crinkling under the grease-laden forage-cap. And yet for three years now he had been training for this moment.

There were many such young Englishmen in 1941, men who, only two years before, had been castigated by their enemies, and even by their seniors at home, as spineless, un-warlike, decadent. They were pink-cheeked, careless young men at whom the ally, the man from the Dominions, looked in apprehension. Then they saw the R.A.F. wings, sewn neatly above the jacket pocket, worn proudly but without ostentation, and they wondered. Then too, perhaps, they might see a purple and white striped medal ribbon, and they would know without any doubt that whatever it took to make a hero, outside of the strip cartoons, these men had.

Loveitt wore no medal ribbons, but he had worked hard for those wings—and harder still to keep them. He had first

---

[1] It was thought at first that the *Rawalpindi* was sunk by the *Lutzow*; it was later established that it was the work of the battle-cruisers *Scharnhorst* and *Gneisenau*.

flown with the Volunteer Reserve in March 1938, won his wings, and been called up in September 1939. Then had followed a period of training with the Royal Navy as a torpedo-bomber pilot, including catapult take-offs and deck landings on an aircraft carrier, after which he and fourteen other sergeant pilots had been told that they were to be transferred to the Fleet Air Arm.

In spite of an innate admiration for things naval, all the pilots had resisted. The Royal Air Force had come first in their lives, and it still came first for them. Besides, in the R.A.F. they were the cream. In the Fleet Air Arm, the ship came first. It wasn't just the thought that the ship, their runway, might be obliged to change course after they had taken off without notifying them, so as to make it almost impossible to find again; that was just another hazard of war. It went far deeper than that. It was a question of status.

There were other reasons, too. The pay of a petty-officer pilot was three-and-something a day less. And you wore your wings on the cuff of your sleeve. Yes, that was the hardest one of all to swallow. Not on your breast, but on the cuff of your sleeve. And not the prized R.A.F. wings, even then.

To Loveitt there was something symbolic about those wings. It wasn't merely conceit, though that might be a part of it. They stood for something—the ambition, the striving, the attainment; and something more even than a combination of these three. They completed his personality. He associated them with his manhood.

The pilots could see the Navy's point of view and were mostly ready to compromise. First they asked if they could keep their R.A.F. rate of pay; this was referred to the Admiralty, and agreed. Then they asked if they could wear their R.A.F. wings on the naval uniform: after all, they had won their wings in the R.A.F., there was no arguing with that, and surely this outward sign could not be taken away from them. An affirmative to this one would have satisfied them all, but this time the Admiralty said no. However, the Admiralty, too, was ready to compromise, and when its offer came it was a handsome one: all the pilots were offered commissions in the Fleet Air Arm.

This was an offer which should have satisfied all reasonable men; but Loveitt, in common with a good many of the others, found that his R.A.F. wings were something about which he was incapable of being reasonable. He had never thought of himself as being of an obstinate nature, but now he became the stubbornest of the stubborn. An old Service phrase, something like 'maintenance of aim', carelessly learnt, tumbled into the forefront of his mind. When the Navy realized it was up against something that to crush would be a denial of its own traditions, it let the defiant ones, Loveitt amongst them, go.

Having given up the chance of a commission in the Fleet Air Arm, Loveitt found that the R.A.F. were little interested in him. He was sent to No. 42 Squadron, at that time flying Wildebeests; but these slow-moving aircraft were already classed as obsolete. There was, too, a surplus of pilots, and under such circumstances a mere sergeant-pilot (V.R.) stood little chance. However, he was at least employed mostly on flying duties, including an attachment to a Coastal Hudson squadron; and during this time 42 Squadron were re-equipped with Beauforts and moved to Leuchars in Fife. Eventually it came Loveitt's turn to be trained as the captain of a Beaufort, and to be given his own crew, loyal, efficient, personal.

Although the route by which he had reached operations had been circuitous, Loveitt found many compensations. Few men were as thoroughly trained as he. Few men in the squadron knew ships as well as he did. And ships were their *raison d'être*. Ships like the *Lutzow*.

The mention of the *Rawalpindi* had thrown Loveitt's mind back telescopically over the last eighteen months or so. He remembered the gallant delaying action the *Rawalpindi* had fought, an old merchant ship, termed for the purposes of war an armed merchant cruiser, hopelessly outgunned by the enemy. The *Rawalpindi* had gone down, but not before it had called British cruisers to the aid of the convoy it was protecting. The message had identified the attacker as the *Lutzow*. A few minutes later, when the enemy force was correctly identified as the *Scharnhorst* and *Gneisenau*, the *Rawalpindi* was already severely damaged and its wireless equipment blown to pieces by a direct hit. British cruisers which rushed to the scene found that the German raiders had fled. It was assumed that the *Lutzow* had taken fright and made for the haven of the Baltic. Anyway, there she had stayed, until now.

Loveitt glanced at the operations room clock, and then at the date on the board behind the wing commander. Nearly eleven o'clock. Not much more than an hour before midnight. Thursday the 12th of June, 1941. He nudged Al Morris, his young, tough, athletic-looking navigator from Nokomis, Saskatchewan.

"Look at the time. Soon be midnight. By the time we get there it'll be Friday the thirteenth."

Loveitt had always revelled in defying superstition. He always went out of his way to walk under a ladder, to look at the new moon through glass, to take the third light from a match. He refused to touch wood or to throw salt over his shoulder—refused, in fact, to make any attempt to curry favour with the arbiters of chance. And yet he had a strong faith in his own luck. Somehow, too, he had managed to reconcile his crew to the daily flaunting of superstition.

"I've got a feeling tomorrow's going to be an unlucky day," whispered Loveitt.

"Unlucky?"

"For the *Lutzow*."

Loveitt kept one ear cocked for the wing commander. They had known early the previous day that there might be a target for them, and some of them, already out on Rovers and sweeps, had been warned to be on the look out for enemy naval units. No one had seen anything, but later in the day it had been confirmed that an enemy capital ship, probably the *Lutzow*, had left Kiel Bay and was steaming north.

From that point on, the squadron had stood by, waiting for a sighting report to come in. The Admiralty had received an Intelligence report that the *Lutzow* had been seen rounding the Skaw at 12.30, escorted by four destroyers, and P.R.U. aircraft searched the Skagerrak the whole afternoon and evening; but still there were no sightings.

At 19.30, in the belief that a sighting was imminent, the A.O.C.-in-C. Coastal Command, Air Chief Marshal Sir Frederick Bowhill, brought his strike forces to instant readiness. The available force consisted of thirteen Beauforts of

42 Squadron at Leuchars and five Beauforts of 22 Squadron on special detachment at Wick.

At 22.00 there was still no news of a sighting, and Bowhill was in something of a dilemma. There could be little doubt that the *Lutzow* was still steering her course, making progress in a westerly direction and then north-westerly towards the shelter of the fjords. It was tantalizing to feel that the pocket-battleship might already be within Beaufort range, might even pass out of range before they could act on any sighting report that came through.

The period of time in which the Beauforts could strike at a target off southern Norway was limited by the rate of progress of the target. Suppose the *Lutzow* were doing 22 knots, as reported by naval Intelligence. At this rate she had probably already been within range for an hour or so and might remain within range for at the most another five or six hours.

From the time of giving the order for a strike to the actual positioning of the force off southern Norway, about three hours must elapse. If the Beauforts were to catch the *Lutzow*, the executive order must be given soon and the Beauforts must be off before midnight. But there was still no sighting report.

Bowhill, seasoned campaigner that he was, was toying with the idea of breaking one of the canons for the employment of strike forces and sending his Beauforts off without a sighting report. If he waited for the sighting, it might arrive too late for the strike force to reach the target area before the *Lutzow* took shelter in one of the fjords. Also, once sighted she might contrive to escape by doubling back on her tracks at high speed. Again, after about 02.00, because of the short night in northern waters at this time of year, there would be grave risk of the strike force being intercepted by enemy fighters.

How did these risks compare with the risks of sending a strike force off in ignorance of the position of the target they were briefed to attack?

Good prior reconnaissance was recognized as being the basis for the successful employment of long-range strike aircraft operating over the sea. The abandonment of this policy threatened all sorts of pitfalls. The estimate of the progress of the *Lutzow* was sheer supposition. The ship might be almost anywhere. Bowhill had in mind that if the sighting report came through while the Beauforts were *en route* for the target area, he could relay the position to them by W/T; but suppose the Beauforts had by this time reached their limit of range and had no endurance left to take them to the confirmed position? It would be many hours then before they could be landed, refuelled and repositioned in the target area.

There was another major risk to be faced. A strike at this distance relied for its success to a large extent on surprise. A long search for a target in enemy coastal waters was extremely dangerous. The Beauforts might be seen and pounced on by fighters before they could find the target.

Bowhill balanced these risks one against the other like an alchemist. Delay might mean a missed opportunity: a chance might present itself to attack the *Lutzow* in the next three to four hours, and only if the Beauforts were already half way to the target area would they be able to take advantage of it. On the other hand, precipitate action might mean an abortive sortie, heavy losses and the inability to take advantage of a genuine opportunity later. But Bowhill was oppressed by the narrow corridor of time in which, assuming the continued progress of the *Lutzow*, the Beauforts could effectively strike. If things went wrong he could always recall the Beauforts, and there might still be time for them to strike again.

It took Bowhill twenty agonizing minutes to make up his mind. But once the decision was made, a plan quickly formed in his brain for narrowing down the possibility of error in the search area.

There were five Beauforts at Wick and thirteen at Leuchars. Bowhill decided to send the five Wick aircraft to a point a few miles south of Stavanger, as being the maximum possible progress the *Lutzow* could have made, and nine of the Leuchars aircraft to a point a few miles south-east of Lister, as being the least likely progress made. The Stavanger aircraft would turn south and sweep down the coast, the Lister aircraft would turn north, and the *Lutzow* would be caught in an aerial pincer movement. The scheme had the additional advantage, from the point of view of confusing the enemy's defences, of positioning two separate flights of aircraft off the Norwegian coast at different points at about the same time.

Four of the Leuchars aircraft would be held in reserve, and these would be used to follow up the first force if a sighting was made. The substance of the plan was communicated to the two squadron commanders by Bowhill himself. At Leuchars, Loveitt listened intently as Wing Commander Roy Faville, C.O. of 42 Squadron, passed the information on to the crews.

"Nothing's been seen of the *Lutzow* for nearly twelve hours," Faville was saying, "but from its position and course then, and previous movements, there's very little doubt that it's making for the fjords north of Stavanger. Once it gets there it can lie up in the daytime, moving only at night and in bad weather, and eventually it'll be able to break out into the Atlantic almost at will. You've got some idea what damage it can do out there. I've had the C.-in-C. on the phone personally. *We've got to get this ship.* That means we've got to get it before it reaches Stavanger. In other words, we've got to get it tonight.

"When last seen the *Lutzow* was steaming at an estimated 22 knots, and it's on that basis that we've computed her present position. She has an escort of five destroyers, one way out ahead, probably minesweeping, and four in a rectangle, two on either side, boxing her in.

"The point we shall be making for is about ten miles south-east of Lister, and if we've had no position report up to the time we make our landfall we shall turn north-west along the shipping lane towards Stavanger. 22 Squadron will be searching southwards from Stavanger, so between us we shall comb the area.

"We'll make our initial strike with a formation of nine aircraft in three vics of three, each vic to proceed independently. I shall lead the first formation, with Philpot[1] on my starboard and Loveitt on my port. When we sight the target, Loveitt will move across from the port side into echelon starboard, and we'll make a normal formation attack

---

[1] Oliver Philpot, the man who, shot down on a shipping strike a few months later, escaped from P.O.W. camp with Eric Williams by means of the fabulous 'wooden horse', and subsequently wrote his story in *Stolen Journey*.

from seaward. The other two vics will take off at ten-minute intervals and will form up and attack in the same manner.

"We've got thirteen aircraft, so that will leave four in reserve." Loveitt nudged Morris at the mention of thirteen. "The reserve aircraft will be prepared to take off later if a sighting report comes through.

"The convoy is still being hunted by reconnaissance aircraft, and it's very likely that we shall be sent a new position by W/T on the outward trip. So, wireless operators, keep your ears open. At the same time we've got to be prepared to do a recce ourselves.

"The most important thing on this trip is going to be the navigation. We've got to be absolutely spot on. The Germans have chosen their time for the break-out of this ship carefully, waiting for a spell of really dirty weather. There's only one bright spot—there's a moon. The Met people say there should be some clear patches, and in these patches visibility will be good.

"We shall only get one chance at this ship, so get right in and drop your fish as close as you can. That's all."

A general hubbub filled the operations room. Navigators sorted their charts, wireless operators collected their identification letters and codes. Wallace-Pannell, Loveitt's rear gunner, was the first to rejoin him, carrying a pannier.

"Got the pigeons all right?" asked Loveitt.

"Yes—and what do you think. Pannier No. 13!"

"Did you have to cheat to get it?"

"No, honestly."

"This is our night all right."

Joined by Morris and Downing, the wireless operator, they made their way out to dispersal. Loveitt had something of an affection for his aircraft. Its letter was W—'W for Wreck' they called it—and when he had first taken it up the flight sergeant engineer had warned him that it was the slowest aircraft on the squadron, five knots slower than any other. But on one of their first trips, coming back from a fruitless search for enemy shipping in Norwegian waters, they had arrived off Aberdeen at dusk just in time to see a Heinkel 113 about to start a bombing run on a British convoy. It was too late to interfere with the bombing run, but, anticipating that the German aircraft would turn out to sea at the end of its run, Loveitt manœuvred his aircraft so as to be in position slightly above the Heinkel and flying at the same speed when the German pilot turned for home. He timed the manœuvre so well that Wallace-Pannell had been given a point-blank no deflection shot from the turret. One good burst sent the Heinkel crashing down into the sea. Its crew were later picked up in their dinghy and taken prisoner. After this incident there was only one aircraft for Loveitt and his crew.

At 23.15, led by Faville, the first three Beauforts of 42 Squadron took off from Leuchars, five miles south of the Firth of Tay, and a few minutes later, having formed up over the airfield, they set course for southern Norway. The five Beauforts of 22 Squadron took off from Wick half an hour later and set course for Stavanger.

The Met people had been right. It was storms and low cloud all the way, with just an occasional break in which the moon shone with unusual clarity—a strong light suddenly switched on in a darkened room, and then as suddenly switched off again. Faville, Philpot and Loveitt flew in tight, disciplined formation—tiring for the pilots and nerve-racking for the crews. Loveitt flew on the dim blue formation light a few feet in front of his starboard wing-tip, darting a glance every few seconds at his instruments.

Sitting in the pilot's seat, on the port side of the fuselage, with the aircraft on which he was formating over to starboard, Loveitt found his head aching and his eyes tiring with the continual transfer of his gaze from one point to the other. He decided to move over into echelon right. He had to get into this position for the attack, so there would be nothing lost in getting there now; and it would have the great advantage of bringing the formation light that he had to watch over to his side.

While Faville and Philpot held their position, Loveitt swung round behind them, taking care to avoid their slipstream, and tucked in on the right of Philpot. As he swung round he very nearly lost contact, and only by opening the throttles quickly did he manage to keep in touch.

For over an hour they flew on, mostly through black rain clouds, keeping their height steady at 600 feet, speed 140 knots, economical cruising. They would need every drop of petrol to complete the round trip and still have something to spare to look for the target.

Meanwhile, at Coastal Command Headquarters in London, Bowhill was watching the progress of the operation, waiting anxiously for news of a sighting. The hands of the operations room clock pointed to midnight. The controller could hear it ticking. It was Friday the thirteenth.

At that moment, as one day passed into another, a Blenheim on patrol sighted the convoy. The pilot picked out the *Lutzow* clearly, one destroyer out ahead, the other four still boxing her in. Within a few minutes Bowhill was studying the report. The convoy was thirty miles due south of Lister, steering west-north-west. Soon it would turn north and follow the coastline, unless it tried some manœuvre to shake off pursuit. But in any case the Blenheim would shadow it. There was no escape for the *Lutzow* now.

Bowhill waited for an amplifying report from the Blenheim, but when it came it held disappointment. The Blenheim was under attack by enemy fighters. It had been impossible to continue shadowing the convoy and contact had been lost.

There was nothing more Bowhill could do now but have the sighting report relayed out to the strike aircraft. If the *Lutzow* held her course they would find her. If she doubled back on her tracks, she would be sighted again sooner or later and the whole sequence of events would be repeated. Altogether, the night was going well.

When the sighting report was relayed, the leading flight of 42 Squadron were already half way across the North Sea. They were perfectly positioned. With a five-degree alteration of course to starboard, they could run in behind the position given by the Blenheim and then turn north-west along the probable track of the *Lutzow*.

As the leading flight covered the last two hundred miles towards the position south of Lister, the tension in the aircraft grew. In spite of the continued blackness, Loveitt had a growing certainty that his luck was going to be in.

"We should reach the position given in the sighting report in about ten minutes," called Morris.

"O.K.," said Loveitt. "Keep your eyes peeled, chaps."

Loveitt watched the leader closely, and a few moments later saw him begin a shallow dive down to 400 feet. The low cloud dispersed for a time, and although there were still heavy black clouds above them, obscuring the moon, Morris fancied he saw lights on the water a few miles ahead of them away to starboard. Loveitt took his eyes off the leader for a moment to look across in the direction pointed out by Morris. He saw at once that Morris was right. But looking across at the lights, with the other two aircraft on his blind side, he did not realize that Faville and Philpot had seen the lights too. Faville began a turn to starboard, Philpot tucked in with him, and both aircraft cut right across Loveitt. Caught up in their slipstream, he was sucked into a maelstrom of agitated air and his aircraft was thrown about violently, out of control. He struggled desperately as he realized that the turbulence was sending him in a steep dive down towards the sea.

When he recovered control they were only a few feet above the water. And they were alone.

Down on the deck, Loveitt looked about him for some sign of the others, but an impenetrable blackness stared back at him. Then he looked for the cluster of lights he had seen from 400 feet. There they were, some distance away, but still to starboard—they couldn't have got so very far off course. It was good to know that, now that they were on their own. He turned gently to starboard until they were heading for the lights.

"What happened?" called Morris from the nose. "I thought we were going in."

"So did I. Did you see them turn?"

"No."

"First thing I knew we were being chucked all over the sky. If we'd been any lower than 400 feet we'd have had it."

"Can you see the lights?"

"Yes."

"Looks like fishing vessels to me."

Loveitt waited until he had circled the lights before he

23

answered. But there was no doubt about it. Fishing vessels it was.

"What do we do now?"

"I'll give you a course that'll take us in towards the coast. We'll get a pinpoint and then make for the shipping lane."

"O.K."

Loveitt got the new course from Morris and turned on to it. Then he called Downing.

"Listen out for the others on the radio, will you? I'm afraid we've lost them. If they find the convoy they're bound to send an attack report. Then we'll get the position."

"Right."

"And Wally—keep a look out for fighters. We must be getting near Norway."

"O.K."

Loveitt climbed back to 600 feet. The last few minutes had been hectic, and he found the height relaxing. They would keep on this course for ten minutes. Better not stay on it longer for fear of crossing the Norwegian coast in the darkness and flying into the mountains. They were still flying mostly in cloud, and in the cloud it was intensely dark. Loveitt knew that Morris would have kept an air plot while they were in formation, but navigating was never altogether satisfactory when you were following another aircraft. Then they had been thrown off course, and although they had picked out the lights of the fishing vessels again, they couldn't have more than a rough idea of their present track. They must get a pinpoint before they started the search for the *Lutzow*.

The rain had found a weakness in the perspex canopy and was dripping on to his knee. The mood of optimism was passing. He began to feel clammy and uncomfortable.

"Ten minutes up," called Morris. "No sign of a landfall."

If they turned in a north-westerly direction now, they must surely be somewhere near the shipping lane. But somewhere near wasn't good enough. If only they could get a pinpoint, they would be certain to find the *Lutzow* if she had held her course.

"We'll have to keep on a bit longer," said Loveitt. "Can we aim to hit the coast at an angle? That'd give us a better chance of getting a glimpse of it as we run across it, instead of bashing straight in."

"Steer 340."

As Loveitt began his turn to port his eyes switched from the turn and bank indicator to the compass. What he saw made him look more closely. The needle was going the wrong way.

He realized instantly what had happened. Rain had dripped on to the compass face and obscured his view. Somehow the cross-piece that distinguished North was the wrong end.[1] Since leaving the fishing vessels they had been flying on reciprocal—away from the coast. The oldest mistake of all. He could hardly bear the thought of it. No wonder they hadn't seen anything.

"I'm afraid I've slipped up, Al. I've been on reciprocal. I know there's no excuse, but there's water dripping in on to the compass, and that must have messed me up. I'm turning through 180 degrees and we'll have to keep going for at least another fifteen minutes now. Sorry, chaps."

"You're turning on to the original course—straight in to the coast?"

"Yes. We'll have to. We've wasted so much time."

"How about going up to 1500 feet? That'll take us over most of the coastal stuff at least."

"Good idea."

They kept going for a full fifteen minutes, the tension growing. The merest glimpse of land and they could plot for themselves the shipping lane, five miles out, where coastwise traffic sailed. But without a sight of land it would be little more than guesswork.

The darkness pressed around them more and more frustratingly. Loveitt's nerve was beginning to fail him. His mind fought to cope with the argument that things had gone awry and that the best he could do was to carry out a search on dead-reckoning and then turn for home.

Suddenly the unseen world beneath them erupted in a fiery rash of explosive. A voice spoke calmly into Loveitt's ear.

---

[1] This was the earlier-type compass, which had two parallel wires, not the later 'T' type which prevented this mistake.

"Bags of flak, skipper. Bursting just below and behind the tail."

"The ships! Where are they?"

Morris called from the nose. "It isn't the ships. In the light of the gun-flashes I can see land."

"Then let's get to hell out of here."

Loveitt turned the Beaufort steeply to port, away from the intense fire from below, back out to sea. Wallace-Pannell called him again from the turret.

"They're still firing at us. We're getting out of range, though. Turn ten degrees to starboard and lose a couple of hundred feet. That should shake them off."

The voice from the turret was controlled and calculating, and Loveitt obeyed it. Wallace-Pannell continued to give evasive action, and soon they passed out of range.

"Where the hell was that?" Loveitt asked Morris.

"I've just worked it out. There's absolutely no doubt about it. That was the airfield at Lister."

Lister! The new Nazi airfield in southern Norway. The latest base for ocean-raiding Dorniers. They had stirred up something now. In a few moments there would be a whole squadron of fighters up after them.

And yet, what a pinpoint! For the last half-hour they had been praying for some sign to tell them where they were. Now they had it, with a frightening exactitude.

"If we can't find the *Lutzow* now, we never will," said Loveitt. "We'll have to chance what Lister can send after us. We'll take some finding in this stuff, anyway. Al, come back a moment and let's have a look at that chart."

Morris came back out of the nose and sat next to Loveitt.

"How much longer can we stooge around?"

The two men were silent for a moment, working out the fuel consumption. They had barely half an hour to spare for a search, allowing the absolute limit of endurance.

Loveitt was recovering from the shock of the sudden barrage, and as he looked at the chart he realized that all they would have time for was a quick sweep up past Lister Fjord to perhaps a few miles north of Egersund. But if the convoy had continued on its north-westerly course after the sighting, this was the area in which it must be.

There was always the chance that the captain of the *Lutzow*, knowing that the convoy had been sighted, and fearing attack, might double back on his tracks and seek shelter at Kristiansand, hoping to lie up there undetected next day and break out again the following night. But having got so far, was the German captain likely to turn back within a few hours' sailing of comparative safety? Knowing that he had been spotted by an enemy reconnaissance aircraft, that this dirty night was his chance to escape, surely he would be making full speed for the fjords beyond Stavanger.

The recce report had estimated that the convoy's speed was 22 knots. But Loveitt knew, from long months of study, all there was to know about ships of the *Lutzow* class. All the pocket-battleships were capable of doing several knots more than 22—certainly 26.

"Work out a new position," he told Morris. "Assume they've been doing 26 knots since midnight—ever since they were spotted by the Blenheim. According to my reckoning that'll put them somewhere off Egersund. We'll just about make it."

Morris went back into the nose to work out the exact position, and Loveitt turned back towards land to hit the shipping lane and strike north-west towards Egersund, turning his back as he did so on the chance that the *Lutzow* might be skulking somewhere in the huge stretch of water behind them. He would keep going on this course as long as he dared.

He brought the Beaufort down until the altimeter read 500 feet, but even Morris in the nose could see nothing. He kept her in a gentle glide, down to the limit of safety, and then even lower than that. Still they could see nothing.

Loveitt and Morris peered ahead, tensed by the low altitude, trying to convert the amorphous shadows into the outline of ships. Wallace-Pannell scanned the darkness behind them for fighters. Downing listened out on the radio.

They kept resolutely in the shipping lane, five miles out from the coast. Even if they flew slap through the middle of the convoy, they would be hard pressed to see it.

After fifteen minutes Downing called on the intercom.

"I've just picked up a message from the leader," he said.

"The others are giving up. They're sending negative reports and they're setting course for home."

"O.K."

Loveitt had hardly digested this when Morris called him. "We're just about opposite Egersund now."

Loveitt held his course for a moment, deciding what to do. The night was completely black. The opaqueness of the perspex struck back painfully at his eyes. The *Lutzow* could not possibly be further north than this. They had missed it, or anyway it had escaped them somehow. It seemed pointless to continue. The other chaps were already on their way home. Their endurance was nearing the safe limit—had in fact already reached the normal prudent limit. He wanted to live. There could be no possible criticism if he gave up now and set course for home.

He turned on to a course of 267 degrees, climbed to 800 feet, and levelled out. 267 was generally about right for the homeward leg on these trips off southern Norway. Morris came back out of the nose and worked out a course for Leuchars. Wallace-Pannell came out of the turret. Loveitt lit a cigarette. All they had to do now was get back.

Ahead of them the night was at first as black as ever, but as they left the coast behind there were again the occasional clear patches where the moon shone brilliantly. A few miles away to starboard, Loveitt could see two bowls of light where the moon had broken through, one a mile or so north of the other. What a pity there hadn't been a few patches like that back in the shipping lane.

The world around them was a darkened stage in which the pools of light thrown by two spotlights accentuated the darkness. Suddenly, into the first of these pools of light, Loveitt saw appear, like the first spot of rain on a dry pavement, a tiny patch of white. It was the wake of a ship.

God and man together had produced a magnificent scene. Loveitt could not move the spotlight, but he had no need to: the light was still, but the subject moved. Entering the stage, with a majestic, splendid haste, a thousand yards behind the first minesweeping destroyer, was the *Lutzow*, boxed in by her rectangle of destroyers, the leading pair lying directly in the path of torpedo attack.

How clever of the German captain to steam twenty-five miles out! He'd never have thought of looking for him there.

From this point on Loveitt was in the hands of the men who had gone before him, of the men who would come after him, of his instructors, of his years of training, of his *esprit de corps*. Yet he was out on his own. The other chaps had gone home. It was up to him. In another hour or two the *Lutzow* would be safe from prying eyes in a Norwegian fjord, sooner or later to break out into the Atlantic. The lives of a thousand merchant seamen, their ships, their precious cargoes, lay for the moment with him.

He sat somewhere outside the aircraft, above the perspex cockpit, watching the actions of an automaton, watching them impassively, uncritically, breathlessly.

It was too late to get the *Lutzow* in the first pool of light. But away to the north, right in the path of the convoy, was the second spotlight. If he kept on his present course, at right angles to the convoy, crossed behind it, kept on for a mile or so away from it on its port side, and then swung round back towards the east, he could time his run to converge on the *Lutzow* in the middle of the second pool of light.

He swung round to the north-west, losing height steadily, making swift, exact, arbitrary judgments of distance, speed and time. He must aim his run right into the centre of the second pool of light, so as to allow for any last-minute adjustments.

He began his run from about three miles, still letting down gently, throttles well back, keeping his speed down to 140 knots. Now he was where he wanted to be, twenty feet above the water, waiting for the ships to appear out of the darkness away to the right. Suppose they had heard his engines? Surely they must have done. Suppose they had altered course in that thick curtain of dirty weather? How would he ever find them again? There were only the two patches of moonlight. If they didn't appear in a moment he would be too soon. But in the same moment the sweeping destroyer emerged from the murk, steaming strongly, holding her course.

He leaned forward in his dress-circle seat, waiting for the *Lutzow*, unseen as yet in the wings of a vast theatre, about to make her entrance into the limes like a great star.

There she was, magnificently unaware of her peril. He knew a moment's surprise at the familiarity of her outline. It was like seeing a famous actress pass by in the street. She was beautiful, and just like her pictures.

It was a part of his detachment that he could pause to admire this hostile, inimical thing.

In the same moment he saw the four destroyers. The forward port destroyer lay right in his path.

He held his course, pulling up gently to the dropping height of sixty feet. That wouldn't be enough to clear the masts of the destroyer, so he would have to fly across its stern. The destroyer would almost certainly be at a distance of a thousand yards from the *Lutzow*. One of the hardest things to do was to judge distance over water, and he had an exact distance measured out for him.

In the next few seconds the convoy would see him and put down a sleeting curtain of fire. It was incredible that he had got thus far undetected. The destroyer was rushing towards him, sixty feet below. He went through his drill again mechanically. Speed and height were just right. He had to be sure that the torpedo would glide smoothly into the water and not break its back. Safely past the destroyer, he would have three to four hundred yards in which to steady the air-craft, aim off at the *Lutzow*, and drop his fish.

He crossed the stern of the destroyer with a sudden sensation of realism and speed. Someone on the bridge fired a Very light at him, perhaps in a sort of belated, impotent belligerence, perhaps simply giving him the colours of the day. The coloured star-shells rose prettily, further illuminating the scene. There was the *Lutzow*, throwing back the intense white moonlight, reflecting the star-shells, for all the world like a huge set-piece at a firework display. The mighty *Lutzow*, a sitting duck.

He lined up the nose of the aircraft to aim the torpedo, allowing one and a half lengths' deflection, aiming for the front half of the ship, forward of her armour plating. He had timed the whole manœuvre perfectly and all he had to do was apply the gentlest pressure with his left foot to the port rudder-bar. The nose swung away to port slightly and steadied exactly as he wanted it. There could be no missing.

He was aiming for the whole squadron. Suddenly the vessel filled his whole screen. One last look at the turn and bank indicator, to make sure that he was dead straight and level, and he steadied himself and the aircraft in one supreme effort of will. His index finger was already curled round the release button. He pressed it deliberately, hardly moving a muscle, holding his breath.

There followed instantly the distinctive tremor as the retaining cable sprang off.

"Hey," called Downing from the fuselage, "you've dropped your torp."

Only then did he realize that he had not spoken a word since the sighting, that only he and his navigator knew.

Suddenly he was back in the aircraft again, ramming open the throttles, holding the Beaufort down desperately, racing past the bows of the battleship, turning and climbing tautly away to port, dreading the barrage that must come It wasn't until afterwards that he knew that, in his dread of the flak he felt sure must rise at them, he had screamed, "It's coming, it's coming," as they rushed past the bows of the *Lutzow* and climbed away.

"You've hit it! You've hit it!" Downing and Wallace-Pannell, alive at last to what was afoot, were shouting over the intercom. Loveitt steepened his climbing turn to port, circled round the leading destroyer, and looked back over his left shoulder at his prey. The giant stalagmite of water that had been thrown up by the explosion was still frozen grotesquely in place, some way down the side of the stricken vessel. Smoke and steam were cascading from her bows. He allowed himself a long, astonished stare at what he had done, and then, fear returning with a rush, he turned and climbed away out of range. The convoy was slowing down, taken completely by surprise. Not a shot had been fired at him.

Loveitt's Beaufort had been taken by the German squadron for a Ju 88 known to be patrolling the area. The torpedo found its mark in spite of a last-minute alteration of helm. The *Lutzow* immediately developed a heavy list to port, and, with part of the upper deck under water, both engines came to a stop. The port propeller shaft was severely damaged, and because of the heavy list the starboard propeller shaft was almost clear of the water. The *Lutzow* was taken in tow by one of the destroyers and the convoy made for the protection of the shore batteries at Egersund.

Meanwhile at 02.25 Loveitt made his attack report, and this was picked up by the other 42 Squadron aircraft. Rooney, a survivor of the bombing attack on the *Scharnhorst* of twelve months earlier, found the *Lutzow* enveloped in smoke, but he dropped his torpedo into the centre of the smoke concentration. No results were observed and he learned later that his torpedo missed. One other aircraft of 42 Squadron found the convoy, but its torpedo failed to release.

Up to this time the five aircraft of 22 Squadron from Wick had had no luck. Two of them had been forced to land back at Wick with turret trouble, and the other three had failed to find the target. The two who were forced to land, however, took off again soon after two o'clock that morning. One of them found the *Lutzow* at 04.23, steering for Stavanger under its own steam, its starboard engine having been started an hour earlier. The ship was making about 12 knots. It was daylight, and this lone Beaufort, forced to drop its torpedo prematurely by concentrated fire from the ships, was shot down by an escorting Me 109 as it turned away.

The *Lutzow*, however, was so severely damaged by Loveitt's torpedo that the commanding officer now decided to turn about and make for a home port. She was not picked up again by reconnaissance aircraft until 16.00 hours that afternoon, and by then she was rounding the Skaw, out of range of our strike forces. She was not seen again until four days later, when photos taken by a P.R.U. aircraft showed her in dry dock at Kiel. She did not leave this berth for six months.

When Loveitt landed he was mobbed by the crews who had picked up his signal, and then rushed off to the operations room and dragged through a dozen interrogations. It was almost as if they were loath to believe that a hit had been scored, so sure did they want to be before they let him go. It was the first torpedo he'd ever dropped in anger; and he'd put the first R.A.F.-launched torpedo into a German capital ship at sea.

Chapter 2

THE ROVER

W HEN the war began there were two torpedo-bomber
squadrons based in the United Kingdom—Nos. 22 and
42, both of which were equipped with the obsolete Wildebeest and were marking time until the delivery in numbers
of the new Bristol Beaufort. This type of aircraft, the natural
successor to the Blenheim, began to arrive on 22 Squadron
at Thorney Island, near Portsmouth, at the beginning of
1940.

The Beaufort was of immensely strong construction, and
at the time of its introduction was claimed to be the fastest
medium bomber in the world. Its two Taurus engines gave
a top speed of 290 miles per hour and a cruising speed of
some 145 knots. The crew of four were well accommodated
in the fuselage. The navigator had a fine view from the
perspex nose, and could pass readily to and from his take-off
position on the right of the pilot. The wireless operator was
comfortably seated in the fuselage directly behind the pilot,
separated from him by armour plating and by the radio
equipment; he, too, could move easily about the aircraft, and
when going into action or under attack by fighters he left his
seat at the radio and manned two free Vickers machine-guns
which were mounted in the waist hatches, one on either side
of the fuselage. The power-operated turret sat on the back
of the aircraft about half way along the fuselage, and the
two gunners could readily swap places to give them a change
and to reduce fatigue. Sitting alone in a turret in daylight,
scanning the sky hour after hour for other aircraft, was a
taut and wearying occupation.

All previous torpedo training had been carried out on the
Swordfish and the Wildebeest, whose cruising speed was well
under a hundred knots, and the method of attack for these
aircraft had been to dive down towards the target from a
comparatively safe height, flatten out, and launch the
torpedo. But the Beaufort built up speed very rapidly in a

33

dive—far too much speed for the successful launching of a
torpedo. It was not possible to lose this speed quickly by
flattening out. So the Beaufort attack had to be made at low
level, both the approach and the drop. Various attempts
were made to remove this tactical limitation, by the fitting of
dive-brakes, and by the introduction of a flying torpedo
known as a 'toraplane', which could be dropped from a
height of 1500 feet and which flew into the water at the
correct angle. But neither method proved itself in trials, and
neither was used operationally. The low-level approach, with
the Beaufort exposed to the full weight of defensive fire for a
long period and unable to take more than very limited
evasive action, had come to stay.

Training in the new method of attack was begun at
Thorney Island in February 1940, and in April No. 22
Squadron moved to North Coates, on the Lincolnshire coast,
a few miles south of Grimsby. Here they flew operationally
for the first time in Beauforts, laying mines in enemy coastal
waters.

The Beaufort was a newly developed aircraft, and like
all other new aircraft it had its teething troubles. Several
crews disappeared unaccountably on these minelaying operations. There were crashes on take-off, some of them fatal. The
pilots began to suspect the engines. But the engines, fully
tried and tested by the makers, were brand new. How could
there be anything fundamentally wrong with such a beautiful new aircraft? The commanding officer of the squadron
did his best to scotch rumour, and to persuade his pilots of
what was often demonstrably true—that the accidents were
due to inexperience.

The Beaufort, in fact, was not an easy aircraft to control.
Torpedo pilots were used to the Swordfish and the Wildebeest, which virtually flew themselves. But the Beaufort was
a very different matter. It was much heavier, it had two
high-powered engines, and its wing area was small. It
carried a torpedo and a crew of four with ease, at a much
faster speed and for a much greater range; but it was a
handful to fly.

Suspicion that there might, in fact, be some serious
mechanical fault in the Taurus engine was heightened to-

wards the end of May when the C.O. himself failed to return from a routine minelaying operation. A fortnight later a court of enquiry was convened, with a brief to investigate the operational efficiency of the Beaufort and its engines. The result was the grounding of 22 and 42 Squadrons for modifications to the Taurus engine. 42 carried out the bombing attack on the *Scharnhorst* of 21st June, their first Beaufort operation of any kind, while the court of enquiry was sitting.

22 Squadron, under a new commanding officer, Wing Commander F. J. St. G. Braithwaite, resumed operations at the beginning of September with a series of bombing attacks on enemy harbours—Flushing, Ostend, Calais, Boulogne. Then, on 11th September, came the first torpedo action. An enemy convoy was sighted at 14.30 that afternoon off Calais, and Braithwaite was asked to lay on a strike. Five aircraft, led by Flight Lieutenant Dick Beauman, one of the two flight commanders, were to rendezvous with a fighter escort over Detling and then proceed to the target. The fighters failed to appear and Beauman decided to set course without them. When the formation reached Calais there was no sign of the convoy either. Beauman decided to sweep north-east to Ostend, and the convoy was sighted on the way. The Beauforts attacked independently. Three of the torpedoes failed to release through electrical faults, but Beauman and the other flight commander, 'Fanny' Francis, pressed home their attacks. One torpedo exploded prematurely when it hit a sandbank between the aircraft and the target: the other torpedo hit and completely destroyed a large merchant vessel. The other Beauforts went in and machine-gunned the escorting flak-ships, and all five aircraft returned safely to North Coates. Nearly everything had gone wrong, yet it had been a highly encouraging start.

Four days later came the first Rover, which became the standard form of routine operation for many months. The Rover was a roving commission, an armed reconnaissance against enemy shipping in a chosen area, carried out by a small number of aircraft working independently, each with its own area of search. It was born of a general shortage of both strike and reconnaissance aircraft, the Beauforts seeking out their own targets in the known shipping lanes.

In addition, the torpedo squadrons had a brief to work out the tactical side of torpedo-dropping with the new type of aircraft. The torpedo training unit at Gosport was awaiting the squadrons' decision on tactics, and training was even suspended altogether for a time.

Meanwhile, the tactics of the Rover soon fell into place, breeding an individualism in pilots and crews which was to become characteristic of torpedo men. Within their wide general terms, the rules of the Rover were strict. Pilots flew at visibility distance from the enemy coast—generally, for 22 Squadron, the Dutch coast—which in good conditions averaged about ten miles. There had to be plenty of cloud cover, so that the Beaufort could quickly escape the attentions of enemy fighters: no one had any illusions about the prospects of a Beaufort when pitted against an Me 109. Besides, the Beaufort's job was to sink shipping, not to become embroiled in aerial combat. If the pilot ran out of cloud cover nearing the enemy coast, his orders were to return to base.

The usual tactics were to search low down near the surface of the water, where visibility was limited but where the Beaufort itself was difficult to see or hear. The Beaufort thus operated as a sort of super-fast motor torpedo-boat, speeding along the surface of the water, often taking a target completely unawares.

While some of the early Rovers were flown at cloud-base height, on the assumption that this made the Beaufort safer from fighter attack as well as increasing visibility, it was found that the Beaufort was easily seen from a distance when flying at this height, and, worse still, could be picked up outside visibility distance by enemy radar. Moreover, once having made a sighting, the Beaufort had to come down low to drop its torpedo, and a quick surprise attack was therefore only possible if the aircraft was flying low already. Low cloud, however, remained obligatory, and all pilots flew with one eye on the proximity of cloud cover.

The essence of Rover tactics was to keep moving. To spend several minutes in the same area, or to circle a target before attacking, was to invite opposition and court disaster. The secret of the successful operation was quick target recognition and an immediate attack. This was the only way to take defences unawares.

But although the tactics soon became stereotyped, the men who flew the Beauforts, sharing though they did the quality of individualism, lone raiders preying on the enemy far from base, were yet of diverse character. First there was the C.O., Braithwaite, 34 years old, tall and impressive, a man easy to respect and admire. He was the ideal squadron commander. Restricted himself by his Group Headquarters to two sorties a month, he knew that there were pilots on his squadron with closer experience of the Rover, and he did not disdain to fly sometimes under their leadership. He was a penetrating judge of character, and was quick to see when a man was showing signs of wilting under the strain of operational flying, or when a pilot was not temperamentally suited to torpedo work. Although early in the war there was no such thing as an operational tour, the shortage of trained crews compelling experienced men (if they were fortunate) to complete over fifty sorties and still have no immediate hope of rest, Braithwaite managed to post men who were coming near to breaking-point to jobs as instructors before the crack-up came. He knew that these men were good material and that every man, whoever he might be, came near to breaking-point sooner or later. Many of these men came back to do great things on a second tour.

Two pilots of widely different personality were Dick Beauman and Sergeant Norman Hearn-Phillips, universally known as 'H-P'. Beauman had all the attributes of the popular hero—dashing, reckless, good-looking, a trifle spoilt, accustomed to success, determined and fearless. He loved his role of lone wolf, was never happier than when he was searching off the Dutch coast, well inside visibility distance, often over the coast itself, prying into Dutch ports, seeking out the enemy. Married to a beautiful girl, with a young son, he had everything in the world a man could wish for. But he was headstrong and impatient, sinking ships was his job and his life, and he wanted to sink one every day. He was far and away the outstanding pilot of the Rover period, and he set a pace which could not but result in a rare competitive spirit on the squadron.

If Beauman had a weakness it was his impetuousness. He always wanted results, and he loved the spectacular. Once, on a visit to Coastal Command Headquarters, he was shown a reconnaissance photograph of the *Bremen* and the *Europa* in Bremerhaven, surrounded by protective barges and torpedo nets. From that time on his mind repeatedly strayed northwards towards Bremerhaven, and more often than not on a Rover he strayed towards that area physically too. He drew plans of the estuary, showing how a torpedo might be dropped, and one night, on a moonlight Rover, he penetrated the harbour. Caught in a vortex of fire and blinded by searchlights, he held on until suddenly he saw the anchored *Bremen* and *Europa* rush lopsidedly into his windscreen. To make a torpedo run was impossible, and he had to turn and climb steeply to avoid ramming the ships. Back at base, the other senior pilots tried to dissuade Beauman from making any further attempt against these ships, urging that it was not only suicidal but impracticable. But still Beauman hankered after them.

Hearn-Phillips had joined the R.A.F. as a sergeant-pilot in 1936. After qualifying as a pilot he was trained first on torpedo and then on general reconnaissance work. He was, perhaps, the most highly trained man on the squadron. H-P kept to the rules. He was a professional soldier, his job was to destroy the enemy, and to preserve himself and his aircraft if he could. He never went much inside visibility distance, except when it was necessary to do so for an actual attack, or when he was led there by the flight leader, when he followed, loyally enough, but sceptically. He kept most of the time about ten miles out to sea, where he was able to spot not only coast-crawling traffic but also any shipping steaming some distance out. When there was no cloud cover, H-P gave up and went home. There was always tomorrow. War was his business, and he took it seriously. He was in charge of an expensive aircraft and a trained crew. On one occasion, after dropping a torpedo that ran almost at once into the shallows, he flew back and studied the coastal charts minutely, marking all the shallow areas where torpedoes could not run, finding that there were some parts of the coast where he need not go in as close as ten miles as there was no depth for shipping or for successfully dropping a torpedo. In this and other ways he increased his chances of sinking ships, and his own chances of survival.

On another occasion, H-P's wireless operator was late for take-off. H-P knew the dangers, but he wasn't going to miss his take-off time. He had no option but to take off without him. H-P liked the chap personally, thought him a good wireless operator and a keen flier. But it was the last chance he had of flying with H-P.

Visitors to the squadron, observers from Group, Press men, were always sent off with the phlegmatic H-P. He had a habit of coming back.

'Fanny' Francis, the second flight commander, was perhaps the one potentially great leader on the squadron. Beauman had that streak of irresponsibility, so that although his achievement and personality were an inspiration, he was too individual for outstanding leadership. But Francis was a born leader, audacious and determined without rashness. He had been a pilot on the torpedo development flight at Gosport up to July 1940, and it was only after a long campaign of agitation that he succeeded in getting himself posted to 22 Squadron—a triumph of pertinacity in itself.

Francis led the first set-piece torpedo attack of the war— a night strike on shipping in Cherbourg harbour. A detachment of six crews was based at Thorney Island for the operation. They arrived there from North Coates about midday, stood by through the afternoon, and were then released until next morning.

"May we go out of camp?" asked H-P.

Hearn-Phillips and Farthing, Francis's navigator, had been stationed at Thorney Island with the squadron in the early months of the war, and they had several friends to call on near by.

"Yes, but don't be late back—you may be flying early tomorrow."

H-P and Farthing went off. Most of the others went to the pictures on the camp. During the evening, a strike against Cherbourg was decided on for that night. One or two stragglers were picked up from pubs in the village by bus, and the rest were called out on the Tannoy. But no one had the slightest idea where to look for Farthing and H-P.

It was only by chance that they returned in time for the raid. H-P had decided that, as the two senior of the N.C.O.s of the party, he and Farthing had better get back early and set an example. When they arrived on the camp they were grabbed and taken to the operations room, where they found that all the crews had already been briefed and had gone out to their aircraft. They were hastily given the colours of the day, and told that they were to rendezvous with some Blenheims over Wittering.

"What's the target?"

"Cherbourg. Shipping in the harbour. The biggest you can find."

They rushed out to dispersal, got the rest of the briefing from Francis, who was making ready to take off with H-P's navigator, sorted themselves out, took off, joined formation and set course. It was the sort of experience that might have unsettled a lot of people—but not the imperturbable H-P.

There was a moon, but it was obscured by cloud and the night was black. The plan was for the Blenheims to go in first and bomb the docks with incendiaries. The fires started by the Blenheims would rage behind the harbour, silhouetting the shipping for the approaching Beauforts, who were to enter the harbour in three waves of two each, at different angles, two from the east end of the harbour, two from the north, two from the west.

On the way across to the Cherbourg peninsula the formation ran into cloud. The aircraft were forced to open out. H-P came down below cloud soon after, and found he was on his own. He kept going, watching for signs of the others, his navigator keeping an independent plot. When they sighted the French coast they realized they had drifted east. H-P turned to starboard and flew along parallel to the coast for a few minutes. Very soon he got his pinpoint from the flak over Cherbourg, some miles ahead. The Blenheims were already over the harbour. H-P had been briefed to go in from the east, and he was approaching nicely from that angle, but as he picked out the breakwater a mile or so distant he saw two Beauforts going in ahead of him. He turned to starboard again with the idea of swinging right round the harbour and coming in from the west, but as he flew along parallel with the breakwater he saw another Beaufort crossing his track, going in from the west. He decided to turn short and fly across the centre of the breakwater, to spread the attack and to keep clear of other aircraft. As he turned for the harbour he saw a red glow on the horizon and caught a glimpse of fires raging in the town.

H-P was the last over the breakwater. The masts of many ships were silhouetted above him against the fires raging on the quay. He was aware of three destroyers and perhaps two or three merchantmen. He picked a destroyer and a merchantman, one behind the other. If the torpedo ran underneath one it would surely come up for the other. As he crossed the breakwater he found he was flying through a curtain of flak, which beat like hail on the metal surface of the Beaufort. He estimated his height on the masts and funnels of the ships, but it was a tricky business and he half expected to run into a ship in the shadows. He dropped his torpedo and opened the throttles. At once the Beaufort began to climb alarmingly. It was the last thing he wanted—to fly up into the flames ahead like a moth at a candle, where he would be an illuminated target for the gunners. He struggled to hold the Beaufort down, spinning the trimmer forward. It flapped loosely. Half the tail, including the trimmers, had been shot away.

H-P managed to extricate his Beaufort from the flak of Cherbourg and to complete the sea crossing back to Thorney; but when he checked the flaps he found they were not working. That meant the hydraulics had gone. But he could fire the undercart down by the emergency cartridge. He pressed the button gingerly. Nothing happened.

He climbed away and called up his wireless operator. "Tell them we're having undercarriage trouble and to get the others in first. Then if we have to do a belly-flop we shan't clutter up the airfield." The wireless operator sent the message, and soon afterwards H-P got a green from flying control. He hadn't seen the others land, but as he had been the last to attack it was probable that they had got back first. He made a good wheels-up landing in the middle of the flare-path. But someone had blundered. As he got out of the wreck, H-P was attacked by an enraged duty pilot.

41

"What the hell did you do that for? How am I going to get the others in?"

H-P had come through a pretty gruelling night, and he might have been forgiven for losing his temper. But that wasn't his way.

"I sent a message that my undercart was damaged, and you gave me a green. Not my fault, old man. I'll give you a hand moving the flare-path."

They moved the flare-path and eventually got the others down. There were only four of them. The sixth aircraft had been shot down over Cherbourg. Four pilots had dropped their torpedoes, but the fifth had got lost and turned back. Reconnaissance next day showed that one merchant vessel had been definitely hit. It had been a warm night for Cherbourg.

After the novelty of this set-piece attack, the crews returned to North Coates and settled down again to the increasingly familiar pattern of the Rover, Beauman, Francis and H-P quickly establishing themselves as the outstanding pilots. The crews only went out in bad weather, and some men took to these conditions less kindly than others.

In October, three new pilots took their places on the squadron who were to rival the established aces and who between them were to win five decorations in the next two years, including a V.C. They were Jimmy Hyde, Ken Campbell and Pat Gibbs. Hyde, an Australian in the R.A.F., had already had his baptism in torpedo work as a second-pilot-cum-navigator with Beauman. He had converted to Beauforts on the squadron, and was now ready to captain an aircraft himself. He proved to be a prudent and orthodox but determined torpedo pilot, as steady and dependable as H-P. Campbell was a 24-year-old Scot from Saltcoats, Ayrshire, who had entered the R.A.F. soon after the outbreak of war from the Cambridge University Air Squadron. He soon stood out as a pilot of unusual aggression and will, with all the latent qualities of the leader. Completing a distinguished trio was Pat Gibbs.

Gibbs was a young permanent officer who had joined the R.A.F. in 1934 through a Cranwell cadetship. He had no ambitions for a military career—it was flying alone that attracted him. He had spent the first year of the war as a torpedo instructor at Gosport, and he had helped to train many of the squadron crews. For many months he had tried in vain for a posting to 22 Squadron, and when Francis left the development unit at Gosport, Gibbs had said to him half-jokingly, "Tell your new C.O. I want to join his squadron". A mere application for a posting was one thing, and might have to take its turn behind countless others—in flying, no less than in other walks of life, the other chap's grass always looked greener than yours—but a request by a squadron commander for a particular pilot had been known to get astonishingly quick results. Francis knew Gibbs well enough, he knew the frustration of endless training flights, and he did not forget Gibbs when he eventually got to 22. Braithwaite soon asked for him. As the number of aircraft in the squadron increased, a third flight was formed. Gibbs was to be 'C' Flight commander.

Gibbs was an experienced and resourceful pilot without ever being a brilliant one. His flying was just about good enough to get him by. But he had spent five years in torpedo work and he had absolute faith in the torpedo as a weapon. His fighting instinct, his desire to strike at the enemy, had long been pent up. He had talked about the coming war throughout the rise of Nazi power, and when it came he had been forced to spend the first twelve months of it at Gosport. He was itching to prove himself in action. The word that occurred to everyone when Pat Gibbs's name was mentioned was 'dedicated'. He was utterly dedicated to the task of sinking ships with the torpedo.

There were thousands of brave men in all branches of the air war, but each individual branch threw up a man possessed of this terrifying selfless dedication, which marked him out from his fellows for all time. Cheshire in bombing. Bader and Johnson in air fighting. Pape in escape. All these men approached the fanatical. The name of Pat Gibbs stands with them.

He was not always an easy man to live with. He was far too sure that he was right about the torpedo to appear other than obsessed, almost bigoted. He was quite prepared to be the only man in step. He believed he was right, and if others

43

disagreed, then they and not he were wrong. It didn't matter who they were, how strong in numbers or in rank, he was always convinced that he was right. This made him not always popular with his contemporaries, and got him into trouble in the end with the brass-hats; but his enthusiasm won many of his seniors and contemporaries and all his juniors over to his side. He was sensitive, aesthetic, highly-strung and imaginative, and he suffered all the agonies of the fight. And for much of the time he was fighting a battle from within, a struggle against what he considered to be misuse, abuse and neglect of the torpedo weapon.

Gibbs took off on his first operational flight soon after joining the squadron, on a daylight Rover as No. 2 to Dick Beauman. It was perfect Rover weather, low cloud down to a few hundred feet, belts of rain, visibility low enough to make them safe from fighter attack and yet sufficient to pick out any ships there might be on the shipping routes. Gibbs felt all the commonplace emotions before take-off—excitement, apprehension, nervous tension, elation, all sharpened by his own perceptivity of temperament. But as soon as he was in the air, his mercurial emotions steadied into a calm awareness of the present. For as long as he flew against the enemy, this was how it was to be.

He flew a few wing-spans to starboard of Beauman, close enough to see his leader waving encouragingly at him. He was comforted by the feeling of comradeship. He was always to prefer being one of a formation, whether following or leading.

The outline of islands off the Dutch coast came as an anti-climax. They looked peaceful and friendly, there was nothing to distinguish them from similar sandy islands back in England. Visibility was three to four miles off the coast, and Gibbs expected Beauman to turn before they reached land. But he flew straight on, over the islands, and then between the islands and the mainland, his navigator continually taking photographs. Keeping just below the cloud base, the two aircraft flew directly past Texel, Terschelling and Borkum, peeping into harbours, watching the shore batteries fire impotently at them, their fire looking deceptively harmless.

To Beauman it was familiar ground; this stretch of coast-line belonged to him. But to Gibbs it was new, and he wondered what it all had to do with torpedo work. The waters over which they were flying were shallow, and any shipping worth expending a torpedo on would be at least five miles off the coast. But at length Beauman tired of the preliminaries and headed out to sea.

Gibbs had followed his leader's twisting, haphazard course as closely as he could, but as they turned out to sea at fifty feet the cloud base lowered, merging with the horizon, and driving rain swept across the windscreen and clung to it like sticky paint. The chances of finding any shipping looked grim. But whatever queer method Beauman used, it brought results, and soon Gibbs saw the aircraft ahead of him waggle its wings as the signal to attack. But where were the ships? Beauman, at least, must have seen something. Gibbs let his aircraft slip back behind Beauman, so that he didn't have to concentrate so closely on keeping station, and at once straight ahead two ships flickered at him out of the white mist, and then he thought he saw several more. Beauman was making straight for the largest ship, a tanker of about 2000 tons. The tanker had an escort of three flak ships. So far the ships had either not seen them in the mist or not recognized them as inimical. Gibbs was 200 yards behind Beauman. He saw the leader's torpedo splash into the water, the splash leaving a pool of white foam from which a track of bubbles hurried towards the target. Gibbs aimed his torpedo into the same splash, feeling now nothing of the tension he had felt at take-off, only a cool efficiency and a sense of heightened perception, as though he were staring at a succession of movie stills. His torpedo was on its way as he began to follow Beauman in a turn away to starboard.

Beauman's attack had completely surprised the convoy and he got through without having a single shot fired at him until he was safely away. But the flak-ships picked up Gibbs as he dropped his torpedo. The guns flashed at him out of the mist, silver tracers rushed past him and exploded around him in black puffs of smoke, and machine-gun fire raked the water beneath him, churning it up like a cauldron. As he turned steeply away to starboard there was the screech of rending metal and then three stupefying explosions inside the aircraft. The Beaufort juddered and jerked, the cockpit filled with smoke, the navigator and tail gunner fell back wounded, and the aircraft staggered on into the mist, out of control.

Shot down on his first operation! The words thundered in his ears, above the roar of the engines and the slipstream. So this was all he could manage for a C.O. who had specially asked for him! Shot down on his first op.

As the smoke cleared in the cockpit, Gibbs struggled to bring the Beaufort under control. Somehow it still seemed to be flying, drunkenly, capriciously, but flying. He had no elevator control, the perspex nose was shattered, and blood covered the maps and charts; but he was still airborne. Soon he found that he could climb on the elevator tabs, which had not been damaged. Aileron and rudder seemed O.K. too. He jerked a quick look back along the fuselage, where 'Ginger' Coulson, his wireless operator, was stooped over the wounded tail gunner. Coulson caught his eye, gave him the thumbs up, and grinned.

It was a tremendous tonic. Suddenly it all seemed frightfully funny. He sat grinning at his navigator, moving the control column back and forth and getting no response, as though it was the biggest joke in the world. They pointed to the holes in the aircraft, and they laughed.

All the way home they kept noticing things, remembering things, reasons why they should be at the bottom of the North Sea. They laughed uproariously.

Gibbs got the aircraft back safely, landing it on a strange airfield in Lincolnshire. The two wounded men were taken to hospital, and the squadron sent an aircraft to fetch Gibbs and Coulson. Beauman met them on the runway at North Coates.

Gibbs was in the news already. The German news bulletins were claiming to have shot his Beaufort down.

The pattern of the Rover continued, varied sometimes by changing the load to bombs, so that inland targets could be attacked if no shipping was found. Most sorties were inspired by the squadron itself, the flight commanders sensing that Rover weather was on the way, and the C.O. pressing

Group to let his aircraft try to find a target. It was a stimulating free-lance role, and the crews loved it. They might spend several days on the ground, watching the sky like countrymen for signs of favourable weather. Then there would be a run of a week or so in which conditions of low cloud persisted. First they would find nothing, then strike and miss, then send off another two or three aircraft and score a hit at the third attempt. All the time they were discussing tactics, especially Gibbs and Francis, who spent most of their time in each other's offices, planning the destruction of enemy shipping, comparing their experience, deciding where they had gone wrong, watching for signs of the enemy's reaction. These two men made plenty of mistakes; but they very rarely made the same mistake twice. They loved their work and were depressed only by failure. Gibbs called the Rover 'the most demanding operation in individual effort, the most satisfying in achievement, and the most thrilling in action'.

Late in October the squadron carried out a high-level night bombing attack on the German liners *Bremen* and *Europa* in Bremerhaven (Gibbs on this occasion doubled his total night-flying hours); and early in November six crews, including Francis, Gibbs and H-P, were detached to St Eval to bomb the U-Boat base at Lorient. But no sooner had they got to St Eval than a perfect target presented itself for torpedoes—an 8000-ton merchant vessel near Ushant which was making for Brest harbour. This was not a Rover, but a planned strike at a specific target. There was no cloud cover, and they would be within range of enemy fighters, but there was no question of turning back.

Francis worked out a plan of attack before take-off. He would go in first himself, with H-P and Gibbs to follow at ten-second intervals. H-P and Gibbs were to watch for any avoiding action the ship might take in the face of Francis's attack, and aim their torpedoes accordingly. When they sighted the target, however, Gibbs decided that H-P had left too great a distance between himself and Francis, thus driving Gibbs back a long way to the rear. Gibbs decided to overtake H-P before they attacked and to swing across into the gap. H-P did not have time to settle down again, Gibbs had very little time to adjust his position, and the three

47

torpedoes dropped in quick succession. But they had under-estimated the ship's speed. All three torpedoes missed astern.

Gibbs felt their lack of success keenly. The whole hazard-ous flight had been in vain, three valuable torpedoes had been lost, and the enemy tanker was steaming on serenely, tantalizingly, while they faced a depressing flight home and an admission of failure at the end of it.

They spent three nights bombing Lorient, without losing a crew, although on one occasion Gibbs's navigator was wounded and Gibbs crash-landed back at St Eval. When the detachment ended, Gibbs had completed six operations in all, and in doing so had broken two aircraft and landed two navigators and an air gunner in hospital. However, 'Ginger' Coulson, the wireless operator, was still with him. Coulson became almost as much a mascot to Gibbs as the toy 'Panda' he always carried in the aircraft.

After a series of bombing attacks on German-occupied air-fields in France, the squadron settled down once again to anti-shipping operations from North Coates. Towards the end of November, Beauman and Gibbs took off together on a Rover. A few days earlier, news had come through of the award of the D.F.M. to Hearn-Phillips. Beauman had be· 1 having a lean time, unaccountably missing a good target twice in recent weeks, and he was thirsting for success. Gibbs followed Beauman, knowing by now what to expect from his leadership.

As they crossed the North Sea the cloud base lowered, and by the time they made their landfall off Texel it was ideal weather. As usual, Beauman spent a good deal of time over land, paid a visit to Den Helder and Borkum, and kept on in a north-easterly direction. Gibbs wondered if Beauman was toying with the idea of having a go at the *Bremen* and *Europa*. Gibbs was having trouble with an engine, and in worsening weather was finding it increasingly difficult to follow Beau-man's random course. The engine trouble persisted, and eventually Gibbs could no longer hold on to the wraith which was Beauman's aircraft. He turned for home.

Meanwhile, Beauman sped on towards the mouth of the Elbe, where he found a large convoy obligingly at anchor. He dropped at a 7600-ton oil tanker, and left it sinking and in flames. After the attack he flew alongside the tanker in order to read the ship's name, while his navigator took a picture showing the tanker belching clouds of thick black smoke with its deck aflame from stem to stern. The news of the sinking was given by the B.B.C. that night at nine o'clock, and the picture of the tanker in flames appeared in the news-papers a day or so later.

It was arranged that Beauman should give a talk on torpedo work in the Home Service twelve days later, on 9th December 1940.

November, as might be expected, produced perfect Rover weather right to the end. Two days after his spectacular sinking of the oil tanker, Beauman was off again on another Rover, making for his usual landfall at Den Helder. The air-craft accompanying him had to return to base with engine trouble, and Beauman was left on his own. Shortly before midday he sighted a convoy off Terschelling consisting of fifteen merchantmen, and he attacked at once. But some-thing was wrong with his approach, because his gunners saw the torpedo splash into the water and dive to the bottom. Beauman got safely clear of the convoy and sent a message back to North Coates, where, as was customary, two more aircraft were waiting for news of a sighting. The pattern for the second pair on these occasions was fundamentally differ-ent. The first pair observed the rules of the Rover. But if they made a sighting which was regarded as worth following up, the second pair were in the position of taking off on a strike at a known target. Their orders might then be to press home the attack, whatever the cloud conditions.

The two pilots waiting were Gibbs and Barry. The morning fog had dispersed under the influence of a warm late-autumn sun, and as they took off there was not more than an occa-sional wisp of cloud high out of reach in an otherwise pale blue sky. The navigation now became doubly, trebly im-portant. On a Rover, it was enough to make a landfall; you soon discovered for yourself where you were from the coast-line. But now, with the position of the convoy known, and the convoy itself alerted by Beauman's attack, their only chance of achieving any sort of surprise was to steer unerringly to the target, taking the distance across the North Sea as one long

c   49

torpedo run, drop their torpedoes in unison, and then run for home.

As they crossed the North Sea and approached the reported position of the convoy, Gibbs and Barry began to feel more and more naked. They were not used to being far from home in this sort of weather. After the earlier attack it seemed certain that there would be fighters about. Gibbs pinned his faith in the navigation. It was unlikely that short-range fighters would be actually circling the convoy. That was too wasteful of effort. What was more likely was that there would be medium-range aircraft acting as convoy escort, with a squadron of fighters alerted at the nearest airfield. At the first sight of the two Beauforts, the escorting aircraft would signal to the ground by wireless, and the fighters would take off. Everything depended on a lightning attack.

The navigation was precise, the visibility was unlimited, and the first thing they saw, before they even saw the coast-line, was a forest of masts and a haze of smoke floating above the horizon. As they swept across the convex sea, the masts were joined by funnels, and then out of the water protruded the hulls of a line of ships.

They were in the right position for an immediate attack, but the visibility was so good that the convoy almost had time to call up the fighters before the Beauforts could cross the ten miles or more of intervening water.

Gibbs counted eight merchant ships in the convoy, steaming in line ahead, and flanked to seaward by a screen of flak-ships, positioned exactly at torpedo-dropping range as far as he could judge from this distance, and directly in the path of torpedo attack. So far there was no sign that they had been seen.

The size of the convoy, the distance it covered, and the way in which it was distributed, suggested to Gibbs a departure from his original plan of attack. Approaching such a large number of ships almost beam on, from the direction of enemy territory and within a few hours of a previous attack, it was extremely unlikely that they could narrow the range much further without being detected. As yet they were still too far away for the convoy to have much chance of picking them up. He decided to turn away to starboard, holding his present distance from the convoy, and manœuvre so as to approach the leading ship from as near to dead ahead as possible. The look-out would naturally be keenest on the ship's starboard side, facing out to sea, and to approach from this side would mean that every ship in the convoy would have an equally good view. But approaching head-on, only the leading ship was likely to see them until the others were alerted.

The biggest ship in the convoy, an 8000-ton merchantman, lay fourth in line. Gibbs decided that if he could get past the first one or two ships unseen, or at least without attracting really heavy flak, he would delay his turn into the attack until just ahead of this ship. But once they were seen and the flak-ships had their range, to delay the attack might result in being shot down without having launched a torpedo; he would turn in straight away and attack the next ship in the line.

They bore down rapidly on the leading ship, flying now on an exactly reciprocal course to the convoy, about a mile further out to sea, flattened on the water. They waited breathlessly for the firing squad to open up. But so far the tactics were successful. No one had seen them.

As they passed the first ship, and then the second, tension turned to curiosity. Were the Germans asleep? Was it possible to fly up and down like this for any length of time? It was almost ludicrous. It was even slightly suspicious, ominous. Had the Germans got a plan too? Could it possibly be that they were holding their fire?

All this time they should have been under heavy fire, the heaviest fire they had ever experienced. Fighters should be on the way to intercept them. Perhaps they were. But the gunners were scanning an empty sky. They were flying down the biggest convoy they had ever seen, picking and choosing a target. It was preposterous.

Gibbs rocked the wings of his Beaufort very, very slightly, fearful of attracting attention, as though his signal to Barry might set off the scores of guns which must surely be trained on them. Then he turned in towards the 8000-ton ship. The signal was almost imperceptible and Barry missed it, carrying on down the convoy as Gibbs turned in.

Gibbs raced across the glittering sea at fifty feet towards

the target, only taking his eyes off it to shoot a glance at his instruments. 145 knots. Exactly right. Below him was the flak-ship whose bows they would cross in a moment or so. Once past that ship they would be within dropping range.

The presence of the two Beauforts burst upon the German convoy as they passed the outlying flak-ship. By this time Barry had realized that he had missed the signal and had turned in astern of the flak-ship to attack another ship lower down the line. Whatever the effect it might have on the attack itself, the immediate result of the splitting up of the two Beauforts was to divide the flak. Now it was flung up at them from all angles, a solid phalanx of fire. It was as though the convoy was clawing at them even more desperately in its fury at being taken by surprise.

Once he had dropped his torpedo, Gibbs did not allow his Beaufort to pursue an even course for a fraction of a second. He pushed the stick forward, pulled it back, banked to port, climbed to starboard, shaking every convulsion he could coax out of the straining Beaufort. The violence of his flying and the fear of the flak combined to drench him with sweat. But the physical effort helped to disperse his fear, and all the time he saw in his mind's eye the run of the torpedo towards its target. Never for one moment did he forget that, flak or no flak, the whole operation depended on and would be judged by that.

He hardly dared to look back at his prey, lest he should have failed. It was easy, when you went straight into cloud cover after an attack, to believe what you wanted to believe, that the torpedo was running well and must have struck home. But today there was no cloud cover. He would have to look.

"She's up!" The triumphant shout of the tail gunner nearly split his ear-drums. Turning quickly, he was just in time to see a column of water falling round the stern of the ship he had attacked. As he sped away on a course for home, black smoke from the explosion still enveloped the stern and rose like a burning funeral pyre to the sky.

Gibbs's aim had been only just on the mark. The torpedo struck the extreme stern of the ship. Another few feet and it would have run harmlessly by. And Barry's attack had shown no result. But on the way back Gibbs and his crew knew the zenith of elation and exhilaration. They were childishly impatient to get back and tell their story. They imagined every scene, the detailed description of how they had done it, the party that night in the Mess.

Meanwhile, Beauman and Hicks had returned from the first attack, rearmed, and taken off again for the convoy about an hour after Gibbs—much to the annoyance of the other pilots on standby, who felt that it should have been their turn this time. They were met by intense but inaccurate fire from the flak-ships, not so lethal as it looked but sufficient to put them off their aim. Both their torpedoes missed. And on the ground at North Coates, Gibbs was rushed to the operations room to make his report, while the two aircraft were refuelled and reloaded with torpedoes.

The A.O.C. Group, on the telephone, wanted to speak to the pilot who had scored the hit. There was no time for congratulations.

"Do you think the convoy's worth another strike?"

"Certainly it is."

"How about cloud cover? Is it sufficient?"

It was not in Gibbs to say no. "Yes, sir—it's . . . it's quite adequate for a quick attack."

So they went off once more, three aircraft this time, led by Gibbs. H-P, still kicking his heels on standby, was quietly furious at being left out this time. He might be forgiven for feeling that Beauman and Gibbs were hogging it a bit. A worthwhile target had been found, H-P was next on standby, he was fresh, and he thought he could get airborne before Gibbs and Barry, who had to go through de-briefing. Time was important, as it would soon be dark. But Gibbs wanted to go, and more, he felt he ought to go, he was the man to go. He knew exactly what the conditions were, he had brought off one attack successfully and he could bring off another.

It was half-past four when the three aircraft took off. They could hardly hope to reach the target in daylight. The attack would have to be made in near-darkness. Soon after take-off the three aircraft split up and proceeded independently. Gibbs had visions of getting two ships in one day. But the gathering darkness frustrated them; they failed to sight the convoy and were forced to turn for home.

By the time he got back to North Coates, Gibbs had completed eight hours' flying; eight hours which had included long periods of low flying, of nervous tension, punctuated by short periods of intense concentration, excitement and danger. Without realizing it, he was very tired. It was a night landing back at base. There was no runway—just a grass field with two rows of goose-neck flares and a chance-light. And Gibbs was still a novice as a night-flier.

He straightened on his approach, and took his hands off the throttle levers for a moment to adjust the cockpit light. The throttle levers slipped back almost at once, and both engines died away. The aircraft sank. Gibbs saw the flare-path in his windscreen tilt and rise above him. He rammed open the throttles, but it was too late. The Beaufort banged into the ground with terrible force, rebounded into the air, and then turned over and over until it struck the ground with a final blinding crash of disintegration. Gibbs's last conscious memory was of the flare-path moving across the sky above him as the aircraft cartwheeled into a Lincolnshire dyke.

Coulson picked himself up in a nearby field, dazed but unhurt. The navigator had broken both his legs. The gunner had severe concussion. Gibbs had head injuries and a broken right arm. It would be many months before he could fly again.

Next morning, Francis recovered 'Panda' from the dyke. Like the rest of the crew, it was bruised and shaken, but lived to fight another day. It was sitting forlornly on the locker beside Gibbs's hospital bed that night.

Gibbs was away from the squadron for nearly four months. Normally, when an absence of even half this length was involved, the pilot was posted away and his place filled. But Braithwaite knew his man. He knew that nothing would hearten Gibbs more in his fight to get fit again than the knowledge that his place was being kept open for him. And in any case, Braithwaite didn't want to lose him.

Two days after Gibbs's crash, on 1st October, Beauman was off again on a Rover, attacking a 5000-ton merchantman off Terschelling, and four days later he was patrolling again off the same coast, this time with Francis and H-P. Francis attacked a 3000-ton ship, but saw no result of his attack. H-P dropped at a merchant vessel off Cuxhaven, but his torpedo missed astern. On his way home he passed Wilhelmshaven, where he caught sight of a Beaufort crossing the estuary, making for the harbour. Already the shore batteries were putting up a lively barrage. H-P saw the Beaufort pressing on through the flak, low down on the water. The pilot of the Beaufort was Dick Beauman. He was never seen again.

It may be that the *Bremen* and the *Europa* had been Beauman's Lorelei. A torpedo attack on these ships in harbour was a rash, suicidal conception, but the squadron knew well enough that Beauman had been obsessed with it. He had completed over fifty operational sorties in less than six months, and his daring and adventurous spirit had taken him into and through many dangers almost comparable. The successful launching of a torpedo against one of these ships would have crowned his career. But long before he could get within striking distance he was shot down.

These were days before there were such things as operational tours, times when gongs, perhaps, were harder to win than at any stage of the war. Beauman, of all torpedo pilots, had engaged himself persistently in a chase which in later years became known as gong-hunting, without winning one.

The squadron was at first incredulous, and then bitter. Beauman had seemed indestructible; and yet they all knew he wasn't the type of pilot who survived wars. But men in other commands were being described as aces, were getting gongs, it seemed, for very much less than Beauman had done. Was there a pilot flying who had so carried the war to the enemy?

Beauman was killed four days before he was to have broadcast to the world. Braithwaite gave the talk instead. It wasn't until many months after Beauman was reported missing that news came through of a back-dated D.F.C.

And what of Beauman's crew? What were the feelings of crew-members towards pilots who exposed them to every imaginable danger?

A man like Beauman attracted men of a similar temperament into his crew. Crews felt no bitterness towards their drivers. Rather they took a pride in their idiosyncrasies. If

55

their pilot was the kind who sought rather than avoided danger, it was a matter for shooting a line rather than for disaffection. Gibbs had been surprised at the fatalistic way in which his crew had accepted their injuries that night in the dyke. For them, a crash which had been their pilot's fault had been all in a day's work.

Being crewed up with a pilot was like marriage. For better, for worse. Till death do us part.

December was a black month for the squadron. Two days after Christmas, 'Fanny' Francis was shot down by a flak-ship during an attack on a 5000-ton merchant vessel. His Beaufort dived into the water and disappeared. In four weeks, all three flight commanders had been swept away.

It was a very different squadron to which Gibbs returned in March. But it was still 22, 'Dinky-Do', the original, the leading torpedo squadron, ever jealous of its reputation and precedence. Braithwaite was still C.O. And new men were making their mark—notably Tony Gadd, one of the new flight commanders, who, like Gibbs, had spent the first year of the war at Gosport; and Ken Campbell, who was revealing something of Beauman's flair for finding and striking at ships. Jimmy Hyde was still going strong; so was Hank Sharman, a square, robust, swarthy, black-haired man who, like Hyde, had begun his tour with 22 on the early raids as a second-pilot-cum-navigator and had eventually graduated to first pilot and captain. H-P had been rested. He had completed over sixty operations, and he had been sent as an instructor to the Beaufort O.T.U. The decision to introduce a limit to the number of operations a pilot could complete before being rested had come just a month too late to save Dick Beauman.

Although Gibbs was now back on the squadron, he was not yet fit to fly on operations, and when, in April 1941, the squadron was ordered to St Eval to watch over the *Scharnhorst* and *Gneisenau*, newly arrived in Brest, Braithwaite left Gibbs behind at North Coates to supervise the maintenance and repair of aircraft, and to act as a filter to spare Braithwaite as much as possible of routine administration while he was away. The squadron remained at St Eval for five weeks, and during this time carried out one of the most suicidal, opportunist and significant torpedo operations of the war.

Chapter 3

THE MILLION-TO-ONE CHANCE

If the presence of the enemy battle-cruisers in a Biscayan port is confirmed, every effort by the Navy and the Air Force should be made to destroy them, and for this purpose serious risks and sacrifices must be made.

WINSTON CHURCHILL, 22nd March 1941

THE events of 1940 had left Hitler and Mussolini undisputed masters of Europe. Britain now stood alone, her continuing independence nothing more than a pinprick in the hide of a vast and subjugated continent. Nevertheless there was scarcely anyone in Britain who did not look forward to the time when the lost ground would be regained and when victorious British troops would set foot on German soil.

In the meantime the base had to be secured, and kept secure. Hitler's invasion plans had already foundered; now he turned to blockade.

By the spring of 1941 it was apparent that the enemy was waging the Battle of the Atlantic in deadly earnest. The war at sea had gone well enough for us at first; but with the German occupation of Norway, the Low Countries and France, and the entry of Italy into the war, the forces available for the defence of our Atlantic lifeline became wholly inadequate.

We had won the Battle of Britain, but the worst was still to come: Hitler was determined to sever our supply line with America and thus starve us out.

Against the might of the Royal Navy Hitler could set only a few surface raiders—plus the U-boats. But the resources of the Royal Navy had to be distributed throughout the world. Hitler could concentrate his raiders where he pleased.

When the war began, the biggest German capital ships in service were the so-called battle-cruisers *Scharnhorst* and *Gneisenau*. These two ships had been ordered in 1934, soon after Hitler came to power. They displaced 32,000 tons, had nine 11-inch guns, and were capable of a speed of 31 knots. There was not a single British ship which they could not

c* 57

either outrun or outgun: those that could catch them couldn't sink them and those that could sink them couldn't catch them. In 1941 the German battle-cruisers were the two most important vessels in the war.

These two ships began their career by sinking the armed merchant cruiser *Rawalpindi* in November 1939. Next, in June 1940, moving up the Norwegian coast under orders to penetrate the fjords around Narvik, they learnt that the aircraft carriers *Ark Royal* and *Glorious* were at sea. They intercepted and sank the *Glorious*. It was shortly after this incident that the *Scharnhorst* was bombed by nine Beauforts in the first Beaufort strike of the war. In the ensuing months, both ships survived a pounding by Bomber Command while docked at Kiel.

By 1941 the Germans were ready to begin the all-out Battle of the Atlantic. Already, in the last seven months of 1940, over three million tons of British, Allied and neutral shipping had been sent to the bottom. At first, in January, the Germans were hampered by the weather. But by the end of that month, the *Scharnhorst* and *Gneisenau* were about to pass through the Denmark Strait into the North Atlantic, and the *Hipper*, sheltering at Brest, was about to break out to the south.

The *Hipper* sank seven out of nineteen ships in a convoy homeward bound from West Africa. The *Scharnhorst* and *Gneisenau*, in a seven-week cruise in the North Atlantic, sank or captured 22 ships totalling 116,000 tons. The total sinkings were 400,000 tons in February and over half a million tons in March.

And the *Bismarck*, the biggest warship in the world, was ready for sea. Hitler believed that when this ship joined forces with the two battle-cruisers in the Atlantic, Britain would be starved into submission in sixty days.

This was the broad German plan. But first, the *Bismarck* had to get into the North Atlantic, and the *Scharnhorst* had to put into Brest to re-tube her boilers. This she did on 22nd March, accompanied by the *Gneisenau*.

The presence of the ships at Brest was communicated to us by the French Resistance, and R.A.F. reconnaissance planes confirmed this intelligence on 28th March.

Already, on 6th March, following the frightful shipping losses of the previous nine months, and in view of the avowed German intention of finishing the war quickly by blockade, the R.A.F. had been ordered, by special directive of the Prime Minister, to concentrate on objectives connected with the Battle of the Atlantic. When the presence of the ships at Brest was known, they thus became the primary objective of Bomber Command.

For over a week after the discovery of the ships, weather conditions hampered our bombers, but even so some 200 aircraft succeeded in delivering attacks. No hits were scored, and even one of the few bombs that did fall near the ships failed to explode. Had it exploded it might have caused superficial damage; as it was, it became the first link in a chain of events which saved Britain from starvation.

Because of the proximity of the unexploded bomb, the *Gneisenau* had to be moved out of dry dock into the harbour while a bomb-disposal team dealt with the bomb. The *Scharnhorst*, already out of dry dock and in the harbour, was tied up to the north quay, protected by a torpedo boom. There was no room there for the *Gneisenau*; and as it would only be a matter of hours before the bomb was moved or rendered harmless, it was decided to run the *Gneisenau* straight out into the harbour, where it could be moored to a buoy, and run it straight back into dry dock when the bomb was cleared.

This was on the 5th April. On the same day, a P.R.U. Spitfire photographed the harbour. This was one of the two or three decisive photographs of the war, comparable, say, with the photographs of Peenemünde and the prototype 'V' weapons.

The *Gneisenau* had left the security of dry dock and lay exposed in the inner harbour of Brest. It might be possible to attack her with torpedoes. A Beaufort strike was therefore planned for dawn next day.

The task was given to 22 Squadron. The idea was at first strongly opposed by Braithwaite, who argued, correctly enough, that such an operation had not more than one chance in a thousand of success.

Braithwaite, like any good squadron commander, looked

at things first from the point of view of his squadron. Normally, one was inclined to resist with all one's power any operational conception which meant sending one's crews on a sortie from which they had not even a sporting chance of returning. There might naturally be exceptions; but even these should offer, except in the most desperate circumstances, something like an even chance of success.

The inability of the R.A.F. to damage targets of this nature with bombs had already drawn from the Prime Minister the comment that it constituted a 'very definite failure' on the part of Bomber Command. These were days of recriminations, and the R.A.F. was suffering severe criticism for failing to develop and produce an aircraft of the dive-bomber type. This criticism was later shown to be unjustified: dive-bombers were successful enough against soft and vulnerable opposition, but against a strong and determined defence their losses were prohibitive. But at this time even Churchill was talking about the Air Ministry's 'neglect' and 'very grievous error'. Now here was a target whose destruction or containing was absolutely vital to the successful prosecution of the war. What could the R.A.F. do about it?

In his strictures Churchill had done the R.A.F. less than justice; but he had appreciated the situation correctly. Serious risks and sacrifices must be faced in an endeavour to destroy or cripple these ships: the sacrifice, for instance, of a number of torpedo-bombers and their crews.

A torpedo attack on a capital ship in harbour could have only one ending. Braithwaite—and the crews of his squadron—knew this well enough. The question was, would there be any real chance of damaging the ship?

The anti-aircraft defences at Brest had been hastily strengthened since the arrival of the two battle-cruisers. Bomber Command had already found that the harbour was one of the most heavily defended targets in Europe. What was the prospect facing a torpedo-carrying aircraft?

The inner harbour of Brest was protected by a stone mole bending round it from the west. At the furthest point the mole was less than a mile from the quayside. The *Gneisenau* was anchored at right angles to the quay, some five hundred

yards from the eastern boundary of the harbour, about equidistant from the mole and the quay. In order to aim a
torpedo, an aircraft must traverse the outer harbour and
approach the mole at an angle to the anchored ship. This
meant exposing itself to crossfire from the protective batteries
of guns clustered thickly around the two arms of land that
encircled the outer harbour. And in this outer harbour, just
outside the mole, were moored three heavily armed flak-
ships, guarding the approach to the battle-cruiser. On rising
ground behind the quay, and in dominating positions all
round the inner harbour, stood further batteries of guns. As
an aircraft approached the mole, over a thousand guns
would be trained on it, 250 of them of heavy calibre. In
addition, it would have to face the guns of the *Gneisenau* and
the *Scharnhorst*.

Nothing, it seemed, could possibly penetrate these defences.
The density of flak that could be put down by these guns
represented an impassable barrier.

But suppose an aircraft did get through. As it approached
the mole, under withering fire, the pilot would have to line
up his aircraft and aim and drop his torpedo *before he crossed
the mole*, so that the torpedo splashed into the water immediately beyond the mole and had the longest possible distance
to run to the target. The distance from the mole to the
Gneisenau was not more than 500 yards. If the torpedo were
dropped inside this range it would be too close; it would not
have time to arm itself and settle down to its running depth.
It would thus pass harmlessly under the target and fail to
explode.

Everything depended on the pilot's approach to the mole
being at roughly the right dropping angle. He would have
only a few seconds from the moment of sighting the *Gneisenau*
to the dropping of the torpedo, and there would be no room
for more than tiny adjustments of course. In those few
seconds, every gun in the harbour would be firing at him,
from behind, from abeam, from dead ahead. The chances of
living through those few seconds to take effective aim seemed
infinitesimal.

And after the drop, what then? The only hope for an
aircraft under such conditions was to stay right down on the

deck, where it might at least escape the fire of some of the bigger guns. But the physical contours of the harbour made this impossible. North of the quayside the ground rose precipitously. The pilot would be forced to pull up and climb away immediately after launching the torpedo to avoid the rising ground ahead. His aircraft would soar above the massed guns and be silhouetted against the sky like a clay pigeon.

But if the impossible happened, if the pilot approached the mole at the correct angle, and lived long enough to aim his torpedo, he had a stationary target ahead of him 250 yards long. A man with resolution, a cool head and the necessary courage could not fail to hit his target.

The forces backing the operation were too strong for a squadron commander, and Braithwaite set about putting a plan into operation and making it work. The *Gneisenau* would almost certainly be protected by torpedo nets. It would be too bitter an ending for an aircraft to succeed in its mission and then for the torpedo to be caught in a protective net. The nets must be ruptured first.

Braithwaite was on detachment at St Eval with nine of the squadron aircraft and crews. These were the only aircraft within striking distance of Brest. Three of the crews were already out on a strike when the request for an attack on the *Gneisenau* came through. Braithwaite decided to send the remaining six aircraft off for a dawn attack next day. Three aircraft would go in first and bomb the torpedo nets, and the other three would follow up with torpedoes. The aircraft carrying the bombs would fly at 500 feet, which would give them virtually no better chance of escaping. They would, however, get the advantage of whatever degree of surprise the operation could achieve. But they would stir the harbour up for those that were to follow.

The crews carrying the torpedoes were to take off first so as to be sure of being stationed outside the harbour when the bombing aircraft went in. The signal for torpedo attack would be the explosion of the bombs.

The crews chosen to carry the torpedoes were Hyde, Campbell, and a sergeant-pilot named Camp. Hyde was the most experienced pilot on the squadron; he had been awarded the D.F.C. only nine days previously. Campbell was on his twentieth operational trip. Camp, a red-headed Irishman, had been on the squadron for some months and had shown great keenness.

The operation began badly. Heavy rain swamped the airfield at St Eval. Two of the aircraft carrying bombs got bogged. In revving up their engines to pull out they only succeeded in embedding themselves more firmly. The plan of attack, such as it was, was thus upset from the start. Hyde, Campbell and Camp got off safely with their torpedoes, but of the rest only Menary was able to take off. There were no standby aircraft available.

Under normal conditions the four aircraft might have been recalled. But there was Churchill's directive. The Battle of the Atlantic was at its height and this might prove to be one of the decisive actions of the war. By tomorrow the *Gneisenau* would be back in dry dock; or both ships might be out in the Atlantic again, ready to rendezvous with the *Bismarck*. Conscious as they were of the slender hope that the four aircraft represented, the men responsible for despatching them, from the A.O.C.-in-C. downwards, knew that the R.A.F. had been called upon and that, no matter what the odds, it could not be found wanting in the will to try.

The four aircraft took off at various times between 04.30 and 05.15. But the weather that had waterlogged the airfield now upset the navigation. Menary, the only man carrying bombs, lost his way completely and eventually dropped his bombs at a ship in convoy near the Ile de Batz. It was broad daylight and he was many miles from Brest. Camp also got a long way off course and did not arrive at Brest until 07.00. He approached the harbour from the south-west as briefed, crossing the Ile de Longue at 800 feet. It had been daylight for over half an hour and he knew he had missed the rendez-vous, but he was still prepared to go in. The weather was atrocious, thick with early-morning haze and mist, but Camp felt that if he could somehow locate the docks the weather might help him to make his approach unseen. He came right down to sea-level, and almost before he realized it he found he was flying between the two arms of land encircling the outer harbour. But the outline was evanescent and he could not get a definite pinpoint. Suddenly his aircraft was boxed in by flak as he came under heavy fire from the flak-ships and shore batteries. He had little idea of his precise direction and it was pointless to go on. He pulled up in a climbing turn to the east and almost immediately found himself in cloud.

Camp was unaware that every gun in the harbour had been alerted half an hour earlier by the arrival of Campbell and Hyde.

These two pilots had reached Brest independently soon after dawn. Both had loitered outside the harbour, waiting for the bomb explosions. Neither knew that two of the bomb-carrying aircraft had failed to take off, nor did they know that the third had lost its way. Campbell, a few minutes ahead of Hyde, began a wide circuit, watching for some sign of the other aircraft. The light was seeping in under the horizon, like a chink in a curtain. It was going to be virtually a daylight attack, and that would surely multiply the already mammoth odds tenfold. Campbell had seen no explosions, but perhaps he was the last to arrive. He had better go straight in.

As Campbell set his compass to steer for the inner harbour, as yet invisible in the mist ahead, Hyde was making his landfall. Suddenly Hyde saw an aircraft flash by beneath him. He just had time to pick out an 'X' on the fuselage, the aircraft letter. He called his navigator.

"Who's in 'X'?"

"Campbell."

"It looks as though he's going in. Has anyone seen anything? Any explosions, I mean?"

"Not a thing."

"He's going in all right. I can't think why."

Hyde continued to circle outside the harbour, waiting for Campbell to come out. He had been a long time on 22 Squadron, longer than anyone. Throughout he had been that rarity, a pilot who coupled dash with steadiness and a strict regard for orders. There had been no explosions, so there could have been no bombs. The orders were to wait for the explosions. No sense in throwing away his life, his air-craft, the lives of his crew, for the sake of putting a torpedo into a torpedo net. They could always come back again later.

Meanwhile, Campbell had brought his aircraft down to 300 feet and was aiming for the right-hand end of the mole. In the outer harbour the cloud base was low and he streaked along beneath it, intermittently in cloud. Ahead of him out of the mist he picked out the flak-ships. There was the mole, a thin line on the water. If the *Gneisenau* was still anchored to the same buoy, he was perfectly placed for a stern attack.

The failure of the plan to rupture the torpedo nets, added to the fact that it was to be a lone daylight attack, meant that the original odds had multiplied themselves into something like a million to one.

Campbell began his dive down towards the east end of the mole. He could see the flak-ships clearly now. Beyond the mole, a massive shadow was resolving itself into the stern of the *Gneisenau*. He swung away to starboard and then back to port, making an angle of forty-five degrees with the *Gneisenau*. He flattened out his dive, 50 feet above the water. The flak-ships were upon him. He raced between them at mast height, unchallenged, squinting down the barrels of their guns. The mole was only 200 yards away. He looked steadfastly ahead, every nerve alert, steadied the aircraft, and aimed the nose deliberately. When the mole disappeared under the windscreen, he released the torpedo.

Aircraft and torpedo crossed the mole independently, the nose of the torpedo tilted downwards towards the water. The defences of Brest were taken by surprise. Still the Beaufort was unchallenged by anti-aircraft fire.

The *Gneisenau* towered above them like a mammoth warehouse. Campbell began to pull away to port to clear the hills behind the harbour, making for the sanctuary of cloud. In perhaps another fifteen seconds they would be safe.

But the peaceful harbour of Brest had been aroused from its lethargy. The Beaufort now had to fly through the fiercest, heaviest, most concentrated barrage that any single aircraft had ever faced or would ever face again. Nothing could live in such a wall of steel.

This was the blinding, withering fire which they had awaited and which they knew must come. Their last sight was of the flashing guns of the *Gneisenau*, lighting the hills behind the harbour, the hills over which they had watched the last dawn they would ever see.

The Beaufort, out of control, crashed into the harbour. What happened in those last moments will never be known. Stabbed by a hundred points of steel, the Beaufort kept flying when almost any other type of aircraft must have been brought down. Campbell himself may have been killed some seconds before the crash came. Scott, the navigator, a contemporary of Al Morris, Loveitt's navigator, may have tried to drag Campbell off the stick and take over. When they lifted the aircraft out of the harbour, it was said by the French Resistance that they found a blonde Canadian in the pilot's seat. Campbell and his gallant crew took the secrets of those last despairing seconds with them.

A few months earlier Scott, as one of the first Canadian aircrew to arrive in England, had been invited to an English home to tea. That home was Buckingham Palace, the hosts the Queen and the two Princesses.

Although Campbell and his crew did not live to see their torpedo run true to its mark, there is no doubt that they knew, whatever their personal fate might be, that severe damage would be done to the *Gneisenau*.

In fact, the damage done was such that had the battle-cruiser been at sea at the time of the attack it would have sunk rapidly. The Germans had to put nearly every ship in the harbour alongside to support it and pump out the water, and it was only with the greatest difficulty that they were able towards the end of the day to get the *Gneisenau* back into dry dock. Eight months later the starboard propeller shaft was still under repair.

Hitler's dream of joining the two battle-cruisers up with the *Bismarck* in the North Atlantic and causing such havoc as to end the war in sixty days, or even in a hundred and sixty days, was shattered. When the *Bismarck* came out, it had to face the Royal Navy and the Fleet Air Arm alone.

Although photographic reconnaissance suggested that the *Gneisenau* (we thought it was the *Scharnhorst* at the time) had been hit, we did not know for many months how serious the damage was. We could take nothing for granted in the war at sea, and we had to go on hitting at this ship for the next ten months. No one, anyway, could easily believe that the million-to-one chance had come off.

Campbell and his crew were buried by the Germans in the grove of honour in the cemetery at Brest. When the news of the strike eventually filtered through to London in March 1942, Campbell was posthumously awarded the Victoria Cross.

Men did not fly together unless they were temperamentally attuned. Only the bravest flew with the brave. The names of Campbell's crew were Sergeant Scott, Sergeant Mullins and Sergeant Hillman.

These men were not automatons. Fear could not be drilled or disciplined out of them. They were human beings, with all the imperfections of their fellows.

One of them Hillman, the wireless operator, had once been human enough to be late for take-off. This was how, three months earlier, he had lost his place in Hearn-Phillips's crew.

Chapter 4

TRAINING AND PSYCHOLOGY

THE 22 Squadron crews on detachment at St Eval returned to North Coates on 8th May and resumed their routine patrolling of the Dutch coast. 42 Squadron, at Leuchars, were covering the Norwegian coast and the Skagerrak. Both squadrons carried out strikes against the *Lutzow* in June, but only Loveitt of 42 was successful.

Two days after the attack on the *Lutzow*, Gibbs hit a 6000-ton merchantman off Texel. He had been patrolling the shipping lane with two other aircraft when, taking his eyes off the Texel coastline to glance seawards, he jumped with astonishment at the sight of a large convoy almost under his wing-tip on the port side. Gibbs turned in at once to attack the leading ship, while Camp and White, in the other two aircraft, picked their own targets. Approaching from landwards, they were either not seen or taken for friendly aircraft. Once again Gibbs was able to get within torpedo range without being fired at; and even when the flak came it was desultory, as though the gunners were not convinced that it was a genuine attack. Gibbs was thus able to aim his torpedo from much closer range than was possible under determined fire.

It was only a matter of seconds from the sighting of the target to the dropping of the torpedo, and the result of the attack was a hit full amidships, fair and square. Gibbs was thus confirmed in his view that the secret of success in torpedo work was to drop from close range. But only if surprise were achieved could one reach the ideal dropping position without being shot down or having one's aim spoiled by the keenness of the barrage.

Camp, the Irishman who had flown into the harbour at Brest after Ken Campbell, was shot down in this attack—the only aircraft to be lost when Gibbs was leading an attack throughout his first tour.

Towards the end of June, the squadron moved to Thorney

68

Island. The daylight Rover off the Dutch islands had been becoming increasingly expensive. It had been one of the most fruitful ways of embarrassing the enemy, consistently delaying his shipping, but the Germans had learnt their lesson, and the protection they were according their convoys threatened to make attacks in daylight prohibitive. 22 Squadron were to carry out operations in the Channel against specific targets, supported by fighters, while a new Beaufort squadron—86—took over the patrolling of the Dutch islands, operating mostly at night. It was the end of an era. Torpedo attacks still took place from the new base, but the presence of shipping on the French coast was rare, and on the few occasions when the squadron did have a chance to strike, results were depressing.

The change in operating conditions, the absence of the atmosphere of 'seek out and strike', the diminishing number of attacks, inevitably had their effect on the squadron's character. Pilots were less dashing, less individualistic. A notable exception was a young Australian who arrived on the squadron with four other pilots in June—Johnny Lander. He quickly proved himself an able and determined pilot, a little inclined to rashness, in direct line of succession to Dick Beauman and Ken Campbell. He was the only one of the four new pilots to survive the summer.

There were many failures during that summer, some under favourable conditions, and the squadron crews could not fail to notice that the R.A.F. were placing increasing reliance on the bomb as an anti-shipping weapon, losing faith in the torpedo, which was expensive to produce, restricted in application, and required long and specialized training for successful use. Blenheims of No. 2 Group were carrying out shipping strikes, and they continued to do so almost until the end of the year, when severe losses forced Bomber Command to call off these attacks. But bombing was successfully continued by Hudsons operating at night. A fourth Beaufort squadron—No. 217—was formed, but except against really big targets the torpedo was out of favour.

One man, at least, retained his faith in the torpedo—Pat Gibbs. He successfully completed his tour, and left 22 Squadron in September 1941 for the torpedo training unit. Lucky as he had been to survive, he still hankered after squadron life, still itched for the chance to prove that the torpedo could succeed. There were rumours that Beaufort squadrons were to operate in the Mediterranean, and Gibbs did not need to study a map to know that this narrow land-locked sea, across which all the supplies for Rommel's Afrika Korps must be ferried, might have been made for the aerial torpedo.

Nervously exhausted by his twelve months on 22 Squadron, Gibbs found the strict, confined routine of a training unit a further irritant. He was a squadron leader now; and his mind was set firmly on commanding his own Beaufort squadron. His chance was to come.

The first Beauforts had been delivered direct to the operational squadrons and the pilots had carried out their conversion courses at their squadron airfields. Some of them had spent a week or so at the Bristol Aircraft Company's factory at Filton, learning how to handle the new machine. But by the end of 1940 the production of Beauforts was sufficient to allow the opening, at Chivenor near Barnstaple in Devon, of a Beaufort operational training unit. Here new crews were formed, trained and welded together as a team. From the O.T.U. they were posted to a torpedo training unit at Abbotsinch, near Glasgow; and then, having completed their training, they were posted to one of the Beaufort squadrons.

When the aircrews arrived at Chivenor, they were already trained flying men. Pilots not only had their wings but had learnt how to fly twin-engined aircraft. Navigators and wireless operator/air gunners had won their wings more recently; most of the wop/A.G.s, in fact, came straight from gunnery school, where the half-wing of the A.G. had only just been pinned on their tunics.

Already the process of selection, of the survival of the fittest, had operated at many stages in their careers, from the first aircrew interview and medical, through the early courses, exercises, tests and examinations, numbers falling at each hurdle, until at last the final course was safely passed and the coveted wings proudly sewn into place. The unending process of selection had operated again as the men were

posted, some to one Command, some to another. This sometimes seemed a haphazard process, and indeed it was often
a case of which Command needed the men and which
operational training unit had vacancies. But, wherever possible, the natural abilities and qualities of the men were
considered. The crews in Coastal Command would have to
face long hours of uneventful flying over featureless sea, with,
perhaps, a vital rendezvous or target at the end of the outward flight. Navigators must therefore be highly skilled,
capable of navigating the aircraft entirely by dead-reckoning,
without pinpoints for many hours; thus many of the navigators who emerged from their training with high ratings
were posted to Coastal Command. Wireless operators, too,
had to be capable of making contact with urgent messages
after long periods of radio silence. Pilots were chosen, perhaps,
for their reliability, their pertinacity, their durability, rather
than for flying brilliance.

These men, products of various training schools dotted all
over the country, converged on Chivenor in the last day or so
before the start of a new course, running into each other in
the train towards the end of the journey.

"Not going to Chivenor, I suppose?"

"Yes!"

The pilots, perhaps, were not unduly concerned about the
composition of their crew. Most of them gave the matter
very little thought indeed. Sometime in the next two months,
they supposed, they would manage to pick up a crew. They
were modest about their flying, could not understand any
man being prepared to trust himself to another in the air, and
did not feel the self-confidence to ask anyone to join their
crew. Most of them, perhaps, had a vague feeling that they
were going to need a good navigator. The navigators, for
their part, mixed easily with the pilots, friendships were soon
struck up, and the way was open for some outside force to
throw two men together.

This force invariably came from the wop/A.G.s. These men
were generally of a lower educational standard and mental
age than the pilot or navigator; they lacked the schooling or
the capacity for study which they would need to pass out as
pilots or navigators. Some of them, of course, were older

71

men, beyond the age-limit for training as pilots. Others had tried hard to attain pilot status, and failed through various shortcomings of temperament or physique. Some, even, had accepted immediate training as wop/A.G.s rather than wait many months for a pilot's course; these had been afraid that the war might be over before they could get into the fight. But for most, the role of wop/A.G. was a wonderful opportunity for fit, keen men of lesser academic achievement to get into the air war.

But although he was content to entrust his life to others, and to play a subordinate role—even to call himself a passenger, which he often was—the wop/A.G., because of the diverse elements of the nation's life from which he was drawn, was endowed with his full share of shrewdness and native wit. He wanted to join the 'Raf', as he called it; he wanted to fly. He was attracted by the glamour of flying, he was fascinated by the spell cast by the R.A.F. wings. When he had those, he would be on top of the world. Of course, he would only have a half-wing. But half a wing was a good deal better than no wing at all. Some said it was better.

He was not deterred by the stories of the carnage done to 'ass-end charlies', as the gunners were known. On the contrary, he revelled in them. He came, mostly, from the big cities, and he often had a score to settle. But . . . he wanted to survive. And he had discovered pretty quickly that there were good aircraft and bad aircraft, and good pilots and bad pilots to go with them.

So instead of the pilot choosing himself a navigator, and then looking for a couple of likely gunners, it was the gunners who chose the crew. More gregarious, perhaps, than the pilot/navigator, they had already struck up strong friendships. When we get to O.T.U., two gunners would say, let's try and stick together. Such men had often been in step, on the same courses, comparing results, hopes and fears, right through their service. Now they looked around for a driver.

They knew pretty well what they were looking for. Most of them wanted steadiness; the appearance of sound, cautious endeavour. They had set out to do a job, and they meant to go through with it, to the end if need be, but for the moment they were less concerned with heroics than with survival.

They all looked for assurance, complete self-sufficiency. The less disciplined might seek out the irresponsible. But differences in character might be so extreme as to be almost grotesque; what mattered most was harmony of temperament. All, without knowing it, looked at a man for the spark of immortality. There were men with whom the thought of death was hard to reconcile. They chose the men with whom they would care to live, but with whom, if it came to it, they felt they might not be afraid to die.

So, almost without realizing it, the pilots and navigators found themselves part of a crew. The pilot, whatever his age, or social or intellectual accomplishment, became the acknowledged leader, and this acted at once as a stimulus to his morale. A leader was wanted, and leadership was born.

The responsibility they bore for others made the pilots extroverts. They might experience nervous tensions, but to display them was fatal. The slightest attack of nerves in a pilot transmitted a thousand harmonics down the fuselage. Lack of moral fibre in a crew often had a tensed pilot at its centre of gravity. A nervous pilot meant a neurotic crew.

Again, all crew-members were aware of this without knowing it in so many words. They were all prepared to do their duty, but that little bit extra that won medals was generally inspired by the pilot. They all dreamt of the purple-and-white medal ribbon beneath the half-wing—most of them had thoughtfully left room for it—but few were sorry when a sticky trip was scrubbed or a pilot turned back.

As a result, although all men in a crew shared the same dangers and experience, there was very little bitterness at the way the pilots had of getting most of the gongs.

This was the pattern of crew relationship to which the men settled down at Chivenor. There were daily classroom lectures, navigational exercises, morse practice, in the air and on the ground. The pilots converted on to Beauforts. Then men flew together as a crew for the first time. Cross-country flights, day and night flying, and everyone learning something all the time, about their jobs, about each other, about themselves. The Beaufort remained a difficult aircraft to master, pilots and navigators were inexperienced, and flying was dangerous. The loss of crews at Chivenor in the summer

73

of 1941 was as bad as and sometimes worse than on a squadron.

That was the word that recurred in every conversation, that stood as the ultimate goal for all these men: the squadron. It was a magic name, and conjured up a seemingly unattainable picture of equality with fully-fledged fliers, of freedom from the taint of trainee. No one feared to go on ops. Not at this stage. All dangers and difficulties would somehow be resolved on a squadron.

When they passed out at Chivenor, the crews went on to Abbotsinch, where they learned for the first time the technique of dropping the torpedo.

First they learned the mechanics of the torpedo itself. It was a self-propelled weapon, driven by an engine which operated two propellers in the tail. These propellers revolved in opposite directions, keeping the torpedo horizontal. Steering was by means of horizontal and vertical rudders in the tail, controlled respectively by a depth gear and gyroscope. There were six main compartments of the torpedo. First was the warhead, which contained the expolsive charge. Second was the pistol, which fired the charge. The pistol could be either contact or duplex. The contact pistol was the type most used. It was not, however, set so as to explode immediately on impact with any object, otherwise it would have exploded on hitting the water. The torpedo had to run some distance before the pistol became fully armed and cocked. But once it was armed it would explode on impact provided the speed of the torpedo relative to the target was greater than six knots, and provided the striking angle, the angle between the torpedo and the target, was greater than eleven degrees. The other type of head, the duplex, was potentially more damaging as it exploded right underneath the target.

Next came the air vessel, which acted as a storage chamber for the compressed air used in driving the engine. The balance chamber, aft of the air vessel, contained depth gear which combined to bring the torpedo out of its initial plunge and to keep it running afterwards at a pre-set depth, which could be varied according to the draught of the ship to be attacked. The balance chamber also contained the fuel bottle which supplied fuel to the engine.

The engine was a semi-Diesel type with variable-speed setting, generally set to drive the torpedo at 40 knots. It would maintain this speed for some 2000 yards, after which, if there had been no impact, it lost way and finally sank. Behind the engine room was the buoyancy chamber, so called because it kept the rear end of the torpedo buoyant in the same way as the balance chamber and the air vessel kept the front end buoyant. This chamber contained the gyro which steered the torpedo, and through it ran the driving shaft from the engine to the propellers. Finally came the tail. When fitted to an aircraft, a wooden device known as an air tail was attached to the end of the torpedo tail, to control the torpedo during its flight in the air before hitting the water, at which stage it detached itself from the torpedo.

At Abbotsinch a brief explanation of the mechanics of the torpedo was followed by a series of lectures and demonstrations on the art of dropping it. Here the vital factors were height and speed, so that the torpedo made a good entry into the water, neither ricocheting along the surface due to being dropped too low or at too great a speed, nor diving to the bottom through being dropped too high or at too slow a speed; correct sighting; and keeping the aircraft steady just before and just after the drop.

If the torpedo entered the water badly, it swerved or set off at an angle. But even after a good drop, the torpedo oscillated in depth following its plunge for some distance before it settled down to its depth setting. It took some 300 yards for the torpedo to settle down. This was called the recovery range, and within this distance the pistol would arm itself. To this had to be added the distance between the actual drop and the point of entry into the water, making a safe range for a drop of not less than five hundred yards. This was the difficulty in Campbell's attack on the *Gneisenau*.

Range was particularly difficult to judge over water, but the tendency was to drop out of range rather than too close. As the ship began to bulge at the pilot when the range closed to less than a mile, experience told him to hold on a bit longer as he could not possibly be as close as he seemed. But as the ship filled his screen, the thought that he might get in too close if he didn't drop soon was in every pilot's mind. And if

75

he was undecided, accurate flak was always liable to make up his mind for him. There is only one recorded operational instance of a pilot dropping too close.

The next problem was sighting. Several torpedo sights were tried, but so many factors had to be estimated by the pilot that most of them preferred to ignore the sight and aim off according to their knowledge of the speed of the ship, the speed of the torpedo, the angle at which they were attacking, and the range. But experience showed that few pilots were capable of estimating the aiming-off angle accurately, and they were continually urged to use the sight. This sight assumed a range of 1000 yards (which the pilot, of course, had to estimate), and a uniform angle on the bow for all attacks (again the pilot had to use his judgment to get into the recommended position). For sighting the target, the pilot set the ship's speed on the sight (having first estimated it). The sight was calibrated to give the correct aiming-off point if the speed of the ship had been estimated correctly—and, of course, if all the other measurements and angles had been correctly judged. But even this rule-of-thumb method was upset if the ship took avoiding action, as it invariably did. Small wonder that pilots tended to rely on aiming instinctively.

But at Abbotsinch, every effort was made to give pilots confidence in their ability to estimate all these factors accurately. Dummy attacks, and real attacks with dummy torpedoes, were carried out daily on a small merchant vessel off the Ayrshire coast. And on board this vessel, photographic and measuring equipment was fitted which, after the attack, told the pilot the accuracy he had achieved in his attack. All the figures which could only be guessed in the air were now revealed. The ship's speed was known. The pilot knew his own speed from his instruments. Height and range were measured from the ship. So were the angle on the bow, the actual angle of aiming off, whether the aircraft had been straight and level for the drop, and most fascinating of all, whether the torpedo had hit or missed, where it had hit, how much it had missed by.

Many of the instructors at Abbotsinch were men who had already completed an operational tour. Braithwaite com-

76

manded the unit when he left 22 Squadron. Hank Sharman was one of the instructors. The chief instructor, Flight Lieutenant Gaine, had taken part in the record-breaking long-distance flight from Cairo to Australia in a Wellesley in 1938. He taught pilots how to drop torpedoes for nearly two years. He himself had not undertaken an operational tour. Some of the instructors taught their pupils to practise violent evasive action before and after the drop. Gaine concentrated on the perfect launching, keeping the aircraft straight and level all though, attempting nothing spectacular, not even breaking away after the drop. He was inevitably dubbed 'Larry' Gaine, after the coloured Canadian boxer, and this in turn was as inevitably corrupted to 'Larry Gains'. His quiet, unassuming manner, his air of detachment, almost of mental isolation, made him a well-loved if somewhat aloof figure. He wasn't one of the boys, he was a regular, he was older than most of the pupils, he very definitely wasn't an operational type.

What would happen to him if he carried out one of his copybook attacks against a shooting target? He wouldn't last one trip.

Later, at Malta, he was to show them.

Abbotsinch gave Beaufort crews their first taste of the thrill of low-flying over the sea towards a moving target. It was a sight that never failed to stimulate them. Even crews nearing the end of their tour, living on their nerves, responded to its intoxication. The course also continued the story of tragic accidents which began for most at Chivenor. Pilots had to be conditioned to being at home near the water. But height was as hard to judge as distance, and even dummy torpedo attacks took their toll.

Chapter 5

THE UNIQUE OPPORTUNITY

It is considered unlikely that the enemy would attempt the passage of the Straits in daylight. If, however, this should be attempted, a unique opportunity will be offered to both our surface vessels and air striking force. . . .

Air Ministry Appreciation, April 1941

THE climax of the work of the Beaufort torpedo-bombers based in the United Kingdom was the afternoon of 12th February 1942, when the battle-cruisers *Scharnhorst* and *Gneisenau*, together with the cruiser *Prinz Eugen* and a tremendous gaggle of supporting craft, having slipped out of Brest the previous night, attempted to force the passage of the English Channel.

This was an operation the possibility of which did not occur to Hitler until late in 1941, which even then was regarded by Admiral Raeder, C.-in-C. German Naval Forces, as not feasible, but which the British Admiralty and Air Ministry had regarded as the only likely outcome of the situation ever since the ships had docked in Brest.

"The naval force at Brest has, above all," said Hitler, at a conference with his naval chiefs, "the welcome effect of tying up enemy forces and of diverting them from making attacks on the German homeland." Hitler was right. Three-quarters of the entire weight of bombs dropped by aircraft of Bomber Command in 1941 fell on Brest.

"This advantage," continued Hitler, "will last exactly as long as the enemy considers himself compelled to attack because these ships are undamaged.

"The whole German Fleet is now needed in Norway, where the Russians may start an offensive and where the British are preparing to attempt an invasion." The British, reeling under the Japanese onslaught in Malaya and suffering severe setbacks in the Middle East, were still thinking in terms of being invaded themselves.

"The *Scharnhorst* and *Gneisenau* cannot be further exposed to chance hits in Brest. Their return through the Channel is therefore desirable."

Hitler's pronouncement was a typical medley of shrewdness and fantasy, and his naval chiefs remained unconvinced.

"Impossible," said Admiral Raeder. "The risk is tremendous."

Hitler brushed all opposition aside. "The return of the ships through the Channel is desirable. We shall rely on achieving complete surprise, moving the ships in bad weather and at night, when the R.A.F. cannot observe us. The British are incapable of reacting quickly. By the time they are ready to go into action the ships will be safely through the Straits of Dover."

As far back as 29th April 1941, a plan, known as Operation 'Fuller', had been concerted between the Admiralty and the Air Ministry. This plan was the natural outcome of the Admiralty's assumption that the German ships, when they put to sea, would do all they could to avoid contact with units of the Home Fleet or with the naval force at Gibraltar. Hazardous as the passage of the Channel might seem, it made certain of avoiding British capital ships; for the enemy's occupation of the whole Continental seaboard from Norway to Spain made intervention by British capital ships in this area impracticable. The enemy, too, would be threatened by shore-based aircraft, though over a much smaller area. It was therefore thought probable that the ships would seek to pass through the narrows at Dover, where they would be most vulnerable, under cover of darkness.

Operation 'Fuller' provided for close day and night air reconnaissance off Brest and up Channel to check the movements of the enemy ships. It also provided, in the event of the passage being attempted, for co-ordinated attacks by all the available aircraft in all five operational bomber groups, for attacks by all available torpedo and bomber aircraft of Coastal Command, and for fighter protection from Cherbourg to south of Walcheren by aircraft of three fighter Groups. Most of these attacks were to be made in daylight; no attacks were to be carried out by bomber aircraft at night. Assuming that the enemy ships passed through the Straits at night, the bomber attacks would be made at the nearest point to the Straits which the ships must traverse in daylight. Passing through the Straits at night, the ships would be met by torpedo attacks by light surface forces and Swordfish aircraft of the Fleet Air Arm, and by Coastal Command Beauforts, for whom the target would be illuminated by flares dropped by reconnaissance aircraft.

If the enemy attempted the passage of the Straits in daylight, attacks were to be delivered with the maximum possible number of aircraft while the ships were in the Straits. But it was considered unlikely that any such attempt would be made.

The original plan for Operation 'Fuller' was stimulated by circumstantial evidence that the German ships might attempt to pass up the Channel between 30th April and 4th May 1941. But it was a false alarm. We did not then know how successful Campbell's sacrifice had been.

On 4th June 1941 the two battle-cruisers were joined at Brest by the cruiser *Prinz Eugen*, which had been in company with the *Bismarck* at the sinking of the *Hood*, but had escaped the *Bismarck's* subsequent fate. Heavy Bomber Command raids continued.

The actual break-out of the ships was meticulously planned. The crux of the plan lay at the beginning. The ships were to leave Brest after dark. The Germans believed that by leaving Brest in darkness they would be secure from discovery. Their plans did not take into account the British use of airborne radar.

The Germans went to fantastic lengths to keep even a suspicion of their purpose from filtering through, even to the men who were to take part. Only the captains of the three ships and a handful of staff officers knew the true plan. A spurious plan was circulated according to which the ships were to leave Brest after sunset on 11th February, carry out exercises between La Pallice and St Nazaire during the 12th, and then return to Brest. Everything was done to support the fiction that the ships were to return. Not a detail was forgotten. High ranking officers in the know left their small kit in their private houses ashore. Reinicke, Chief of Staff to Admiral Ciliax, Commander of German Naval Forces in Brest, had to borrow shirts, collars and underwear for the next seven weeks.

The British watched the situation grimly. In spite of the German belief that the operation could not succeed if their enemies got wind of it, the British were certain, as certain as anyone who does not himself command the initiating action can be, that the ships were about to break out. Intelligence reports indicated that repairs to the ships had been almost completed. It was known that exercises had been carried out by all three ships in the open water. On 25th January they were all photographed in the harbour. Reconnaissance showed the number of supporting craft at Brest to be increasing. Strong flotillas of E-Boats were concentrated in various Channel ports. There were reports of unusual activity at occupied airfields in France. The *Tirpitz* was moved from Kiel to Trondheim—possibly as a diversion. The Admiralty were convinced that a break-out was imminent: everything pointed to an attempt being made in the next no-moon period. On 2nd February, the Admiralty issued an appreciation on the probable departure of the ships. It began guardedly, but gained in confidence as it proceeded. "The Brest ships cannot be fully efficient yet," it said. "Although they have led a charmed life the Germans must be anxious to get them away to a safer harbour."

After a general survey of the tactical situation and of the possible routes of escape, the writer of the appreciation came to the point.

"The short-cut for the German ships is via the English Channel. It is 240 miles from Brest to Cherbourg, and another 120 miles from Cherbourg to the Dover Straits. Whilst ships could make the passage from Brest to Cherbourg, or from Cherbourg to the Dover Straits, in the same dark period, they could not make the complete passage from Brest to the Dover Straits in one dark period.

"They are aware of our mining activities in the Dover Straits, and they recently lost a destroyer there. It is therefore highly probable that they would time their passage through the Straits for about high water.

"At first sight this passage up the Channel appears hazardous for the Germans. It is probable, however, that, as their heavy ships are not fully efficient, they would prefer such passage, relying for security on their destroyers and aircraft, which are efficient, and knowing full well that we have no heavy ships with which to oppose them in the Channel. We might well, therefore, find the two battle-cruisers and the 8-inch cruiser with five large and five small destroyers, also, say, 20 fighters constantly overhead (with reinforcements within call), proceeding up the Channel. . . .

"Our bombers have shown that we cannot place much reliance on them to damage the enemy, whilst our Coastal Command T/B aircraft will not muster more than 9.

"Taking all factors into consideration, it appears that the German ships can pass east up the Channel with much less risk than they will incur if they attempt an ocean passage to Norway, and as it is considered the Germans will evade danger until they are fully worked up, the Channel passage appears to be their most probable direction if and when they leave Brest."

Admirable in almost all respects (it appears to do less than justice to the work of Bomber Command over many months, though it cannot be denied that the damage inflicted was mainly superficial and at enormous cost; and there were some 40 Beauforts, not 9) this appreciation forecast the details of the so-called 'Channel Dash' with astounding accuracy. But although it made no specific mention of it, it was coloured by the assumption that the idea in the German naval mind must be to pass through the Dover Straits in darkness.

The executive order for Operation 'Fuller' was made next day. The Admiralty's dispositions were already made, and they ordered their striking forces to deal with a break up Channel. The only units available were six destroyers and six motor torpedo-boats. Six Fleet Air Arm Swordfish, under Lt.-Comdr. Eugene Esmonde, who a few months earlier had led the first torpedo attack on the *Bismarck* and who had subsequently survived the torpedoing of the *Ark Royal* in the Mediterranean, were moved from Lee-on-Solent to Manston, in Kent, on the 4th. All available aircraft in Bomber Command were bombed up and brought to four hours' notice. And there were three squadrons of Beauforts: Numbers 42, 86, and 217. The redoubtable 22 were mostly on embarkation leave, waiting to go to the Far East; the ground crews were already aboard the troopship at Liverpool. A war on the other side of the world that they were never to drop a torpedo in was to cheat the fabulous 22 of their rightful prey.

For a variety of reasons the Beauforts were not concentrated in one place. 42 Squadron was at Leuchars; a detachment had been stationed at St Eval in December and January, but had been sent back to Leuchars when the *Tirpitz* moved from Kiel to Trondheim on 22nd January. The squadron had fourteen aircraft available. 217 Squadron, which had been engaged on special night torpedo operations in the Channel, had seven aircraft at Thorney Island, near Portsmouth. 86 Squadron, the third Beaufort squadron, only recently operational, and with a high percentage of inexperienced crews, was stationed at St Eval, together with a small detachment of 217, again mostly new crews. Also at St Eval was a small holding unit for the scattered 22. Commanding this unit was Johnny Lander. The 22 Squadron aircraft were already undergoing modification for tropical conditions at Filton, and were thus not available. The number of serviceable Beauforts at St Eval was thirteen.

On 8th February, photographs of Brest taken by our reconnaissance aircraft showed the *Prinz Eugen* and the *Scharnhorst* in the harbour and the *Gneisenau* moored at Lanveoc. The photographs also revealed the presence of four large destroyers and a number of small torpedo-boats and minesweepers. Meteorological and navigational information confirmed that as from 10th February the general conditions in the Channel would be reasonably favourable for an attempted break-through in darkness. On the 15th there would be no moon and the tidal conditions at Dover would favour a passage between 04.00 and 06.00 hours. The photographs, and the meteorological and navigational data, together with the mass of evidence already available, convinced Air Chief Marshal Joubert, C.-in-C. of Coastal Command, that there was a very strong indication that a break-out up Channel was likely to be put into execution at any time after Tuesday, 10th February.

Joubert issued an appreciation on 8th February, addressed to the C.-in-C.s of Bomber and Fighter Commands, outlining the background to his convictions and describing the action he was prescribing for his own forces. A routine patrol which had been carried out regularly for the past seven months was being maintained from dusk to dawn at the entrance to Brest harbour. Two other routine patrols, one between Ushant and I. Bréhat and the other between Le Havre and the Somme estuary, were also being maintained in the hours of darkness. Night anti-submarine sweeps of the Bay covered the probable line of exit of the ships and thus backed up the patrols. The Beauforts at St Eval and Thorney Island were to be responsible for night operations in the Channel. The Beauforts at Leuchars were to be held back for a daylight strike in the North Sea in case the night attacks in the Channel failed. The plan was to be co-ordinated with the operations of Fighter and Bomber Commands and the attacks of the Swordfish.

On 9th February Joubert stopped all leave for Beaufort crews, and recalled from embarkation leave six experienced crews of 22 Squadron. This might have been an appropriate moment to warn all aircrews of the threatened operation. But, presumably for security reasons, this course was not taken.

On 10th February, with the courage of his convictions, Joubert took the risk of ordering the Beauforts at Leuchars to fly south to North Coates. They would no longer be in a position to watch over the *Tirpitz*, but they would be able to strike a much earlier blow if the Brest ships came through the Channel. Joubert was putting all his eggs in one basket. But North Coates was snowbound, and the physical move of the Leuchars squadron was delayed.

In Bomber Command, all available aircraft had been ordered to stand by day by day as a striking force for the operation. The result was that all training and operational work, other than raids on Brest, had come to a complete standstill. Such conditions could not be imposed on the Command indefinitely, and from 10th February 100 aircraft were kept at two hours' readiness, the remainder nevertheless being available at short notice. Bomber Command, of course, expected to be given reasonable warning of the approach of the ships and the time of attack.

Meanwhile, the final German plans for the attempt had been laid. Adolf Galland, the German fighter ace, was in charge of the air defences for the operation. He had at call a total of some 280 aircraft, mostly Me 109s and F.W. 190s, with about thirty Me 110s. The majority of these aircraft were based at airfields around Le Touquet, but there were smaller concentrations near Caen and Amsterdam. Fighters from the Le Touquet area returning from action after three o'clock in the afternoon were to carry on to the Amsterdam sector, where they were to land and refuel and return as soon as possible to the ships. Over the whole route there would be a minimum of sixteen and a maximum of thirty-two fighters providing the air umbrella, but these figures could be considerably stepped up in the Straits. The myth of an east to west convoy was circulated and the German pilots were kept in ignorance of what was afoot.

The German weather forecast for 12th February indicated that the weather in the Channel would deteriorate rapidly during the morning. All was ready for what the Germans called Operation 'Thunderbolt/Cerberus'.

Immediately darkness fell on 11th February, seven destroyers formed up at the entrance to Brest harbour to escort the ships, and promptly at 20.00 hours the *Scharnhorst*, *Gneisenau* and *Prinz Eugen* left their berths and began to make their way out of the harbour. But as the ships moved off, there was an air-raid warning. Like naughty children caught out of bed, the ships hastily put about and returned to their berths. By the time the twelve Wellingtons and eight Stirlings of Bomber Command were overhead, the bedroom was quiet and the ships apparently tucked in for the night.

The Wellingtons and Stirlings dropped their bombs, without damaging the ships, and their crews naturally reported no change at Brest when they got back. But as soon as their backs were turned the harbour sprang to life again, and the ships, now behind schedule, eventually formed up outside Brest at 22.45. Had the Bomber Command raid been half an hour later the alarm might have been raised.

The German plan to achieve surprise by slipping out of Brest under cover of darkness had not taken into account the extensive patrol system undertaken by Coastal Command. As the convoy formed up outside Brest, a Hudson was flying the 'Stopper' patrol, the stopper in the bottleneck that formed the entrance to Brest harbour. This patrol was maintained continuously throughout the night by four aircraft in relays, one at a time. The night was intensely black, but the Hudson was fitted with A.S.V.[1]

Unfortunately, this Hudson had already flown to the south-east extremity of its patrol, and was now covering the south-west. It did not detect the German ships. It was not until the relieving Hudson was nearing the end of its patrol that either aircraft came within A.S.V. range of the ships. An examination of the recorded tracks of the second Hudson and of the ships reveals that this aircraft passed within nine miles of the German squadron. Unaccountably, no A.S.V. contact was made.

The German ships, like the genii, had escaped from the bottle. But they still had to traverse the area covered by the Ushant-to-the-Channel-Isles patrol. Here again, the aircraft carrying out the patrol met with misfortune, in the shape of the breakdown of its radar. The aircraft returned to base. No relief was sent, partly because of a shortage of aircraft, partly because, since 'Stopper' had reported nothing, it was held that the ships must now be well south of the patrol line if they had sailed, in which case they would be picked up by the third and last patrol opposite the Sussex coast.

But again there was misfortune. This aircraft was recalled because of a threat of fog at its base. Had it continued its patrol until first light, as was usual, it might well have detected the German vessels.

The daylight patrols were flown by aircraft of Fighter Command, but they went no further south than the mouth of the Somme. Thus for nearly twelve hours the German squadron continued its progress up the English Channel, miraculously undetected; twelve hours during which the Beaufort crews slept, and, when morning came, went about their workaday tasks. One of the crews at St Eval took off on a routine sweep of the Bay, many miles away from the German ships, which had passed due south of St Eval soon after midnight. Other aircraft at St Eval were carrying out a training programme. At Leuchars, three crews were waiting to

[1] Air to Surface vessel—radar equipment carried in aircraft to detect the presence of shipping at a distance.

fly a routine patrol, standby strike aircraft and crews were at readiness, and a training schedule was pinned up in the crew room. At Thorney Island, only four of the seven aircraft were loaded with torpedoes; the others were fitted with bombs.

The Beaufort crews, aware as they might be, from the cancellation of leave, of a certain mounting tension, had still not been told of the significance of the hour. These men had been subjected to continual nervous strain for many weeks. The presence of the three capital ships at Brest, and of the *Tirpitz* at Trondheim, cast a long shadow. In every man's mind was the thought, the fear, that a similar operation might be ordered to that in which Campbell had died so gloriously. They knew, too, that if the ships came out they would be the spearhead. But they had only a vague, phantasmal idea of what might be required of them. The absence of 22 Squadron not only deprived the torpedo force of its *corps d'élite*, but it affected all the other torpedo squadrons in that the inadequacy of the force for the task required of it made systematic training impossible.

Scattered and inexperienced as the torpedo force inevitably was through the uncertainty of enemy action and the demands of overseas theatres, the remaining crews, through being kept in ignorance of the portents, were denied the much-needed stimulus of a known operation.

The crews of 42 Squadron at Leuchars were aware, without having been specifically told, that there was a plan afoot for the squadron to move to North Coates. But they paid no more attention to this rumour than to many another. On the evening of 11th February they were issued with Arctic clothing, which news-hungry men at once interpreted as presaging a move to Iceland, or worse. Then, early on the morning of the 12th, all the air crews were called to the operations room, where they were told that they were to fly south that morning. North Coates was still snowbound, and Joubert had decided to move the squadron to a conveniently situated airfield in Norfolk.

The C.O. of the squadron, Wing Commander M. F. D. Williams, had only just taken over his command; he had not had time to settle in, choose a crew, or get to know his men.

Thus at a vital time the squadron commander was without a crew of his own. He decided to fly south with the man who had been acting as C.O. for the previous three weeks, Squadron Leader W. H. Cliff, the senior flight commander, and choose himself a crew later. Cliff had been in charge of the detachment at St Eval. He had been with No. 36 torpedo-bomber squadron in Singapore up to the previous summer, when he had been invalided home with the ubiquitous tropical skin disease, prickly heat. A few months after he left them, his squadron was wiped out in its first engagement. In the tense atmosphere of expectancy on 42 Squadron he was out of the fire for the moment, but still well in the frying-pan.[1]

The orders were to get all the serviceable aircraft together and fly them down to Coltishall in Norfolk. The crews were mystified by the change in destination, but the instructions were clear enough and their mood changed at once from querulous apathy to animation.

"Coltishall!"

"That's a fighter airfield!"

"What's up with North Coates?"

The whispering stopped as the station commander continued the briefing: "Those are the orders. You can't go in to North Coates because it's snowbound."

"What about our torpedoes, sir?" put in Cliff. "There's no torpedo servicing unit at Coltishall."

"That's being sent down from North Coates by road. It'll be there by the time you land. It's only a short detachment, probably not more than a day or so, so all you'll want is your small kit. Collect your maps and weather forecasts and get away as soon as you can."

"Can you tell us what we're going there for, sir?" This from the two Australian pilots, Birchley and Archer.

"Sorry. That's all the information I've got. Off you go."

A quick check revealed that there were fourteen serviceable aircraft, of which eleven were fitted with torpedoes. There were no spare torpedoes at Leuchars, so the remainder would have to be armed up by the mobile unit at Coltishall.

---

[1] Eleven days later, on 23rd February, Cliff's life was saved by a homing pigeon after he had ditched in the North Sea. The incident is fully described in *Down in the Drink*.

The weather forecast was bad for most of the way, and by the time some of the later crews reached the map section there were no more maps of the route. Sticking to the formation was going to be important.

The fourteen crews had got into their aircraft and started up the engines when the whole move was cancelled. They went back to the crew room, complaining loudly, suffering from nervous irritation, genuinely disappointed and yet secretly relieved. So it had all been just another flap. Those dates in St Andrews could be kept after all. Cliff began to remake his plans for a birthday party that night. He was 27.

Within a few minutes they were told the move was on again. This time they got away—at 09.00 hours, Greenwich Mean Time.

The weather was unpleasant all the way down, with much low cloud and rain and only occasional clear patches. Somewhere off the north-east coast of England the formation ran into a balloon barrage flown by a coastal convoy. Most of the aircraft regained formation within a few minutes, but one aircraft, piloted by a young Canadian named Ralph Manning, lost contact. Manning's crew happened to be one of the crews for whom there had been no maps, and not surprisingly they failed to find Coltishall. Now there were thirteen. They landed at Coltishall at 11.30.

Meanwhile, radar plots of enemy air activity were being telephoned through to Fighter Command operations room at Stanmore, starting at about 08.30. Routine fighter patrols were reporting activity by E-Boats. A special patrol was ordered. Soon after nine o'clock the enemy began jamming our radar stations, intermittently at first, and then persistently. The jamming was much the same as usual, and attracted little notice at first, but received more attention as it increased. The result of the special patrol was awaited and no further patrols were ordered. At length, when the Spitfire pilots landed from the special patrol, they reported having seen a number of vessels, one of which had a tripod mast and superstructure. This information met with a certain scepticism, but the interrogation was intensified. Finally the pilot who had made the report was handed a book of silhouettes of enemy ships, from which he picked out a German capital ship. But before this stage in the interrogation had been reached, two other Spitfire pilots on a routine sweep had sighted and attacked two Me 109s, whose pursuit had taken them right over the German squadron. Although they were not aware of any threat that the ships might come out, the significance of what they saw was not lost on these two pilots, and, hastily abandoning the chase, they sped back to base and reported what they had seen. The time was 11.20. The German ships had covered well over 300 miles undetected and were steaming at 30 knots past Beachy Head into the Straits of Dover.

At the time of the sighting the German ships were about equidistant from the seven Beauforts at Thorney Island and the six Swordfish at Manston. The Beauforts at St Eval, blissfully engaged on their training programme, had for the moment been left far behind. The Beauforts of 42 Squadron were about to land at Coltishall. Even the Beauforts at Thorney Island were unprepared for an early attack. But although nearly half the day was already gone, there was still fully six hours' daylight. All the Beauforts could be got into position to make an attack, if not a co-ordinated one. The entire strength of Bomber Command could still be brought to bear. Much valuable time had been lost, but the unique opportunity was still there. The next six hours would be the testing time.

For the six Swordfish at Manston, the time lost was more serious. These aircraft, carrying exactly the same torpedo as the Beaufort, with a crew of three, were single-engine biplanes with a cruising speed of 87 knots and a restricted range. Fortunately, the sighting report found them well placed provided they attacked at once. But any delay might mean that the ships would pass out of range.

No. 825 (Fleet Air Arm) Squadron had been re-formed at Lee-on-Solent only a few weeks before as a six-aircraft squadron, following the sinking of the *Ark Royal*, in which the squadron had previously served. Four of the six crews had served on the *Ark Royal*. The squadron had been earmarked for service in northern waters, and the advance party had already gone to Scotland when, on 3rd February, the day after the Admiralty appreciation, Esmonde was asked whether he would care to take on the task of attacking the German ships should they attempt the passage of the Straits. It had, of course, been taken more or less for granted that any such attempt would be made at night.

The squadron had only just re-formed and had had no time to work up to operational fitness. But it had in Eugene Esmonde a remarkable commander. Esmonde had joined the Royal Air Force in 1928 on a short-service commission. He had served with the Fleet Air Arm (this was before its transfer to the Admiralty in 1937). During his service alongside the Navy he had acquired something of the stance, physical and mental, of the naval man, which had never left him. When his short-service commission expired in 1933 he joined Imperial Airways and flew Class 'G' flying-boats on the Hong Kong-Malaya run. He remained on the reserve, but in April 1939, tiring of civil flying and believing that a war was imminent, he left Imperial Airways, relinquished his R.A.F. commission, and joined the Fleet Air Arm. He now had some 6,500 flying hours behind him.

Esmonde was a small, dapper man, with a strangely wide forehead, and the perky look of a bird. A sea-bird. He had keen, bright, prominent eyes that, like a bird's, were never still. He was a wonderful pilot, with vast experience, a man not afraid of severity, but absolutely fair, and a superb leader. He was the sort of man that men would follow anywhere, even when they didn't much want to. No one could imagine Esmonde in trouble in the air. It was his element. An Irishman, born at Thurgoland, Yorkshire in 1909, he was now 33 years old. He was a man who was always at his best, but who had already shown outstanding qualities of coolness, determination, resource and leadership under fire.

The crews had been briefed before they left Lee-on-Solent that the German ships were expected to attempt the breakout during the next period of no moon. They were thus the only air crews let into the secret. They arrived at Manston on 4th February, and they carried out occasional Channel patrols in the days that followed, though for most of the time heavy snow on the airfield kept them on the ground. During this period they suffered a good deal of leg-pulling about their ancient-looking 'Stringbags' from the R.A.F. fighter-bomber boys at Manston. One piece of information they gleaned was that there were F.W. 190s operating over Belgium. But they were not seriously alarmed. The German fighters would never smell them out at night.

At 10.55 on the morning of the 12th Esmonde was warned, on the strength of the radar indications of unusual activity in the Channel which were being registered at Dover, that there might be a suitable target for him. This was nearly half an hour before the actual sighting.

"Are you prepared to go in daylight?" The question came from Vice-Admiral, Dover.

"Yes. Of course."

Esmonde ordered the squadron to readiness and had the torpedoes set to run deep. The Swordfish were thus the only aircraft ready to attack when the sighting report came through.

Esmonde received confirmation of the target at 11.30, and shortly afterwards the crews were called into the operations room for briefing by the intelligence officer.

"Well, chaps, they've come out at last—in fact, they're half way up the Channel. You are to take off as soon as possible and make contact at the nearest point, which we estimate at the moment as being somewhere off Boulogne. The three capital ships are escorted by a large number of destroyers and E-Boats, with strong fighter cover, mostly Me 109s. You in turn are to have strong fighter protection. You'll have top cover from three Spitfire squadrons from Biggin Hill, and you'll have two squadrons of Spits from Hornchurch as close escort. You'll rendezvous with the fighters over Manston at 12.25."

Then Esmonde spoke to the crews on tactics. Had they been an experienced squadron, worked up and in practice, Esmonde would have led them in a formation attack, the aircraft fanned out to form a crescent, converging together on the bows of the target. This way, whichever way the ship turned, it must turn into a torpedo. In the existing weather conditions of low cloud down to a thousand feet they would have attacked on radar, diving through the clouds, flattening out at the last moment, dropping the fish, and skidding away. The squadron, when at a highly operational state, had carried out this form of attack with success in the Mediterranean. But such an attack required a considerable degree of training and confidence; in the circumstances it was out of the question.

"We shall fly all the way at between fifty and a hundred feet," Esmonde told them. "Firstly to avoid the ships' radar, secondly because of the weather. There's low cloud down to a thousand feet and below, and since we want to stick together, at least on the way out, we'll be safer on the deck than anywhere else.

"We shall make a low-level approach and drop, in line astern.

"I'd better put it to you that we're volunteering for this job. We'll think about the chances of getting back when we've dropped our fish.

"Well, chaps, what about it?"

He was asking them if they were coming.

It was bad enough attacking only one capital ship, without an escorting screen. But there were three big ships, with a huge concentration of smaller craft and strong fighter cover. It meant a thick anti-aircraft barrage on the way in, irrespective of any fighter attack. The crews were more worried about the ack-ack than about the fighters. The Swordfish was so manoeuvrable that they felt they could evade the attacks of the 109s, as they had in the Med. They felt they stood more chance than the Beauforts with the fighters. The ack-ack was the trouble.

But once you got this far, there was no turning back. You were committed. Nine days ago, back at Lee-on-Solent, you might have found some excuse to get out of it. It was too late now. At this stage, it took more moral courage to stand down than to go. Besides, when a C.O. like Esmonde took a job on, you didn't let him down.

The crews were about to leave the operations room when Esmonde was called back by the controller.

"Can you hold for a bit? Some of the fighters are going to be late."

If Esmonde was frightened of anything, it was that the

ships would pass through the Straits before he could intercept them, and that the Swordfish would thus be involved in a stern chase. If they took off now, they would be flying in a south-easterly direction, to cut the enemy off opposite Calais. But the ships were steaming at 30 knots. If the take-off were delayed for only half an hour, the ships would reach the same latitude as Manston before the Swordfish could cut them off. The smallest further delay, a few minutes spent in searching for the convoy, would mean a stern chase. When you had a ship going away from you at 30 knots, and you were in a Stringbag doing less than 90, and you had a 30-knot wind against you, as they would have today if they had to fly north-west, you might be a long time catching it. Once, in the Mediterranean, he had chased a ship for nearly an hour without noticeably closing the gap. The Swordfish had a radius of action of only 200 miles, and in the end he had had to turn back. On a day like today, while you were struggling to over-take the target, they could pick you off one by one before you even got within torpedo range.

With the wonderful manœuvrability of the Swordfish, it was worth chancing the fighters in order to shorten the trip.

The controller was waiting for his answer, the phone held in front of his body, his free hand covering the mouthpiece. The man holding on at the other end was waiting for his answer too.

"We'll press on."

The controller went straight back to his phone. Esmonde and the crews went out to their aircraft.

The six Swordfish took off at 12.20 and formed up over the airfield. Although bad weather covered most of south-eastern England, Manston was clear. The squadron began circling over Ramsgate, waiting for the first Spitfires to appear. At 12.28 they were joined by one of the Biggin Hill squadrons, consisting of eleven Spitfires. Esmonde now had a fateful decision to make. If he waited for more fighter cover, would they lose the opportunity of getting in the Swordfish blow? The weather was bad, their endurance was short, and there was the old threat of the stern chase. If they could damage one of the big ships, and slow the convoy down, they would be giving the Beauforts a chance to concentrate their attack.

The convoy had been last reported at a distance of 23 miles from Ramsgate on a bearing of 140 degrees. Esmonde set course at 12.30, with the eleven Spitfires in attendance—one squadron of fighters instead of five. (In fact, the other two Biggin Hill squadrons made their way to the target independently and engaged at least some of the enemy fighters, shooting down two for the loss of one Spitfire, and so contributing indirectly to the defence of the Swordfish. But more than this was going to be needed.)

The first three Swordfish, led by Esmonde, flew in line astern and the second three in vic formation: a long thin neck followed by a compact body, in the manner of geese. The Spitfires hovered at 1000 feet, just below cloud, throttled right back, finding the utmost difficulty in keeping the slow Swordfish even in sight. The cloud base began to lower. Visibility was patchy, sometimes as much as four miles and sometimes down to a few hundred yards.

They had been on course for only ten minutes when they saw the enemy fighters, stubby and angular with their abruptly squared-off wing-tips. This must be the new German aircraft of which they had heard rumours at Manston, the deadly F.W. 190. There were Me 109s as well—some fifteen to twenty fighters in all.

In the second Swordfish, flying about 200 yards behind Esmonde, piloted by Sub-Lt. Brian Rose, was the youngest man of the eighteen, Sub-Lt. Edgar Lee, the observer. He was 20. The crew of a Swordfish all sat in open cockpits, the pilot first, protected from the slipstream by a windscreen, then the observer, so close behind that he could tap the pilot on the head without leaning forward, and then the gunner, whose free gas-operated machine-gun fired in an arc of nearly 180 degrees, astern of the beam. All the crew wore flying-helmets and goggles. Lee, youthful, fair-haired, of medium height and light build, was standing up in his cockpit, secured to the floor of the Swordfish by a wire attached to the seat of his harness, so that he couldn't fall out. In action, the observer was expected to watch for the direction of attack and call out evasive action to the pilot.

The enemy aircraft seemed to dive almost straight out of the clouds on to the tail of the first three Swordfish. Esmonde,

Rose and Kingsmill, the three pilots, pulled up to 100 feet to give themselves room to manœuvre. The Spitfires in turn fell on the German fighters, but they quickly lost contact with the Swordfish and became involved in a general dog-fight. For all the ferocity of the Spitfire attack, there seemed to be a large number of F.W. 190s to spare to deal with the Swordfish.

The method of attack of the F.W. 190s was to come in from astern one after another, firing as they came.

"Hard a-port!"

Lee, standing up in his cockpit and facing aft, waited until the attacking fighter had lined himself up, and then shouted out the evasive action. Williams in Esmonde's aircraft, and Samples with Kingsmill, were doing the same. Several Me 109s joined in the attacks.

"Hard a-starboard!"

Lee saw another F.W. 190 almost on their tail. A sharp turn to starboard, and the German fighter shot harmlessly by. Lee tried to vary his evasive action so as to keep the aircraft roughly on course.

The manœuvrability of the Swordfish, even with a torpedo on board, was outstanding, and its unusually slow speed obviously puzzled the German pilots. They kept on coming in from astern, but they overshot each time as the Swordfish turned. For several minutes the Swordfish crews managed to avoid most of the fire. Meanwhile, the three gunners fired their single machine-guns when they could—a pea-shooter against the four-cannon two machine-gun F.W. 190s.

Eventually the German pilots changed their tactics. Some of them continued to come in from astern, but others attacked simultaneously from the beam; a co-ordinated attack from two points. As you turned away from the stern attack, you exposed your tail to the attacker from the beam.

"Hard a-starboard!" Lee shouted to Rose to turn head-on into the beam attack. The fire from astern passed harmlessly by, and the fighter attacking from a-beam broke off in surprise, just in time to avoid a head-on collision. Every time the German fighters came in simultaneously from astern and a-beam, Lee repeated these tactics, risking a collision, but each time the German pilots pulled out just in time.

The F.W. 190s were now throttled right back, all guns
firing, desperately trying to get their speed down to that of
the Swordfish. For seven or eight minutes the Swordfish were
subjected to incessant attacks, and incredibly the six aircraft
survived. But in one of these attacks, Rose's aircraft was
caught in a barrage of crossfire and Johnson, the gunner,
beating the attacks off as best he could, suddenly slumped
over his gun. The light-weight Lee was unable to drag
Johnson off the gun to take his place. Johnson was evidently
either unconscious or dead.

A black smoky haze, residue of the smoke screen laid by
the E-Boats to screen the capital ships, clung to the water and
helped the Swordfish to stick roughly to their course. Now,
ahead of them and on the port bow, their outlines blurred
and confused by the smoke, were the ships they had come to
attack. All six Swordfish were still there.

They were now running into heavy fire from the German
squadron, first from the destroyers and E-Boats, and then
into a splash barrage put down by the 11-inch guns of the
battle-cruisers. Although the German ships were firing right
in amongst them, the German fighters kept up the pressure
with continual attacks from a-beam and astern. It seemed
impossible for the Swordfish to continue to make progress
through the hail of fire.

Lee, looking forward at the German ships, saw the C.O.'s
aircraft, 200 yards ahead of him, suffer a direct hit from a
heavy-calibre shell. The whole of the port lower mainplane
outboard of the main strut fell away into the sea. A moment
later the aircraft was trailing smoke and fire. But Esmonde
still held on.

In the fierce intensity of the barrage from the ships, the
German fighters began to thin out. Lee took his eyes off
them for a moment as Rose tried to line up on the target.
Lee estimated their distance from the ships as two miles. In
less than two minutes they could drop their fish and get away.
Ahead of him he saw Esmonde lining up on the second ship
in the line. It was impossible in the conditions of smoke haze
and low cloud to identify the ships; all they could do was pick
out the capital ships, steaming in line astern in the centre
of the squadron, from the others. It was only later that Lee

97

learned that the leading ship had been the *Gneisenau* and that the second ship, the ship they had attacked, was the *Scharnhorst*.

They were still 3000 yards out, but ahead of them Esmonde seemed to be positioning himself for the drop. It was too early to drop yet if they were going to make sure. A moment later Esmonde's torpedo dropped away. Rose and Lee saw it enter the water; then they looked up again at Esmonde's aircraft. Now they saw why Esmonde had dropped. Enveloped in flames, still under fighter attack, the Swordfish crashed in a steep curve into the sea.

Esmonde had gone, but the torpedo he had been so determined to drop was still alive, running towards its target. And the five Swordfish he had led were all behind him.

A second later Rose flew directly over the spot where Esmonde had crashed. He could see no sign of life on the water. He was much too near the German squadron to circle the wreck, and he shook himself with the realization that the leadership had passed to him. He went on closing steadily. Ahead of him, through the smoke and haze, he could make out the outlines of the second big ship in the line. Behind him, Lee was still giving orders for evasive action as the German fighters continued to make sporadic attacks; but Rose was compelled to fly a fairly straight course in order to get into position for the drop. Although very few of the fighters were now attempting to press home their attacks, the air was still full of F.W. 190s and Me 109s, and the flak was hurtling at them from all quarters of the compass—even from behind, where the escorting screen was now firing inwards from the perimeter of the convoy. When they were about 2000 yards from the target, Rose and Lee felt a bump beneath them, followed by the smell of petrol. The main petrol tank had been hit. Petrol poured out along the fuselage, drenching the machine. Rose switched immediately on to the auxiliary tank. Its capacity was only fifteen gallons. It wouldn't get them home, but it would be enough for the drop, and enough probably for them to clear the escorting screen after the attack.

"I'm pressing on."

Lee heard Rose shout back through his voice pipe, and

then there was a tearing sound in the forward part of his cockpit and he heard Rose groan. A cannon shell had struck the bulkhead between Rose and Lee, and a shell splinter severely wounded Rose at the base of the spine. Rose fell forward over the stick and the ship ahead of them suddenly seemed to climb above them and then shoot away to the left. The world ahead of them collapsed into a maze of kaleidoscopic images. When the water was a pane of glass that they were about to peer through, Rose pulled back desperately on the stick, struggling to keep the Swordfish airborne.

"Make a final run and drop the fish," called Lee. Rose's injured back robbed his muscles of their power, and both men were almost overcome by fumes from the escaping petrol. Another burst from an F.W. 190 tore along the fuselage like a dotted line. The engine was faltering, coughing and then picking up, developing less than full power. Rose aimed off at the *Scharnhorst*, dropping his torpedo at 1200-yards range. Lee looked back and saw it running well. In the act of dropping they sustained another burst of fire from a fighter. Rose, now nearly unconscious, turned the aircraft away blindly. Lee looked over his shoulder and saw Kingsmill, in the third aircraft, settling down to make his run.

The moment Rose dropped his torpedo, the German fighters let him go and turned their attention to Kingsmill. It was a chilling display of flying discipline. As they staggered away from the target area, Lee was astonished to see two F.W. 190s flying in the wake of Kingsmill with their wheels and flaps down. For a moment he looked around incredulously for an aircraft carrier. Then he realized that this was their way of reducing speed in order to get in a long burst at Kingsmill. One of the F.W. 190 pilots paid dearly for his enterprise. Bunce, Kingsmill's gunner, aimed point blank at the German fighter and sent it crashing down into the sea.

But already Kingsmill's aircraft had suffered serious damage. A direct hit from one of the battle-cruisers' guns had landed on top of the engine, shooting away the two top cylinders. The engine and the upper port wing caught fire, but miraculously the engine still developed enough power to keep them airborne. All three of the crew had been severely wounded during the fighter attacks, but still Kingsmill

99

managed to keep the stricken Swordfish on course. Kingsmill, too, picked the *Scharnhorst* for his target. Half blinded by flames and smoke from the blazing wing above him, fearing that the petrol tanks might explode at any moment, Kingsmill knew that he could not have more than a minute or two of airborne time. He kept the aircraft steady and dropped the torpedo at 3000 yards range, holding on long enough to see it running strongly. Then he turned with difficulty away from the battle-cruiser, back towards the escorting screen. The flames above him crackled in the slipstream. As soon as he was clear of the German squadron, he would ditch. Ahead of him he saw what appeared to be a flotilla of British motor torpedo-boats. If he could ditch the aircraft near them, they would still have a chance. As he was easing the stick back to drop the tail on the water, the boats sent a fusillade of machine-gun fire at him. They were German E-Boats. The Swordfish was now a streamer of fire as it wallowed along inches above the water. Kingsmill kept her going until the engine finally cut. He pancaked at once on to the sea and looking up saw that the upper wing was gutted and the dinghy blackened and burnt. The three wounded men struggled out of the blazing plane and jumped into the icy sea. But half a mile away were the silhouettes of the motor torpedo-boats, which had just completed their attack. Kingsmill and his crew had nothing with which to attract their attention, but the blazing aircraft had acted as a flare, and soon the three men were safely aboard.

Before Kingsmill went into the attack, Rose had turned away in an endeavour to escape over the destroyer screen before ditching. Each time he tried to pull the nose of the Swordfish up to gain height, the few gallons left in the auxiliary tank drained away from the feed and the engine began to splutter and cut. They passed straight over one of the destroyers at fifty feet. Rose was in a fainting condition but Lee looked down and saw several German sailors standing about on deck, watching them. Every gun on the destroyer was firing at them. Within about three hundred yards of the screen, the engine cut finally and Rose roused himself for the ditching.

"I'm putting her down!" Rose shouted back at Lee, his

voice only an echo of its usual robustness, but still far louder than the elements; the only other sound was the swish and sough of the wind in the stay-wires, the thunder of the guns and the clatter of the flak. Rose looked ahead and his eyes focused on the motor torpedo boats, three to four miles away. He had to get clear of the destroyers, and he had to make a good ditching to give them time to get Johnson out. Rose brought the Swordfish down expertly, scraping the tail on the swell and then cushioning in. The dinghy inflated automatically and began to float away. Lee grabbed at it and held it firmly while he tried to help Rose out of the front cockpit. Rose had no strength in his arms, and Lee had to let go of the dinghy in order to lever Rose out with both hands. Rose helped by swinging his weight out over the water. Eventually he fell into the sea. Supported by his Mae West, he struggled over to the dinghy and held on.

Now Lee turned to the task of freeing Johnson. He was convinced that Johnson was dead, but he shrank from the thought of leaving him to go down with the Swordfish. Lee was already exhausted from his efforts to free Rose, but he knew that there was no time to spare. The burst petrol tank had filled with water, and the aircraft was full of holes and sinking rapidly. Lee undid Johnson's harness and struggled to lift him out. But the water was now up to his chest and the aircraft was sinking. It was a question of going down with it himself or letting Johnson go. Lee was absolutely certain in his mind that Johnson was dead, but he tried again to drag him out, finally convinced himself that it was hopeless, and floated off the aircraft as it went down.

The damaged Swordfish had sunk in less than a minute. As Lee kicked himself free, he looked back towards the target area and saw the second flight of Swordfish crossing the destroyer screen, still flying in loose vic formation, taking violent evasive action, but proceeding steadily towards the German capital ships. Lee was the last Englishman to see them. None of them returned, there were no survivors, and nothing is known of their fate.

Lee turned to the task of lifting Rose into the dinghy. Rose was now completely paralysed, and every time Lee tried to hoist him up, the dinghy overturned. The water attacked

Lee's limbs with an icy force, but the exertion helped him to keep up his circulation. The spray breaking over the dinghy was freezing into icicles on the air-chamber. Eventually, by levering himself on the rope anchor, Lee managed to push Rose up from underneath and topple him over the rim of the dinghy. Lee clambered in after him. Rose was now unconscious, and Lee collapsed across him, utterly exhausted.

Lee was still conscious, but his mind was numb. His subconscious mind knew that the ships on the edge of the screen were firing at the dinghy, and he sensed that the heavy swell was their only protection, the German gunners getting only an intermittent sight of the dinghy. But he was unable to stir himself. The mist and smoke and flame of the afternoon had penetrated his mind.

Suddenly he was a schoolboy again, back in that warm summer of 1939, studying for his exams. He had been entered for Dartmouth, through the Late Entry scheme, for a regular commission in the Fleet Air Arm; and he remembered clearly the face of the doctor who had examined him, and the numbing shock of what the doctor had told him.

"Colour blindness. I'm sorry. You haven't a chance."

Then the war had started, and a few months later he had heard that the Fleet Air Arm were accepting aircrew recruits again. Taking a chance that war-time records might be incomplete and that standards might be lower, he had made another application. He had talked it over first with his father.

"I'm going to have another go at the Fleet Air Arm, Dad. I just can't concentrate on studies any more."

"Don't be a fool. Don't make the mistake I made. Wait at least until you've finished your exams."

"You didn't."

"My father advised me against it."

"And you took no notice."

His father had been reluctant to accept defeat.

"How about your eyes?"

"The school doctor says my sight's perfect. Apparently it's been getting better every year. I haven't had to wear glasses since I was fifteen. It must be all right."

So he had applied to join the V.R., and got as far as the

medical. And there sat the same doctor, gazing at him curiously.

"Ever had a Fleet Air Arm medical before?"

He felt his heart pounding and the colour flooding his face. He was quite unprepared for being faced with the same doctor, and equally embarrassed by the question.

But the doctor must have examined hundreds of people since last time. Thousands. He couldn't possibly have recognized him.

"No."

He tried to look composed and nonchalant, but felt that the lie was written all over him. The doctor held his gaze for a moment, and then wrote something down on his pad.

"Ever had anything wrong with your eyes?"

Again he felt the colour flooding his face and neck. The doctor must be on to him. Why else should he start off with these two questions? Any others he could have answered truthfully.

But they were white lies, surely. If he told the doctor about that other medical, it might prejudice this one. And if there was really anything the matter, he would never get past all the tests.

The naval doctor had asked no more questions. Lee had passed the tests. All for this. His pilot unconscious or dead. His gunner certainly gone. His C.O. shot down in flames. And the impotent agony of being shot at in a dinghy.

The firing, however, although unpleasant, was erratic. They were soon out of range of the escort's small-arms fire, and the heavier shelling was throwing up the water some distance away.

Lee's mind slowly began to thaw, and he realized that if Rose's life was to be saved he must get help quickly. The dinghy was half full of water, and he tried baling it out with his flying-helmet. Then he remembered the survival pack. He fumbled for a rocket, recognizing the long thin stalk and the rectangular box at the top. His frozen fingers ripped at the friction tape unfeelingly. He was still in a semi-exhausted state, and this coupled with the heavy swell now gave him his most nightmare moment. He saw that the rocket was pointing straight into the face of the unconscious Rose. He steered it away just as the rocket sent up its first coloured shell.

Looking to the north-east for a sign of the German squadron, he saw that the battle was leaving them behind. Two bombers, which he took for a Stirling and a Manchester, dived out of the clouds in flames, followed by an Me 109 and then a Spitfire. All kinds of aircraft, British and German, were falling into the water, like debris from a vast explosion. Lee wondered if under these conditions the rocket would be noticed. He rummaged around for the aluminium dust sea-marker, but he threw it out carelessly into wind, and it blew back over them, coating them with a fine silvery dust, the colour of steel. Lee used the empty sea-marker tin as a bale.

After an hour and a half in the water, Lee heard the throbbing of an engine, and suddenly, out of the mist that seemed to surround them, he saw the motor torpedo-boat, incredibly close. It was flying the skull and cross-bones. Rose, roused by the noise of the engine, looked up and saw the flag.

"Good God, it's a Hun."

So they were going to be on the wrong side of the fence. The two men resigned themselves to capture. At least they were going to be pulled out of the drink.

"Hold on there!"

The motor torpedo-boat was alongside, brushing against the dinghy, and someone was shouting at them in English. Lee hung on to the side, but the sea was choppy and he had to let go. He was appalled at his weakness. One of the A.B.s then jumped without hesitation into the icy sea.

"All right, haul them on board—I'll hold the dinghy."

They hauled the two men up on deck and carried them below. Rose lapsed again into unconsciousness. Lee could hear the crew discussing whether they should attempt an attack on the German squadron. He was almost past caring; but it would be a pretty poor do to have to make two such attacks in one day.

The motor torpedo-boat continued at high speed. Lee had no idea whether the chase might still be on. He refused the rum they offered him. It was a thing he had never been able to stomach. Oh yes, he knew what they would be thinking: a pretty poor sort of naval character, this.

Of the five survivors, Lee was the only one unhurt. After being thawed out in hospital at Dover, he was taken to see Admiral Ramsay, Flag Officer Dover, in Dover Castle, where he learned that Kingsmill's crew, although severely wounded and in hospital at Ramsgate, had also survived the attack. Brian Rose recovered from his injuries, but was killed in a flying accident in 1943.

Lee went back to Manston that night to sort out the kit of the missing men. It was a poignant ending to a day the details of which no 20-year-old could ever forget. The men at Manston who had jeered kindly at the old Stringbags now honoured Lee. The mess was hushed as he entered, and he was given the reception that he and Esmonde and all the others had earned.

What had the sacrifice been worth? Was it an act of callousness to send six Swordfish against three German capital ships, with all the protection they could call on as they sped along the coastline of Occupied Europe?

Up to this moment of the war the Fleet Air Arm Swordfish had enjoyed remarkable success in this form of attack. Twice they had dropped against the *Bismarck*, successfully and without loss. In the Mediterranean they had been the only torpedo-bombers available, and, although operating mostly at night, they had sunk many thousands of tons of Axis shipping. At Taranto and Matapan their success was already legendary. The German squadron, with fighter cover, was a different proposition; but then the Swordfish were to have cover too.

The Swordfish crews were taken by surprise by the number of fighters employed against them. They were extremely unlucky in being intercepted so soon: at the time of the interception they had another thirteen minutes' flying ahead of them before they could expect to reach the target. Yet every Swordfish reached the outer screen, about two miles from the capital ships, and three of them certainly dropped their torpedoes. The other three had only a mile or so to go to the dropping point when last seen.

No man was more experienced in this type of work, no man was a better flier, than Esmonde. His decision to leave without the escort must be regarded as altogether above criticism.

In any case it bears the closest inspection. No one expected to sink these ships, either in the Swordfish or the Beauforts that were to follow. But Esmonde and the men of the Swordfish expected to get at least two hits. That was how they assessed their chances. Two hits, at the least.

When Esmonde marched out to his aircraft, men who knew him had never seen his face so grim. He expected to hit the German ships. He did not expect to return.

Esmonde was posthumously awarded the V.C. The four officers who survived were awarded the D.S.O. and the only surviving gunner the C.G.M. The twelve men besides Esmonde who gave their lives were mentioned in despatches.

Most of the men of the torpedo-bombers in 1942 were men waiting for death. Those who knew they were to attack the *Scharnhorst*, *Gneisenau* and *Prinz Eugen* in the Channel did not expect to survive. Thirteen men in a war is not very many. But on the evening of 12th February 1942, for the 20-year-old Lee, the only man of an entire squadron to return to base, the world seemed empty.

Chapter 6

THE BEAUFORT ATTACKS ON THE
SCHARNHORST AND *GNEISENAU*

BECAUSE of the comprehensive system of reconnaissance
patrols, it had been a reasonable assumption that any
attempt at a move of the German ships from Brest would be
quickly apprehended; therefore the major concentration of
Beauforts was situated at St Eval, directly opposite Brest.
These aircraft commanded an arc stretching from Brest itself
to the Cherbourg peninsula. But when the ships were sighted
they had passed out of range of the St Eval aircraft, and there
was no prospect of getting them into position to attack for
some hours. The flight from St Eval to Manston spanned
practically the entire width of the south coast. The development of a mass attack by all the available Beauforts could
therefore patently not take place before the late afternoon.

The choice facing Joubert threatened to be of the heads-
you-win-tails-I-lose variety: either he could hold the Beauforts at Thorney Island and Coltishall for a co-ordinated
attack with those from St Eval, letting the convoy escape
further and further north meanwhile, with the prospect of the
weather closing in as an added stimulus to his anxiety during
the nerve-racking hours in which the Beauforts held their
fire; or he could violate one of the basic principles of air
power by splitting his force up into penny packets, letting
each formation of Beauforts attack independently in its own
time.

The tactics to be employed by a force of torpedo-bombers
against a target of this nature had been carefully worked out
over the years. But tactics were one thing, practice was
another. Of the available crews, the number who had undergone full torpedo training including mass attacks could be
counted on the fingers of one hand; even these had no experience of making such an attack under fire. In the prevailing
weather conditions it might be difficult for one squadron
alone, or even for one flight, to make a concerted attack.

Common sense argued the abandonment of broad principles for the needs of the hour.

With the passing of time the whole situation might change. The Beauforts were like a centre-forward caught on the wrong foot. In the time they took to transfer their weight to the right foot, the chance might be gone. Better hit the ball first time.

When the position of the German ships was reported, the nearest Beauforts were those of No. 217 Squadron at Thorney Island, numbering seven and constituting the rump of the squadron. Joubert decided to use this unit as a spearhead, to carry out an early torpedo attack with the idea of at least inflicting some damage on the ships and delaying their progress. If this could be achieved, more time would be given for the two main Beaufort forces at St Eval and Coltishall to get into position to launch their attacks.

The commanding officer of 217 Squadron had failed to return from a bombing attack four days earlier, and the man acting as C.O. was Squadron Leader George Taylor, D.F.C., A.F.C. It was to him that Joubert's decision to use 217 as the spearhead, the maiming force, filtered through. "There are three big enemy merchantmen in the Channel," he was told. The filter, for reasons of its own, had drained off the names of the warships and turned them into merchantmen. Taylor was given the approximate position. "Speed eight to ten knots. You are to send off all available aircraft immediately to attack with torpedoes. How soon can you get off?"

Taylor had seven aircraft in all, but only four were fitted with torpedoes. These four had been at Manston on detachment until a few days previously, working in co-operation with fighter aircraft in night attacks on enemy shipping in the Channel. For the purpose their wireless equipment had been removed and special R/T equipment fitted. The other three aircraft were fitted with bombs, and it would take an hour to change the load. In any case, one of them had an electrical fault and would not be serviceable for at least an hour.

"We should be able to get airborne in about an hour and a half, sir."

"Nothing like soon enough. Why can't you get off right away?"

Taylor explained about the load-changing and the electrical fault.

"Well, you've got four aircraft serviceable and fitted with torpedoes—get them off first. Then send the others as soon as they're ready."

"I'd sooner we went together as a squadron," said Taylor. "I think we'd do better in a concerted attack, and we'd have more fire-power for protection."

"Sorry, Taylor. We can't accept any delay. Every available aircraft must be got into the air at once. Get the others to follow on later. As soon as possible, too. It's vitally urgent. The instructions are to rendezvous at Manston at 13.40 hours, pick up your fighter cover and proceed to the target from there. Got that?"

Taylor repeated the instructions back and then called his crews together. It had been his intention to lead the squadron himself, but when he was ordered to send the aircraft off piecemeal, he decided to remain on the ground to ensure that the work of getting the aircraft ready was pressed forward. He had no other officer whom he could reasonably put in charge.

The rendezvous time had of necessity been arbitrarily fixed, and when the first four Beauforts, led by Pilot Officer Tom Carson, a fair-haired open-faced young man of fine physique, great keenness, and a barbed but kindly wit, took off at 13.25, it was apparent that they would be some twenty minutes late at Manston. Their time of take-off was phoned through to Group Headquarters as a matter of routine, and when it was realized at Group that the Beauforts were going to be late, it was decided to send wireless messages to the Beauforts and to the fighter escort instructing them to by-pass Manston and proceed direct to the target. The messages included a new course, position and speed of the ships, this time the speed given being 27 knots. The messages were sent by the normal means to both aircraft—R/T (speech) for the Spitfires and W/T (morse signalling) for the Beauforts. But Carson's four Beauforts were the aircraft that had recently returned from the detachment at Manston. They still had the special R/T equipment mounted in place of their usual W/T. The Spitfires received the diversion and went straight to the target, but Carson's formation, whose R/T frequency was altogether different from the Spitfire R/T, received no message and carried on to Manston.

The four Beauforts reached Manston at 14.00 hours and began circling the airfield. As they approached, they saw a number of Spitfires in the circuit, and they concluded that their fighter escort had waited for them. But these Spitfires had been briefed for other tasks, and they would have nothing to do with the Beauforts. Carson and his formation circled for some time, puzzled by the aloofness of the Spitfires. Eventually, as the conditions in the circuit became more confused with the arrival of further aircraft, Carson's formation got split up. One Beaufort, piloted by Flight Sergeant Mark Banning, a Canadian, managed to stick with him, and Carson decided to set course for the target.

Carson was working to a position given him some two hours earlier, with a rate of progress since then of eight to ten knots. He thus set course for a position nearly fifty miles south of the true one. It was a pity that Carson didn't discover the little deception that had been practised on him at this stage; it was the sort of wry joke he would have enjoyed. Had he received the wireless message from Group, he would have gone straight to the correct position and no doubt identified the 'three merchantmen'.

Carson and Banning swept back and forth for some time off the French coast, but they were much too far from the ships to have any chance of sighting them, or even of getting an A.S.V. contact, and, finding nothing, they returned to Manston, where they landed at 15.35.

While Carson and Banning were searching for a fictitious target in a miscomputed position, all the other five Thorney Island aircraft were making fair progress. The three aircraft which had been left behind, piloted by Flight Lieutenant Finch, Pilot Officer Stewart and Sergeant Rout, had taken off at 14.30, exactly an hour after the others, after having been correctly briefed on the composition, course and speed of the enemy convoy. They circled Manston as ordered and then proceeded to the target. They had been told to expect fighter cover but no close escort, and they wasted very little time over Manston, setting course at 15.00. From bringing up the rear of the Thorney Island detachment they thus became the vanguard. And on the ground at Manston, Aldridge and Lee, piloting the two Beauforts which had lost Carson in the circuit over the airfield an hour earlier, had been told for the first time the true nature of their target, had obtained fresh instructions, and had set off again on their own, only a few minutes behind the formation led by Finch. When Carson and Banning landed at Manston at 15.35, the other five Beauforts were nearing the target.

Finch and his formation of three aircraft found visibility deteriorating as they approached the estimated position of the convoy, and Finch decided that they would carry out their attacks singly, each pilot choosing a target for himself. Every aircraft in this formation had A.S.V., and no difficulty was experienced in finding the German squadron, which spattered the radar screen with blips like rain.

Of all the men of the Beauforts who attacked the German ships that day, 'Ginger' Finch was perhaps the most adventurous, the most audacious, the most impulsive, the most contemptuous of danger. Only a few weeks before, with Aldridge, he had won the D.F.C. in a bombing attack on a powerfully escorted convoy of eight merchant vessels off the Dutch coast. Finch had been leading a formation of three aircraft of which Aldridge had flown No. 3. Going for the largest ship, Finch machine-gunned it on the way in, released four bombs from mast height and scored direct hits with three of them, being himself badly shaken by the explosion of his own bombs. Coming in last, emulating his leader, and undeterred by the sight of No. 2 in the formation being shot down into the sea a few yards in front of him, Aldridge had also scored direct hits, but had pulled up so late that his wing-tip was severed by the bracing wires of a mast. When the ground crews heard that the German warships were out, they said that if anybody got them, it would be 'Ginger' Finch. And the ground crews knew.

The three Beauforts approached the target from an angle of 90 degrees on the port beam. Straight ahead they saw the *Gneisenau*, steaming along apparently slowly in the middle of a tremendous line of ships. But there was no sign of the *Scharnhorst*.

In turning to avoid a previous attack, possibly that of the Swordfish, the *Scharnhorst* had been forced out of the narrow mine-swept channel. Her manœuvre had successfully avoided the attack; but, in turning back to regain the swept channel, she struck a mine.

The *Scharnhorst* was in serious trouble. The lights failed, the wireless went dead, and, leaving a trail of oil behind her, she came to a standstill. While she was licking her wounds, the *Gneisenau* and *Prinz Eugen* thundered by.

Stewart and Rout saw Finch waggle his wings and peel off into the attack, swinging away to port to run up on the bows of the *Gneisenau*. The escorting destroyers began laying a smoke screen, and the two pilots lost sight of their leader. Then they saw why the German convoy hadn't opened fire.

"Two Me 109s dead ahead!"

The German fighters were between the Beauforts and the convoy, and they opened fire at once from dead ahead with a long point-blank no deflection burst of cannon and machine-gun fire. Both aircraft were hit, but they held their course. The German fighters pulled up to avoid a head-on collision and banked steeply to line up behind the two Beauforts. Stewart and Rout were now about 2000 yards from the ship they had selected as their target, the *Prinz Eugen*.

Away to the left, 'Ginger' Finch was about to launch the first torpedo to be dropped by Beauforts against any of these ships in the open sea. It was the first blow to be struck by Joubert's 'maiming force', the spearhead of the Beaufort attacks to come.

Finch was seen to go right in close before dropping his torpedo. He never came out.

Meanwhile, Stewart and Rout were running up towards the *Prinz Eugen*, anxious to complete their attack before the Me 109s could line up behind them. The German cruiser seemed to be leaving hardly any wake. Stewart decided to aim not more than half a length ahead. In spite of the efforts of the destroyers and the confusion of the smoke screen, he had a clear view of the whole length of her beam. He pressed the tit and felt the torpedo go.

"Two 109s on our tail!"

The controls shook as the turret guns regurgitated their food from the ammunition pans. Stewart opened the throttles and began to pull away to starboard. A noise like hail on a tin roof, metallic and unresonant, told him that the German fighters were on the mark. Stewart looked above for shelter, but the cloud base was 1000 feet up. He felt like a man caught in a cloudburst without his raincoat. He would be drenched before he could reach shelter. He put the nose down again, jinking and zig-zagging. Still the tail guns puked away.

"One of them's going down!" The guns were still firing, not at the falling aircraft, but at the one that kept coming in. Streams of tracer were flying past the front cockpit and snuffing out ahead of them, like shooting stars. Suddenly Stewart saw land rushing at him out of the mist. He swerved away to starboard, and a moment later there was a long rattle from the turret.

"He's going! I think I hit him! He's going!"

When they got back, they counted twelve hits in the Beaufort; one bullet had gone through an airscrew, and the tail-plane was severely damaged. They were credited with the first 109. No one was hurt. Stewart's tail gunner had seen the torpedo running towards the target, but no one had been able to follow it when the fighter attack developed.

Behind Stewart, Rout made his attack independently, his first taste of action, under pressure from fighters throughout. He kept his Beaufort down to sixty feet, concentrating on the drop, shutting his mind to the scrap that was going on behind him. He was hit in the hand by a cannon-shell splinter, but he kept his numbed finger on the release button. The wireless operator, manning the side guns, was hit in the arm and the leg by machine-gun bullets, and the gunner was blinded by splinters from a hit on the perspex dome of the turret. Still Rout kept the Beaufort on course. When he judged that he was little more than half a mile from the *Prinz Eugen*, he dropped his torpedo. As he pulled away to starboard it seemed that in every direction in which he might turn a destroyer barred his way. For a full minute he flew around uncertainly, changing course several times, but each time he was met by a fresh hail of fire from escorting craft. The Beaufort was hit several times and a fire broke out amidships. The whole aircraft was filled with the suffocating stench of burning rubber. The fire was in the flare-chute, and the wireless operator and gunner, forgetful of their wounds, attacked it fiercely and beat it out. They were ten minutes inside the destroyer screen before they finally got out, boxed in by flak the whole time. Incredibly the Beaufort kept going. When they finally got clear, Rout set course for Manston. They were a long way off course for a time, but they eventually landed there safely.

Aldridge and Lee, in the two Beauforts which had lost Carson's formation and landed at Manston, reached the target area at about 15.40, directly after the attacks made by Finch, Stewart and Rout. The fight these three crews had put up had a direct bearing on the opposition encountered by Aldridge and Lee: they were not molested by fighters. In addition, the German squadron had run into thicker weather, making fighter interception more difficult. Aldridge and Lee were actually inside the destroyer screen before they sighted the leading ship, the *Gneisenau*. The two aircraft attacked together, dropping their torpedoes from 1500 yards. Both torpedoes were seen to run strongly, but in the thickening mist neither crew was able to follow the trail all the way.

When the thirteen aircraft of 42 Squadron landed at Coltishall from Leuchars, Williams and Cliff were told at once of the break-out of the ships. "They're working on a co-ordinated attack at Group," they were told. "Grab yourselves a quick lunch and report back here."

Over lunch, Williams and Cliff discussed the tricky problem of who was to lead the squadron. Williams had many years' experience of torpedo work in Swordfish aircraft, but he was new to the Beaufort and to 42 Squadron, and he had no crew. Cliff had been on the squadron for several months, and he knew the men.

Williams hesitated. Today was the kind of chance that came to a regular officer perhaps once in a lifetime. But he had to ignore personal ambition and make the right decision for the squadron. In this weather, with a strange crew, and the whole squadron, perhaps even other squadrons, following . . .

The two men eyed each other across their uneaten lunch,

the one hopeful, persuasive, sure of his point, the other uncertain, already feeling the pangs of envy. At length Williams broke the silence.

"All right. You go."

Cliff got up from the table. "I'll go and ring Group. I'll find out what's on and then get the crews together."

"How many aircraft have got torpedoes?"

"There were eleven when we started. We lost Manning on the way down, and he had a torp up, so that leaves ten. Manning may turn up, of course, but it's ten for the moment. My aircraft's u/s and I shall have to take someone else's. That leaves nine—three sections of three."

"I'll round up the stragglers and see if I can chase up the mobile torpedo unit," said Williams. "We'll get your nine off and then I'll see if I can mount another strike with the other five."

Cliff went back to the operations room and rang Group. He was put straight through to the A.O.C.

"Hullo, Cliff. The present position of the ships is the Straits of Dover. You will rendezvous over Manston at 14.45 with a formation of Hudson bombers, who will lead the way and drop their bombs as you go in, to distract attention from your attack. Aircraft of Fighter Command will be at Manston to escort both you and the Hudsons. After the attack return to North Coates. Got that?"

Cliff had been a torpedo man since 1936, and his mind was working strictly to the book.

"Are we to cripple or sink?"

"What?"

"Are the orders that we attempt to cripple or sink?" This was the first question that came to Cliff's mind. It was a question of whether to concentrate all the nine aircraft on the same target, or to split the force into individual flight attacks on all three ships with the idea of inflicting general damage and slowing down the whole convoy. Cliff knew that there were other Beaufort squadrons about somewhere, and as it seemed that any idea of a mass attack had been abandoned, the other squadrons might be able to go in later and administer the *coup de grâce*.

"Good God, man, the ships are out of Brest. Isn't that

115

enough? Go out and attack anything you see. There's nothing at sea but the enemy. Go out and do your best."

"We're not lining up with any of the other Beaufort squadrons?"

"No. The Thorney Island Beauforts are being used as the spearhead and we can't wait for the Beauforts at St Eval. Sorry we can't give you a more accurate position, but it's vital that you get out there and do your best. Good luck."

Cliff lowered the receiver slowly. The A.O.C.'s words were revolving fiercely in his head, with a kind of centrifugal force which every now and then tossed one of them out, so that he was left with nothing more than a jingle. "The ships are out of Brest, go out and do your best."

As he left the control tower he ran in to Williams. "We're due to rendezvous over Manston at 14.45," said Cliff.

"I'll get the crews together," said Williams. "Who are you going to take?"

"I'll take the officer pilots. It's an arbitrary way of deciding, and it should work out about right." The nine crews were called out on the Tannoy, and Cliff briefed them on the tarmac in front of the control tower.

"The target is the German battle-cruisers *Scharnhorst* and *Gneisenau* and the cruiser *Prinz Eugen*." Cliff paused, watching their faces, but he could detect no change in expression. "They're steaming up the Channel, escorted by thirty plus destroyers and other craft."

The silence lasted another second or two, and then there was a shout of laughter and Cliff found himself surrounded by a sea of amused, grinning faces. Salmon and Gluckstein![1] But they were lying crippled by thousands of tons of bombs in Brest! Who was Cliff trying to kid?

Cliff had to raise his voice and insist on being taken seriously. When the men realized he was in earnest, he got silence easily enough. He told the crews what the A.O.C. had told him. The Hudsons were going in with bombs ahead of them. They would pick up a fighter escort at Manston. They were to land at North Coates afterwards. There was nothing at sea but the enemy. They had to get those ships.

---

[1] The two battle-cruisers were dubbed 'Salmon and Gluckstein' during their long stay in Brest by the crews who watched over and attacked them.

Already, before the general briefing, he had told Johnny Dinsdale, a chubby, cheery New Zealander and the other flight commander, to lead the vic on his right, and Charlie Pett, who had flown in the formation behind Ray Loveitt on the *Lutzow* attack, to take the vic on his left. Now he gave the other pilots their positions. Then he described the plan of attack.

Although the A.O.C. had spoken in only the most general terms of the actual attack, Cliff had decided that the situation called for splitting his force and giving each sub-formation a separate target. The arithmetic of it was easy. There were three ships and three sub-formations. They would approach from abeam and take a ship each. He described the plan to the crews, and concluded: "The ships have got a fighter escort, so don't be caught napping. We'll fly out on the deck. We'll break to starboard after the attack and re-form. Land at North Coates."

The mobile torpedo unit failed to arrive in time, and Williams and Cliff adjusted the torpedoes themselves, setting them to run at eighteen feet. They had been topped up at Leuchars that morning and no doubt would run well enough.

The nine Beauforts took off individually between 14.20 and 14.30, formed up over the airfield, and set course for Manston. It was a grey-white afternoon, with visibility deteriorating as they crossed the Thames Estuary. But as they approached Manston it cleared, and ahead of them they saw the sky alive with Hudsons and Spitfires, all going round in one huge circle 2000 feet over Manston airfield. Cliff led the Beauforts straight across the middle of the airfield, and then began circling in the same direction as the rest, a left-hand circuit, but at a lower altitude, just below 1500 feet, keeping his eye on the Hudsons, waiting for them to set course. He tried to form up behind the Hudsons, but each time he did so the Hudsons pulled away and tried to form up behind the Beauforts. Cliff could only conclude that some mistake had been made in the briefing. In the end he gave it up.

None of the aircraft betrayed any intention of leaving the circuit, and after a time Cliff began to get impatient. There were now some fifteen or sixteen Hudsons and twenty to thirty fighters in the circuit, besides the nine Beauforts, all flying

117

round like aerial chairs at a fairground, aimlessly, endlessly, waiting for something to happen. The only thing likely to happen, thought Cliff, was that the fighters would run out of petrol. He called MacDonald, his navigator.

"Can we call them on the R/T?"

"Radio silence was ordered, sir. We'd better not."

The circuit was getting tighter and tighter and seemed to be more and more crowded. Nearly half an hour had elapsed. Cliff went from impatience to irritability. Out there in the Channel the German ships were getting away.

Cliff had been told that the handful of Beauforts at Thorney had been used as the spearhead. The Beauforts from St Eval might be too late. It did not need much imagination to realize that the strike of 42 Squadron might constitute the main hope of stopping the ships.

"I'm going to use the R/T."

"All right, sir."

"Hullo, Hudson leader. Hullo, Spitfire leader. Beaufort leader here. What are we waiting for? Over."

There was no answer. Perhaps it would be better to call Manston control. But when he called he again got no answer.

"Manston's a fighter airfield," said Tessier, the gunner. "They work on a different frequency. Unless they've been told to listen out on our frequency they won't get us."

"And I suppose that goes for the Hudsons and Spitfires?"

"I expect so, sir."

"Good God."

Cliff looked at his watch. Half-past three. He had had enough. As an experiment he turned through 180 degrees and began to fly a right-hand circuit. The whole formation of fighters and bombers did the same.

Cliff turned to his navigator. "See that? Maybe they'll go on doing what I do. I'm not waiting any longer, anyway. Give me a course for the Dutch coast south of Den Helder."

Macdonald gave Cliff the course to steer, and Cliff turned on to it. It was only a rough estimate of where the ships might be. What Cliff had done was to fix on a position a few miles north of what he considered the maximum possible progress of the ships. They could hardly be further north than Den Helder. If there was no sign of the ships when he got there, he could safely turn to starboard and run in a south-westerly direction down the track of the ships till he came to them.

Cliff began to let down, until as the Beauforts crossed the coast they were only a few feet above the water. This would avoid detection by the German radar.

"Anyone following us?"

"*Everyone's* following us!" called Tessier excitedly.

But the fighters had only seemed to follow them, and only five of the Hudsons actually set course.

As soon as they left Manston behind, the weather began to close in on them. There were scurrying low clouds at 100 feet, which the squadron rushed briefly through, like a train through a tunnel. There were patches of fog, and visibility in the clearer patches varied from two miles down to 500 yards. The ships were going to take some finding.

Ten minutes after they set course, Tessier called from the turret.

"I've just seen the Spitfires go over."

"Let's hope they're there when we get there," said Cliff.

Cliff stuck to his plan, and when the formation was two-thirds of the way to the Dutch coast, he saw the outline of a ship loom up out of the mist on the port side. He recognized it almost at once as a destroyer. She was on fire forward.

Cliff called immediately on the R/T. "Don't attack. Don't attack." But on his left, Pett had already broken away and was turning towards the destroyer. "There they are, Red leader," called Pett. He had not heard Cliff's call. A moment later Cliff lost sight of him in the fog and low cloud. When Pett found himself on his own he wheeled round, recognized the ship he had gone after as a destroyer, and turned back to try to join up again with the squadron. He never found them, or the German ships, and although he spent some time searching he eventually went back to North Coates alone. He did not drop his torpedo. The destroyer he had so nearly attacked was H.M.S. *Worcester*, a British destroyer which was on its way back from a daring torpedo attack on the German convoy. The appearance of a Beaufort flying straight at them at low level out of the mist, and breaking away at the last moment, convinced the men on the destroyer that a torpedo had actually been dropped against them. But Pett's torpedo was still slung under the fuselage when he landed at North Coates.

Pett's mistake in diving on the destroyer was understandable in the confusion that existed. "There's nothing at sea but the enemy," he'd been told. But in fact, five British destroyers from Harwich, the only surface force available, had intercepted the German squadron and carried out torpedo attacks, taking advantage of the cover afforded by the bad visibility. Even so, none of the destroyers was able to get closer than 2500 to 3000 yards, and no hits were made.

About this time the Germans, too, were in some confusion. The *Scharnhorst* was at first thought to be so badly damaged by the explosion of the mine as to need a tow into a Dutch port, but she was eventually got under way again shortly after three o'clock. Meanwhile Ciliax, Reinicke and the fighter controller were transferred to the leading destroyer; but this developed engine trouble and the German admiral again decided to make a move. While the three men were being taken by cutter from one destroyer to another, both destroyers were attacked by our bombers. The admiral and his chief of staff sat unprotected in the cutter, severely jolted by the explosions. A moment later, to their exasperation and chagrin, the *Scharnhorst*, now under full speed again, steamed straight past them, unaware of their plight. Before the transfer from one ship to another was complete, they were bombed by a Dornier 217. It wasn't only the British whose plans were in disarray.

Meanwhile Cliff and his eight remaining Beauforts were ploughing on through worse and worse weather towards the Dutch coast. Five miles from the coast they turned to starboard on a course that would take them right through the German convoy. As they turned, Cliff had a brief glimpse of the coast, and then it was lost again in the mist. He had been right to press his claims to lead the squadron. The navigation had been spot on and he had complete confidence in his crew. There was enough to think about on a day like this without being worried by uncertainties about one's crew.

He watched the other Beauforts follow him round in the turn and settle down on the new course. Eight aircraft including his own, in line abreast as though on parade.

Cliff's eyes swept right and left for a moment, gathering his Beauforts around him. Then, as he sat back again and looked to the front, he was electrified to see a destroyer bearing down on them, dead ahead.

"Is it one of ours or theirs?"

The destroyer itself gave the answer by directing a barrage of flak and light anti-aircraft fire at the Beaufort formation. Ahead, a second destroyer screen was coming into view. Cliff put the nose of the Beaufort down to try and get even lower and the others manœuvred to follow. In a moment they must see the big ships.

"There they are!"

Cliff followed Macdonald's pointing finger and saw a bulky grey shape almost dead ahead, slightly to port, perhaps three miles away. For all the time he had spent on ship recognition, Cliff was uncertain which ship it might be. But he could pick out the heavy superstructure, truncated funnel and clinker shield, and he knew it was one of the big ones. It was only later, a long time later, that he discovered it had been the *Gneisenau*. As they approached, a second big ship appeared out of the mist, a mile or so behind the *Gneisenau*. He later learned that this was the *Prinz Eugen*. There was no sign of the *Scharnhorst*.

In the original plan of attack, the assumption had been that they would approach the three ships broadside on. But now there were only two big ships, both dead ahead. "Carry out individual flight attacks," called Cliff. "Flight leaders, choose your own target. I shall take the leading ship."

The flak from escorting craft was getting more accurate, and Cliff swung away to starboard, with Birchley and Archer keeping tight formation. Cliff saw the sub-formation led by Dinsdale pass right underneath him and then carry on in a wider sweep so as to attack the second ship, the *Prinz Eugen*.

On Cliff's left, Norton and Gee had found themselves slightly to port of the big ships when they sighted them. When Cliff gave the order for individual flight attacks, Norton and Gee decided to turn to port and make their attack on the leading ship from the direction of the Dutch coast. As well as taking them out of range for the moment of the escorting craft, most of which were placed to seaward of the cruisers, it meant that the *Gneisenau* would have to face the prospect of attack from both beams simultaneously.

As the eight pilots manœuvred their aircraft into position to attack, each had to turn almost directly away from his target before swinging round for the torpedo run, and each found the utmost difficulty in picking out the big ships again in the grey light against the grey sea. Cliff, Birchley and Archer were the first to attack. The scene that confronted them, as they sped across the water towards the leading ship, changed suddenly from a colourless leaden canvas into a glittering scene of movement and colour against a backcloth of dull grey. The battle-cruiser had its heavy guns depressed and was firing eleven-inch shells at them, shells which were bouncing on the sea ahead of them like ducks and drakes and sometimes ricocheting straight up above them, sometimes throwing up great gouts of water which covered the aircraft with salt spray. All colours of flak and tracer, from crimson to yellow, from turquoise to the brightest green, were pouring from every quarter of the compass, some directed at them, some at the other Beaufort formations, some at the bombers which Cliff knew were overhead only from the huge silver splashes of water jerked up around the ships by falling bombs. Cliff had an impression of every kind of aircraft he had ever seen flying round the sky with deadly purpose. In the diminishing afternoon light the gun-flashes glowed like lighted matches in a packed football stadium. Three or four patches of fiery red, aircraft that would never fly again, were incandescent on the sea. Cliff brought the aircraft under tense control and prepared for the drop. He shut the erupting world around him from his mind and telescoped his gaze into that solid bulk ahead. He aimed off deliberately half a length ahead of the German battle-cruiser, waited until he judged his range as 1200 yards, and then let her go.

The deck of the *Gneisenau* rushed at him out of the haze as he bucked and reared his aircraft with violent jerks of the steering column. There was nothing he could do now but sit tight and pass across the stern of the ship at the lowest possible height. Suddenly he realized that he was still doing only 140 knots, that he had forgotten to open up his throttles after dropping the torp. He felt for the throttles and engaged fine pitch without taking his eye off the *Gneisenau*. He thought he had never seen so highly polished a quarter-deck. A second later the ship was behind him; and then his ear-drums were assaulted by the racket of machine-gun fire.

"What the devil's that?"

"They're shooting at *us*—I thought I'd shoot back." Tessier had got in a burst at the deck of the battle-cruiser from the tail. Cliff kept the throttles wide open and climbed away to starboard.

"Are the other two there?"

"Archer's been hit. Birchley's all right. They're both right behind us."

When the two Australians saw Cliff's torpedo drop off they dropped their own torpedoes instantly, almost in the same splash. But as they started to take evasive action a shell from the *Gneisenau* blew off the perspex top of Archer's turret and burst inside the fuselage, severely wounding the rear gunner and filling the aircraft with smoke and dust. Although half-blinded, Archer pulled the nose of the Beaufort up straight away and managed to keep control. He broke away to starboard, following Cliff, but when he learned of his gunner's injuries he set course for Manston, where he landed safely. Coming away from the *Gneisenau* the flak was still intense, and Cliff and Birchley got separated. They eventually made their way independently to North Coates. All three torpedoes had been seen to enter the water evenly and to run in the direction of the target, but no hits were observed and the *Gneisenau* turned back on course.

The formation on Cliff's right, led by Johnny Dinsdale, had to run down half the length of the convoy before turning in to attack the second big ship, the *Prinz Eugen*. In doing so it had to fly through a continuous barrage from escorting vessels. The cruiser was protected by four destroyers, and in order to press home his attack Dinsdale had to lead his formation through intense fire from the escorting screen. In spite of this all three aircraft got through safely, and Dinsdale dropped his torpedo at an estimated range of 1000 yards. Kerr dropped a moment later, but Dewhurst's torpedo failed to release. Dewhurst's gunner, however, kept his eye on Dinsdale's torpedo and saw it run to within two hundred yards of the *Prinz Eugen* before Dewhurst's steep turn to starboard on the breakaway obscured his view. Again no results were observed.

When Norton and Gee, on Cliff's left, broke away to port with the idea of making their run from the Dutch coast, they were attacked at once by Me 109s. Gee's wireless operator was hit, and Francis, his navigator, went back to take over on the side guns. Norton and Gee became separated, and in the mêlée that ensued both pilots lost sight of the *Gneisenau*. But the men on the guns fired steadily and accurately, visibility nearer the coast was extremely bad, and the fighters, although still menacing, failed to shake Norton and Gee from their purpose. Gee was one of the keenest pilots on the squadron. He was among the more serious-minded of aircrew; he didn't drink, and he took little interest in women. The run of aircrew thought him a little old-fashioned, over-precise, perhaps a trifle fussy. Because of his mannerisms they dubbed him 'Aunty', a nickname which stuck to him throughout his Beaufort days. But they recognized in him a man with the potential qualities of leadership. Norton, too, was as keen as any, and he had an experienced crew. His wireless operator, Downing, had been Loveitt's operator on the *Lutzow* attack. Yet these two pilots, shaking off the German fighters, making contact with the convoy again, picking out the *Prinz Eugen* this time, and flying through everything that the convoy could send at them, dropped their torpedoes with the same results as the rest of the squadron—'results unobserved'. The nightmare phrase to all torpedo-bomber pilots: all too often the euphemism for a miss.

Carson and Banning of 217, following their abortive sortie earlier in the afternoon when they had been sent out to look for the 'three big merchantmen', had landed back at Manston, where they, in their turn, learned for the first time the true nature of their target. It hardly seemed possible that they could have missed such an assembly of craft until they realized that the speed they had been given—eight to ten knots—was twenty knots slower than the actual speed of the convoy, throwing them many miles to the south. Banning found that he had to refuel; the following aircraft always used more petrol than the leader, because of the continual changes

Top: Norman Hearn-Phillips as a young trainee pilot in 1937. The aircraft is an Audax.

Bottom: Hearn-Phillips's Beaufort I L9791 after forced landing on 17 September 1940. (See pages 41-42)

Top: Perfect 'Rover' weather in the North Sea – low cloud and mist – and Dick Beauman gets a tanker.

Bottom: Sqn Ldr Pat Gibbs (2nd left) and crew, 22 Squadron: from left, Flt Sgts Coulson, Stephenson, Peirce. Gibbs later became Wg Cdr, D.S.O., D.F.C.

Top left: Group Captain (later Air Vice-Marshal) J. St G. Braithwaite, C.B.E.

Top centre: Ken Campbell.

Top right: Sqn Ldr W. Hedley Cliff, D.S.O., 42 Squadron.

Bottom: The *Gneisenau* in dry dock at Brest after being torpedoed by Ken Campbell (consequent V.C.). See Chapter 3.

Top: Convoy attack off Norway, 3 December 1941. The 2,500-ton *Nordlicht* has just been bombed by 42 Squadron, with smoke from the explosion drifting astern. Note shells landing in foreground.

Middle left: The men who torpedoed the *Lützow*. From left, Ray Loveitt, Percy Wallace-Pannell (seated), Al Morris and C. T. Downing, 42 Squadron.

Middle right: Eugene Esmonde.

Bottom: Arthur Aldridge (left) and crew, 217 Squadron: from left, Vince Aspinall, Alan Still, Sgt Grimmer, who was replaced by Sgt W. R. (Bill) Carroll pre-Malta.

Top: Beaufort N1182 at Portreath on 26 January 1942. Loading prior to flight to Gibraltar. From left: Lawrie Evans, Dick Marshall, 'Dodge' Doggett, 'Tommy' Tompson, RNZAF.

Bottom: SHQ RAF Sumburgh after the C.O.'s torpedo exploded, 20 March 1942. (See page 143)

Top left: Beaufort I AW196 of 86 Squadron.

Top right: Beaufort IIA DD870 of 86 Squadron.

Middle: Ralph Manning's Beaufort II after the *Prinz Eugen* strike, 17 May 1942 (see page 160).

Bottom: German 2cm (ie, 20mm) flak gun. Note 'kill' marks on barrel.

Top left: Beaufort N1170, Sidi Barrani, 26 March 1942. Lawrie Evans and Dick Marshall inspect wreckage. Evans comments: 'Dick is wondering how many months it will take to deduct the cost of his kite from his aircrew pay!'

Top right: Beaufort I N1165 of 39 Squadron, showing desert conditions in March 1942.

Bottom left: Tony Leaning.

Bottom centre: Johnny Lander.

Bottom right: Pat Gibbs.

Top: 39 Squadron's Beaufort I N1094, the aircraft in which the author was injured on 1 June 1942.

Middle left: Sgt Lionel Dafforn's Beaufort IA DD974 showing damage received on the 15 June 1942 strike (see pages 184-5).

Middle right: 42/47 Squadron tourists. From left, unknown, De Sousa, Adams, Poaps, Hearn-Phillips, McKern, Kerr, Egypt, October 1942.

Bottom: Beaufort IIA DD898 of 39 Squadron over Malta.

in throttle setting necessary to keep station. But Carson cal-
culated that he still had ample petrol in his tanks for the
round trip. Besides, he was angry. He could laugh at the
thought of himself, out there in the Channel with Banning,
peering through the mist for a fictitious target while Salmon
and Gluckstein got away. It was priceless. But he was
indignant at what he interpreted as a lack of confidence in
the squadron crews. What reason could there be for suppress-
ing the truth at this stage other than the fear that the crews
might go out and drop their fish in the open sea and then
come back with a yarn? Good God, one didn't even believe
those stories about the enemy. It was more likely that someone at Group, over-zealous for security, had husbanded his
secrets to the point of secretiveness. In any case it had been a
deplorable waste of time and effort, and he must do his best
to make up for it.

He was on the ground at Manston for only twenty-two
minutes. At three minutes to four he took off again and set
course for the target. He would find them this time.

Carson reached the estimated position of the German
squadron forty-five minutes later. It was a quarter to five on
a mid-February afternoon, and already the light was beginning to fail. The visibility was bad and it was raining. Carson
carried out a search with the aid of his radar equipment, and
he soon picked up echoes of the German ships. By the time
he found the convoy it was just after five o'clock. The
Gneisenau and *Prinz Eugen* were now shadowy, insubstantial
wraiths, indefinite against the grey sea. The rain beat fiercely
against his windscreen and wispy clouds gave him only an
intermittent view.

For a time he lost the ships altogether, but sporadic bursts
of gunfire helped him to memorize their position. He turned
towards the two big ships, still seeing little more than the
occasional flash of an 11-inch or an 8-inch gun. When he was
about 2000 yards from the ship he chose as his target there
was a splashing cascade of water beneath him and in the
same instant he felt the starboard wing lifted up with uncon-
trollable force, until the Beaufort was turned over on its back
like a beetle, still grotesquely clutching its torpedo. Then,
before Carson could grapple effectively with the controls, a

second explosion lifted the wing again until the aircraft had completed an involuntary roll.

"Bombs! Exploding bombs!"

Carson steadied the aircraft, and there straight ahead was the *Gneisenau*, less than a mile away. The next stick of bombs might finish him. He pressed the torpedo-release button, waited the interminable seconds, and then opened up his throttles and pulled out. The flak was thick and accurate and his port wing was badly holed. For a moment he thought the engine had gone. He had a sudden clear view of the *Gneisenau* and its towering superstructure, and then the mist and cloud and smoke gathered again around them and neither he nor his crew had any chance to see the torpedo run. But in the gathering gloom they escaped the attention of fighters, and they broke away safely and returned to Thorney Island.

At about the time that Carson was setting course for home, Banning, having refuelled, was taking off again at Manston. Although the light was now almost gone, and the German squadron enveloped in rain, mist and low cloud, Banning, with the aid of his A.S.V., found the ships without difficulty. Conditions for a torpedo attack were almost hopeless, but nevertheless Banning managed to find a clear lane, and he began a run up on the *Gneisenau*. The German gunners, too, had their eyes accustomed to the near-darkness, and Banning had to fly through an intense and heavy flak barrage. Banning had never dropped a torpedo before, but he was briefed to fly at 70 feet at 150 m.p.h. and aim ahead of the ship. The German squadron was getting out of range of its fighter protection, and Banning was able to watch his torpedo run. The tracks of ship and torpedo were converging, and Banning watched breathlessly. But when the torpedo had covered nearly two-thirds of the distance, the wheel of the *Gneisenau* was put hard a-port, and Banning could judge in a moment that the change of course would allow his torpedo to run away harmlessly astern. Bitterly disappointed, his throat parched and the blood still heavy in his head, he climbed away and set course for base.

The nine Beauforts of 42 Squadron and the seven of 217 Squadron, like the Swordfish, had failed to arrest the progress of the German ships. So far, not a single torpedo hit had been scored. And in addition to the torpedo-carrying aircraft, nearly 250 bombers had been employed in three separate waves throughout the afternoon. Bomber Command at this time had a total available strength of some 300 aircraft, of which about 250 were regarded as suitable for this type of operation. A number of Wellingtons were unable to take off owing to a snowbound airfield, reducing the final total to 242. This included the 100 bombers which had been specially ordered to stand by at two hours' notice. The bomber force, meagre enough in comparison with that available only a few months later, yet represented a formidable threat in terms of load-carrying capacity. If only one aircraft in ten could score a hit, the progress of the ships must be retarded. But there was ten-tenths' cloud in the Channel, never higher than 1000 feet and often as low as 500; and even these conditions were getting worse all the time. Most of the 242 bombers despatched reached the vicinity of the German squadron, but only about one in six were able to drop their bombs. Many were unable to locate the ships at all. Others found the ships but were unable to attack in spite of repeated attempts to gain sufficient height; each time they tried to do so they found themselves in cloud and lost sight of the ships. The one advantage of the weather from the crews' point of view was that it screened them from enemy fighters and to a large extent from flak. But of the 242 bomber aircraft, only 39 were known to have dropped their bombs at the German ships—and not one of these scored a hit; 188 either failed to locate the target or were unable to attack owing to the conditions. Fifteen bombers failed to return.

The last hope lay with the twelve Beauforts at St Eval.

The day began prosaically enough at St Eval with one air-craft being sent out on a routine patrol of the Bay of Biscay. But their geographical position made the crews at St Eval by far the most conscious of the ever-present threat of the three ships anchored in Brest harbour. When those ships came out—and surely they must make a break for it some day—the Beauforts at St Eval would be in the front line. Whether the ships attempted to break out into the Atlantic or up the

Channel, it would fall to the Beauforts at St Eval to strike the first blow. It was in this atmosphere that the crews at St Eval went about their daily tasks.

No. 86 Squadron, which constituted the major Beaufort force at St Eval, consisted largely of newly trained crews, recently posted from operational training. The squadron had been formed at North Coates, shortly after 22 Squadron moved down to Thorney Island, and for some months it had been in a non-operational and then a semi-operational state. Among the Beaufort squadrons it was something of a Cinderella. The reputation of 22 at North Coates had been hard enough to follow anyway; but then had come a protracted period of conversion, of training, and of torpedo practice, while the other Beaufort squadrons were adding to their laurels. To sharpen their inferiority complex, a Canadian Hudson squadron, No. 407, operating on the same station, was making the most of its opportunities in regular bombing sorties at night against enemy shipping operating off the Frisian islands. During this training period, while 86 Squadron was working up to an operational state, a number of crews were lost, some in accidents, others inexplicably in training flights over the North Sea. The squadron was further weakened by the posting overseas of a number of fully trained crews in the closing months of 1941. (Many of these crews subsequently distinguished themselves with No. 39 Squadron in the Middle East.)

The squadron became operational in November 1941, and in the following month an advance party under the squadron C.O., Wing Commander Charles Flood, moved to St Eval, in the general reshuffle when 22 was withdrawn for overseas service. The move was completed in January. The squadron's first torpedo strike took place on 2nd February, against a 5000-ton tanker with two armed trawlers as escort. Three crews took part. One crew accounted for the tanker and the other two failed to return. The squadron lost another crew next day. Three crews, led by Flood, carried out a daring and successful bombing raid on a Guernsey port. The inferiority complex was almost gone.

Also at St Eval was the detachment of six crews from 217 Squadron and the 22 Squadron holding unit, including the six crews recalled from embarkation leave. There were thirteen serviceable aircraft, less the one sent on the Bay of Biscay patrol. (Joubert has said that if he had known about the enemy jamming activity, he would never have allowed this aircraft to leave the ground.)

Of the twelve aircraft, six were manned by crews of 86 Squadron, three by crews of 217, and three by recalled crews of 22. The ground crews and administrative staff of 22 Squadron actually sailed from Liverpool later that day.

The twelve crews chosen were caught in various states of unreadiness. Etheridge, the senior pilot on the 217 detachment, had just landed from a training flight. The 22 Squadron crews were trying to organize an early lunch, with an eye to being stood down for the afternoon. As they waited to be served, the Tannoy blared.

"The following crews report to the operations block. The following crews . . ."

The sound of one's pilot's name spoken over the Tannoy system never failed to quicken the pulse and to conjure pictures in the imagination.

"There goes our early lunch."

"Be just our luck to go for a Burton on embarkation leave."

"You've been recalled, chum—haven't you heard?"

"Go on—tell me there's a war on."

They threw their plates and irons down and walked back to the control tower.

The aircraft were to fly to Thorney Island in two flights of six, led by Charles Flood. Etheridge and the three 22 Squadron crews were included because of a desire to stiffen the formation with experienced men. Only the officers were told of the escape of the ships—and they were ordered to keep their peace. The N.C.O. pilots and crew members knew only that they were to go to Thorney Island and that they might be doing a strike from there.

The Beauforts took off shortly before one o'clock and landed at Thorney Island ninety minutes later. Now the aircraft had to be refuelled. The pilots and navigators were briefed together in the operations room. The gunners were briefed in the signals briefing room. The formation was split into four flights of three. Etheridge found himself in the flight

on the extreme left, to be led by Flight Lieutenant White of
22 Squadron, the flight being made up by another 22 man,
Sergeant Fricker. Etheridge and Fricker were to stick to
White, and White in his turn was to follow Flood, who was
flying the only aircraft equipped with A.S.V. They were to
rendezvous with a Beaufighter escort over Coltishall.

As the pilots and navigators trailed out of the operations
room, thick with Irving jackets, Mae Wests and flying-boots,
drooping with navigation bags, they ran into the gunners.
For a moment the crews mingled in confusion. Then, still
shuffling towards their aircraft, they sorted themselves out
into crews. The gunners had been given frequencies and told
that the operation would be controlled by W/T from
Chatham. They were still in ignorance of the target.

"What's it all about?"

"The big boys are out." The fact that no one had yet told
the gunners was accepted without comment, as being in the
natural order of things.

"The big boys?" The gunners echoed this with an incredulous inflection, discerning the truth of it in almost the same
instant. There was a resigned yet purposeful look about these
men, even about their gait, which the gunners knew. Their
eyes looked ahead without seeing. This, perhaps, was how a
condemned man walked to his death. In the end, willingly.
Let's get it over.

"The big boys? Then what are we doing up here?"

"We'd have been better off back at St Eval."

"We wouldn't—they're right up off the Dutch coast."

"What?" The long-drawn-out, steep cadence, baring the
teeth. "Wh-a-a-at?"

"How the hell did they get there?"

"Who's been sleeping?"

"*Someone's* dropped a clanger."

And then, from the sergeants of a certain squadron: "It
wouldn't have happened if 22 had still been about."

No one, least of all the men of 86 and 217, thought for one
moment of disputing this.

"Hitler must have known 22 were on their way."

"He'd never have brought them out otherwise."

"Bloody Jerries know everything."

"This is one trip we *shan't* get back from."
And they were in their aircraft, and away.

They took off shortly after four o'clock, nearly half an hour after the unsuccessful attack by Cliff and the nine Beauforts of 42 Squadron. They were to rendezvous at Coltishall at five o'clock.

On the ground at Coltishall Wing Commander Williams, C.O. of 42 Squadron, following Cliff's departure, had soon discovered that there was no prospect of the mobile torpedo unit reaching Coltishall before dark. This left him with only one aircraft equipped with a torpedo with which to mount a second strike—and this one unserviceable. The torpedo could not be moved from one aircraft to another without proper apparatus and expert hands. So every effort was made to get the u/s aircraft ready. The pilot—Pilot Officer Wilson —and the crew were told to stand by. (The navigator of this aircraft, Sergeant Andrews, was to play a fateful part in a similar operation against the *Prinz Eugen* three months later.)

Williams had not altogether forgotten Manning, the Canadian, the man who had disappeared on the way down from Leuchars that morning. Manning and his crew, without maps, and without the wireless verification tables necessary to ask for a bearing, had criss-crossed the flat fen country trying to pick out Coltishall. Eventually they found Horsham St Faith, near Norwich, and landed there to get a map. Manning and his navigator went to the control tower, but they found the whole place in disorder. All they could get out of the controller, who had problems of his own, was a wave of the hand and the information that Coltishall was 'five minutes over there'.

After wasting all of a further hour, examining each airfield they saw for a sight of the Beauforts, and actually—like a persistent fly never allowed to settle—landing at and being chased out of three, they eventually found Coltishall. Here they learned at last what the flap was about.

Manning's instructions were to take his crew to the Mess for tea and to return in half an hour. In the meantime his aircraft would be refuelled. He and Wilson were then to take off and position themselves over the airfield at 17.15, in order to

join up with 86 Squadron, who, it was said, were to rendezvous over the airfield at that time (17.15 was the time given).
"We don't know where they're going or what they're attacking," said the controller at Coltishall. "Follow 86 Squadron,
go where they go and attack what they attack." Manning and
Wilson raised their eyebrows at each other and made their
way out to their aircraft. At 17.10 the last two armed Beauforts of 42 Squadron were ticking over at the bottom of the
runway at Coltishall.

As Manning and Wilson were getting into position for
take-off, Flood and his formation of twelve Beauforts flew
over the airfield. The roar of the approaching formation was
drowned for Manning and Wilson by the surge of their own
engines as they cleared them at the bottom of the runway.
As they turned into wind, they heard a sudden thunder of
engines and looked up to see the formation fly directly overhead.

The pilots in the formation were scanning the sky for their
fighter escort. If they saw the two Beauforts turning into wind,
it meant nothing to them. They were looking for Beaufighters.
The crews began to chatter on the intercom.

"Where are the Beaufighters?"

"Where were they coming from, anyway?"

"Can you see anything of them on the deck?"

"Not a sign of them. A couple of Beauforts, that's all."

"Either they're wonderfully well dispersed and camouflaged or they're not here."

Even over the coast the visibility was bad, and the general
weather conditions were now thoroughly unpleasant. In half
an hour it would be dark. The German ships must already be
north of Amsterdam. Flood led his Beauforts once round the
airfield and then set course.

Manning and Wilson took off at once, but the runway in
use pointed inland. By the time they had turned towards the
east the twelve Beauforts had disappeared into the late
afternoon gloom. The two crews had no information about
the position of the target, no briefing except to follow 86.
After a short and fruitless pursuit, they landed back at
Coltishall.

One of the twelve aircraft in Flood's formation was forced

to turn back with electrical trouble; but the eleven remaining Beauforts carried determined men. They knew nothing of the attacks of the other Beaufort squadrons. They were unaware that they represented the last hope in a disastrous day. But they knew, from the course, speed and position they were given, that the German ships must be escaping more or less unscathed. These men lacked nothing in the determination to press home an attack. If they lacked anything, it was torpedo experience. Only Etheridge and the three 22 Squadron pilots had ever dropped a tin fish in anger.

By the time the formation reached the estimated position of the German squadron it was nearly a quarter to six. The unseen sunset behind them threw a wan, colourless afterglow, a millionth of a candlepower which at sea-level would be darkness. Flood's radar operator could get no contact on the A.S.V. Then a wireless message came through to say that one of the ships might be thirty miles to the south-west of the main squadron. This was the damaged *Scharnhorst*. Flood began to sweep down the estimated track of the enemy ships. At five-past six they sighted four German minesweepers. The minesweepers each fired three-star red recognition signals, bathing the sea in light and shattering their long-accumulated night vision. Then came the flak.

Flood gave the signal to break formation, and each crew began searching for the capital ships. All they could find were destroyers. Sleeting barrages of rain, snow, hail and low cloud protected the German convoy and frustrated the Beauforts. Many of the crews found it impossible to see anything. Individual aircraft continued to sweep astern of the minesweepers in the hope of finding the main enemy force. But even if the ships were sighted, it looked impossible to keep anything in view for long enough to develop a torpedo attack. Most of the formation decided that any chance they might have had of making an effective attack had vanished, and set course for base.

When White, leading the sub-formation on Flood's extreme left, swung away to look for the capital ships, Etheridge and Fricker tried to follow, but they soon lost sight of him and of each other and found themselves alone. Fricker began a creeping line ahead search, east to west, west to east, east to west, a mile further south each time, looking for the convoy. Once his gunner sighted an escort vessel, but when Fricker turned back to look for it he could see nothing. They realized that they must be somewhere on the fringe of the German convoy, but there was no clue to the direction of the centre of it. They carried out a square search, saw nothing, realized that conditions were impossible, and turned for home. Unsure of their position, and unable to get wireless assistance because of the general congestion of the ether, they aimed to hit East Anglia and then coast-crawl down to Thorney. Suddenly they heard the 'squeakers' on the R/T and saw a barrage balloon so near that they could almost have leaned out and used it as a punch-ball. They were in the Thames Estuary. It wasn't until half an hour later, when they picked out Brighton's piers, that they pinpointed their position. Their petrol was now desperately low. At last the searchlights picked them up and directed them to Thorney. They had failed, failed even to find the German squadron, and had lost themselves on the way home. They decided that they must be just about the worst crew in Coastal Command. But when they landed they found they were the only crew apart from the C.O. to get back to Thorney. (The others landed back at airfields all over the country.) They were interrogated next morning, and then travelled back to St Eval by train, via London, lugging their parachutes through the London tube, hatless, still in their flying-kit.

When Etheridge found himself alone, he could see the bursts of flak shining through the mist around him, but the ships remained invisible. He knew he must be somewhere near the Dutch coast, and he thought that if he could check his position in relation to the coastline he could set course again for the target area and have a reasonable chance of approaching the German ships at right angles, so as to be in position to attack if he got the merest glimpse of super-structure. He knew he could not hope to see much more. After a minute or so the navigator called out that they were over the coast. Holland was bare and flat and apparently dis-interested. But as they circled to get a pinpoint, the Beaufort was suddenly surrounded by flak. In the light of the gun explosions they saw the sombre outlines of a flak tower, standing alone in the sand, like some medieval fortress. Etheridge set course for the convoy. Again the first indication he had that he was over the ships was the bursting of flak in the cloud above and around him. Twice more Etheridge repeated the trick of orientating himself on the Dutch shore and running up to the convoy. Each time he was shot at by shore batteries and by the ships themselves, although he couldn't see them. As he approached the ships for the third time, his Beaufort was hit by flak. The hydraulic system was severed, the wireless operator wounded, and the radio put out of action. Etheridge realized that he would have to give up. It was hopeless. He'd better make the best of it and at least try to make sure of getting home.

Etheridge's navigator gave him a course for Norfolk—the quickest way back. There were plenty of airfields there, it was flat, and in that area they must be used to aircraft limping home at night, from experience of Bomber Command. As they crossed the coast Etheridge recognized Lowestoft. He switched his navigation lights on, and soon a searchlight pointed the way for them. The signpost was extended by further searchlights, until eventually they flew over an airfield. Etheridge tried to get the undercarriage down, but he soon abandoned the idea. Better to make a straight belly-flop. The navigator recognized the airfield as Horsham St Faith— a grass field, ideal for their purpose. Etheridge made his approach correctly and began to hold off. Just before he breasted the aircraft into the ground he remembered that he hadn't jettisoned the torpedo. It was too late to do anything about it now. Without flaps he'd never have the lift to go round again. Maybe the torp wouldn't have released anyway. All he could do was sit tight and wait for the blinding light and the darkness. But the torpedo eased his landing, acting as a skid on the frozen airfield. The aircraft was hardly damaged at all. Just a slight grazing of the belly and bent props and no more.

Etheridge, too, told his story next day. For his persistence he was awarded the D.F.C.

White, the leader of Etheridge's sub-formation, and Matthewson, the leader of the formation on the right, like Finch, like the second flight of Swordfish, like the seventeen aircraft of Fighter Command and the fifteen of Bomber Command, were never seen again.

The last Beaufort attack on the *Scharnhorst*, *Gneisenau* and *Prinz Eugen*, like those that had gone before, had failed.

The escape of the German ships was and still is regarded by the Germans as a great victory and by the British as a humiliation. The news was greeted in Britain by widespread dismay and indignation, and a court of enquiry was ordered. Enemy capital ships had sailed through the English Channel for the first time for two hundred and fifty years, and the man in the street, brought up to believe in the inviolability of his moat, couldn't understand how it could have happened.

How did it happen?

Firstly, the Navy, because of its commitments elsewhere, and because of the dominance by the enemy of European coastal waters from Norway to the Bay of Biscay, was power-less to interfere—except to the extent of a few destroyers and motor torpedo-boats. Even these small forces were greatly feared by the Germans, and this was a contributory reason to the decision to leave Brest in darkness and make the passage of the Straits in daylight, when attacks by light naval forces against a well-escorted convoy would have less chance of success.

Secondly, there was the weakness of our strike forces. Thirdly, there was the weather. These and these alone were the decisive factors. A lot has been said and written about mistakes. Mistakes there certainly were, plus an absolute catalogue of imperfections which may or may not have been avoidable; but it is extremely doubtful whether any of them materially affected the issue.

The ships should never have got so far without being detected. They should have been discovered by the night patrols. The day patrols should have extended further west. (If the crews of the patrolling aircraft had known that the departure of the ships was considered imminent, they might, being only human, have been doubly vigilant.) But suppose, some time during the night, or in the early morning, that the ships had been discovered. Is there any reason to believe that the outcome would have been different?

Although the ships were not identified until they had been at sea for thirteen hours, the entire strength of Bomber Command was employed against them before dark, the Fleet Air Arm Swordfish made their attack, and of the 28 Beauforts available, sixteen had had their opportunity and failed before the weather became impossible—which suggests that the last twelve, if their attacks could have been delivered, would have been no more successful.

Co-operation between fighters and strike aircraft was imperfect, and this was blamed on the lack of preliminary warning. Wasn't it bound to be so without intense training? Was there, in the harassed months of 1941 and early 1942, ever the opportunity for such training? Would a few hours' notice really have improved co-ordination to any decisive extent? All that can be said is that it would probably have given the Swordfish time to make their attack with a full complement of five squadrons for cover and escort, and might possibly have given the bombers a chance to drop a few armour-piercing bombs in the better conditions that prevailed earlier in the day. How effective close escort of the Swordfish might have been was shown by the fighters that attempted it. In any case the evidence is that the majority, perhaps all, of the Swordfish were eventually shot down by flak.

The bombers could not hope to do more than superficial damage without armour-piercing bombs; these had to be dropped from a height of at least 4000 feet. But for most of the day the cloud base was 1000 feet or less, and the bombers had no blind-bombing devices as yet. So most of the bombers carried general-purpose bombs, which could never achieve penetration, though it was hoped they might cause some damage by blast. A few aircraft were fitted with armour-piercing bombs in the hope that breaks in the cloud might enable high-altitude attacks to be made; but none found their target. The conditions were hopeless for bombing. Dive-bombing, even if we had had the aircraft to do it, would have been impossible. Galland claimed that the bad weather favoured the R.A.F., basing his claim on the premise that bomber crews welcome cloud as cover, whereas cloud is anathema to the fighter; the truth is that the weather robbed Bomber Command of the chance of playing other than a secondary, diversionary role in the operation, while at the same time providing the odd crumb of comfort in making the bombers harder to shoot down.

Under these conditions, the most important striking force was the Beauforts; but compared with the bombers they were a tiny force. Unlike the bomber, which could seek out and find land targets, torpedo aircraft had to await the presentation of a suitable target. To maintain a force of torpedo aircraft sufficient to deal with any situation would have been uneconomic.

Denuded as this small force was by the demands of overseas theatres, inexperienced as were most of the crews, and undeveloped as were their tactics, they were yet the only force with a chance of dealing a crippling blow. But even if there had been time to co-ordinate the Beaufort strikes, and even if all the crews had been of long experience, there would have been little prospect of delivering a concerted attack under the conditions of bad visibility and low cloud. (The changing of the leadership of one squadron, and the loss of the leader of another on a minor strike four days earlier, might have been avoided; but in the event the crews were fortunate in their leaders and responded with numerous acts of individual gallantry.)

What happened to the torpedoes? Even allowing for the conditions, which in any case were not much worse than those under which Beaufort crews had been accustomed to fly on Rover operations, how did the torpedo-bomber force manage to miss these immense targets?

None of the pilots had dropped before against targets moving at such speed. The pace of these ships was something outside their experience. Distance over water is notoriously difficult to judge, and even at two miles' range targets of this size seemed to tower above low-flying aircraft. Whatever the crews' own estimates of range, German reports suggest that most of the torpedoes were dropped from a distance of at least a mile. At this range, a torpedo travelling at 40 knots would take $1\frac{1}{2}$ minutes to reach its target. And since the ships were steaming at over 30 knots, they would cover nearly 1500 yards in the time it took the torpedo to run. The length of the battle-cruisers was 741 feet—about 250 yards. So to hit the target in a beam attack, assuming it held its course, the torpedo pilot must aim six lengths ahead. Even at a range of half a mile—and no one got in as close as this—the torpedo would have to be aimed three lengths ahead. No wonder the ships were not hit. The torpedoes missed astern, or the fast-moving ships, faced with only one torpedo at a time, were able to avoid them by changing course.

Would the Beaufort crews have done any better had they been forewarned? Was there anything to be lost by letting the air crews of all commands into the secret?

Security and Intelligence played a vital part throughout the war. We expected to have a breathing space between the discovery of the break-out and the passage of the ships through the Channel. This was regarded as long enough to brief the air crews. The Germans, too, kept everyone in ignorance of what was afoot, but it did not noticeably impair their resolution or zest. Yet it may be doubted whether we should have lost anything if everybody had been told the facts from the start, even though this might have meant that the enemy was less in the dark about the measures we were taking. Inadequate as they were in practice, they were not unimpressive on paper.

The Swordfish crews knew what they were at Manston for, and yet they, like the Beauforts, failed. Their losses, compared with those of the Beauforts, are explained by their greater vulnerability, and by the fact that their attack had to be made at a point where the enemy could develop his maximum defence in air cover and escort craft.

It may be argued that the knowledge of an action to come, however desperate, acts as a stimulus to valour. It is possible, too, to argue the reverse.

The operation has been held to be a defeat for air power. But air power as such was hardly applied—except in defence by the *Luftwaffe*. A large number of aircraft were thrown into the fray, but it wasn't an application of air power. The sinking of the *Prince of Wales* and the *Repulse*, though, was only two months old, and comparisons were inevitable. The true lesson was that successful air attacks might be made on capital ships provided their defences could be saturated. When the flak remained unsilenced and the fighters went unchecked, this type of attack was, to say the least, uncertain and precarious.

Yet the British public was right to be astonished at the passage of the German ships through the Straits of Dover in daylight. The Admiralty and Air Ministry, in possession of vast Intelligence unavailable to the public, were themselves surprised. And this in spite of the fact that, from the global view of war natural to the insular mind, they had foreseen and feared the event six months before it had even occurred to the enemy.

The break-out was a striking demonstration of the advantages of being the first to take action, even when that action could be closely foretold. As was demonstrated later in the invasion of Europe, even when an operation was long-awaited and dreaded and all one's dispositions had been set to meet it, the side in the position of initiating the action could still achieve surprise.

The move of the ships enabled Bomber Command to concentrate at last on the aerial bombardment of Germany. Now, even the bombs that missed these ships fell on German soil. And when, only sixteen days later, the *Gneisenau* suffered two direct hits and lost ninety of her crew in a Bomber Command raid on Kiel, the answer had been given to the Admiralty appreciation that "our bombers have shown that we can place little reliance on them to damage the enemy". *Gneisenau* never went to sea again.

The *Scharnhorst*, too, which hit another mine on its way to Wilhelmshaven, was out of action for some months, and on 23rd February the *Prinz Eugen*, on her way from Kiel to Trondheim, was torpedoed by the submarine *Trident* and lost about twenty feet of her stern together with her rudder. But both ships survived to give us trouble later in northern waters.

Admiral Raeder himself said that the German Navy "in winning a tactical victory had suffered a strategic defeat". This is a comfortable summing-up for the British, and not without its aptness. Roosevelt, in a cable to Churchill, recorded his conviction that "the location of all the German ships in Germany makes our joint North Atlantic naval problem more simple". From Brest they had threatened all east-bound Atlantic convoys, enforcing two-battleship escorts.

Their position astride our vital communications had been abandoned apparently for nothing. But to have sunk the *Scharnhorst* or *Prinz Eugen* would have been an immense contribution towards redressing the balance of naval power, of inestimable value later to our Russian convoys. The escape of the German ships was a serious defeat. More than anything it was a defeat for the torpedo-bombers. They never had quite the same chance again.

Raeder's conclusion, when adopted by us, smacks rather of the team knocked out of the cup saying "good, now we can concentrate on the league". It would have been a great achievement to pull off the double.

But even had we been given the time of departure twenty-four hours in advance, the *Scharnhorst*, *Gneisenau* and *Prinz Eugen* must have got through. Without in any sense belittling the German achievement, which stands for all time as an impudent and embarrassing feat of arms, we had no chance of preventing it in the prevailing weather conditions with the resources at our command.

Chapter 7

THE ATTACK ON THE *PRINZ EUGEN*

IN spite of the damage done to her off the Norwegian coast by the submarine *Trident* on 23rd February, the German cruiser *Prinz Eugen* succeeded in reaching Trondheim. But having done so, all she could look forward to was a makeshift repair which might enable her to struggle back to Kiel.

In the spring of 1942, the German plans for this operation were being laid. The *Prinz Eugen* was fitted with a 'jury' stern-piece at Trondheim. But her cruising speed and man-œuvrability were inevitably reduced, and the Germans decided to attempt to divide the British reconnaissance and strike effort by running the newly repaired *Lutzow* from the Baltic to Trondheim simultaneously with the move southwards of the *Prinz Eugen*.

Following the Channel Dash, Hitler had concentrated almost his entire remaining naval strength on the Norwegian coast; the *Tirpitz, Admiral Scheer* and *Hipper*, and the damaged *Prinz Eugen*, constituted a perpetual threat to our Russian convoys. But these ships were kept under continual surveillance by reconnaissance aircraft. And the Beauforts of 42, 86 and 217 Squadrons swarmed north to watch over them, to Leuchars, to Wick, and to Sumburgh in the Shetlands, waiting their chance to strike.

The use of airfields as far north as possible was dictated by the location of the German ships. But the operation of Beauforts from Sumburgh was a hazardous undertaking. The airfield was situated on a spit of land with the sea on two sides and a 1200-foot hill less than three miles from one end of the runway, with a smaller hill in line with the other end of the runway and close to the edge of the airfield. To add to the difficulties, the weather in these northern latitudes was notoriously capricious, and forecasting was uncertain.

On 20th March, six aircraft of 42 Squadron took off from Sumburgh in the late afternoon on a special strike off the Norwegian coast. They failed to find their target, and during the search lost contact with each other in falling darkness and worsening weather. Birchley and Archer, the two Australians, got back to Sumburgh, but Birchley overshot the runway and wrecked his aircraft on the rocks. Archer landed safely. Two other aircraft crashed into the Shetland hills, the two gunners surviving one crash and one of the gunners the other. All three survivors were badly injured. Another aircraft landed safely at Wick after being diverted from Sumburgh. The strike had been led by the C.O., Wing Commander Williams. Williams himself found Sumburgh all right, but misjudged his let-down over the hill. The trick on black nights was to come in high and make a steep descent. Williams allowed his speed to drop off too much and his aircraft stalled and flopped from side to side. Eventually it crashed at the end of the runway and ploughed off into the rough ground, disintegrating as it went. While still moving at speed it struck a small frame building dignified by the title 'S.H.Q.'. Inside the headquarters building sat an airman, making use of the only facility offered by the building to its off-duty staff. Out of the dust and wreckage stepped the C.O., followed by the rest of his crew. Williams, a dapper little man at any time, banged the dust off his uniform and set out primly after his rapidly retreating crew, sparing himself time to bid the paralysed airman good evening. The sound of his commanding officer's voice had an electric effect on the airman; he pulled up his trousers and ran. Sixty seconds later the torpedo went off.

Thus the weeks of tragi-comedy passed until, early in May 1942, the standbys became longer and more frequent. Intelligence reports of an impending sortie by the *Lutzow* became more insistent, and the *Prinz Eugen*, her temporary repairs completed, was known to be making ready to return to Kiel. Naval activity in the Norwegian fjords was observed by our reconnaissance aircraft almost daily, and the indications were so strong that two Russian convoys which were about to sail were postponed. Nothing was to stand in the way of our air effort against these ships. The primary target was regarded as the *Prinz Eugen*, with the *Lutzow* as target No. 2. Plans for torpedo operations against these ships, however, received a setback early in May when it was decided

to withdraw 217 Squadron and send it to Malta to be ready
to take part in the June Malta convoy operation. Two Beaufort Squadrons however remained, 86 at Sumburgh and 42
at Leuchars.

Wing Commander Williams, C.O. of 42 Squadron, was
utterly determined to get these ships. Because of the short
time he had been on the squadron, he had given way to Cliff
when the Brest ships had escaped through the Channel. His
decision to pass the leadership to Cliff that day, undoubtedly
justified, was a bitter one for a commanding officer to have
to make. The escape of the ships still rankled. In the first
fortnight in May, Williams threw himself unreservedly into
the task of bringing his squadron to that state of training and
confidence which it had lacked the previous February.
Williams's crew had been with the squadron for a long time.
Andrews, his navigator, had been in the second wave on the
Lutzow attack of June 1941. He had finished his first operational tour shortly after the Channel Dash, in which he had
been in one of the aircraft which had taken off from Coltishall late in the day and lost 86 Squadron in the gathering
gloom. But when it came to a posting at the end of his tour,
Andrews recoiled. He was happy on 42 Squadron; it was his
whole life. His pilot had already been posted, but Andrews
asked if he could remain on the squadron. There were no
heroics about it. He felt more apprehensive about his fate on
a training unit than with the experienced pilots of the
squadron on operational flying. Out of loyalty and comradeship the two gunners in Andrews's crew decided to make the
same request. Williams, it will be remembered, needed a
crew. He was pleased enough to get three such well-tried and
experienced men. On his first trip with them he deferred to
some extent to their experience; but after that he was the boss.

On 6th May, following a rumour that the *Prinz Eugen* was
out, six aircraft of the squadron carried out a sweep of the
Skagerrak. They found nothing; and within a few hours the
cruiser was seen again in Trondheim harbour. It was a false
alarm. But the concentration of aircraft in north-eastern
Scotland continued. Beaufighters and Blenheim squadrons
were on their way to act as escorts. Williams, anxious to keep
his men in trim, went out of his way to organize practice

formation flights. Too much flying might be the cause of an occasional crack in morale, but more often the cause was too little.

The first formation practice, with a Beaufighter escort, was carried out over the Firth of Forth on 9th May. The difficulties of keeping station in a turn, especially for the outside aircraft, were considerable. They had a much greater distance to cover, and if the leader made anything more than a shallow, flat turn, the aircraft on the edge of the formation lost contact, and sometimes lost sight of each other, so as to be in grave danger of collision. All this was carefully re-hearsed on the 9th, simulating the conditions of an actual attack as far as possible, and again two days later. On the second occasion, the two outside Beauforts collided. One went straight into the drink with the loss of all its crew; the second Beaufort, its nose sheared off by the tail of the first aircraft, so that a 150-m.p.h. gale blew violently through the fuselage, spun down after it. Three hundred feet above the water the pilot regained control. He flew straight back to Leuchars and landed safely, his aircraft standing for two days in a hangar, the object of wonder. The pilot took another aircraft up on air test half an hour later.

Nightly during this tense standby period, the crews of 42 Squadron gathered in the Sergeants' Mess, where they drank beer and discussed the coming operation. The morale of the squadron had never been higher—until this collision.

Williams had now been on the squadron long enough to have impressed his personality on it. He was a respected and popular C.O. But on occasions like this there was always somebody ready to draw the inference that if the C.O. hadn't been so mad keen on his bloody practice, Sergeant So-and-So and his crew would still have been with us.

There was no tradition of not talking about a crew that had gone. Not, anyway, in Coastal Command. The accident threw a pall over the Mess party that night, but slowly the tongues were loosened by the beer. Exactly what had caused the accident? Who was to blame?

Englishmen, with an innate respect for class distinctions, for differences of rank, would never have the temerity to criticize a wing commander within his hearing. They were as quick to size up a man as anyone. But they found it natural and easy to be led, and thus they were easy to lead. This was not always so with Dominion crews. If they happened to have been on a squadron longer than a C.O., they might not always prove to be the easiest of subordinates at first, although they quickly responded to personality and leadership. Added to this was a natural and highly developed individualism which was at once their weakness and their strength.

There were a number of possible causes of the accident. The most likely was an error of judgment on the part of the crews concerned. But a contributory cause could have been bad formation flying by the leader, in that too tight a turn was made. In a Sergeants' Mess hushed with horror, this was exactly the accusation which Birchley and Archer, the two Australians, levelled at Williams.

It was a critical moment in the fortunes of the squadron, but Williams took it calmly. It was a fantastic situation—a commanding officer arraigned before a whole squadron. Only the tensions of the moment, the equal responsibility that N.C.O. pilots bore, the friendships that sprang up within a crew between commissioned and non-commissioned officers, the high morale of the squadron, could justify these parties. Under no other circumstances could such an incident have arisen. But the routine barriers between men of different rank were suspended, or anyway attenuated, while the party was on. It wasn't any use pulling rank at this stage. No use to bluster. Misguided or scandalous as the charge might be, it had to be answered.

Williams acted like a man who was sure of his ground. Across the Mess floor, amongst a group of men who had sensed the electric atmosphere but did not yet know the reason for it, Williams spotted Andrews, his navigator. He called him over.

"Yes, sir?"

"What sort of turn did I make today?"

"Perfectly normal turn, sir."

"Sure?"

"Yes. I was watching the turn-and-bank indicator. It was just a normal flat formation turn."

Williams turned to the two Australians.

"Satisfied?"

The incident was not referred to again. But in his handling of it, Williams had cemented the squadron round him, the Australians as well. Williams, for his part, decided that the squadron was as near the top line as it was ever likely to be. He ordered no more formation practices.

Day after day the squadron stood by, almost throughout the hours of daylight. Towards six o'clock, by which time it was too late to organize a strike and reach the Norwegian coast before nightfall, they were stood down. Then the crews got together in the Mess, talked shop, planned the destruction of the *Prinz Eugen*. Williams had left them in no doubt whatever that when the time came, the attack would be pressed right home.

On 16th May, Andrews, who was suffering from a cold, went to sick quarters for something to clear it. The N.C.O. in charge insisted that Andrews see the M.O.

"You can't fly with a cold like that," said the M.O. "I'm putting you on light duties for forty-eight hours." The doctor was already filling in the forms.

"It's all right, Doc. We're only on standby. Don't take me off flying."

"Standby? You can't be on standby either with a cold like that. I'm putting you on light duties, my lad. No standing-by."

"But we've been on standby for weeks, Doc. Nothing's likely to happen. If you could just give me something to help clear my head, I'll be O.K. to-morrow."

"We'll see. For the moment I'm grounding you."

"But I'm the C.O.'s navigator, Doc. There's a big strike coming off. The C.O. will go mad if he hears I'm grounded."

"I'll talk to the C.O." The M.O. picked up the phone. "I've got your navigator down here, sir," Andrews heard him say. "Bad head-cold. Puts him out for flying for a couple of days, I'm afraid."

Andrews couldn't hear what Williams was saying, but he could judge from the cadences that came across to him and from the look on the M.O.'s face that he was putting up a fight. At length the M.O. got a word in.

"Well, I'm the M.O., and I say he can't."

The M.O. listened again for a moment.

"Very good, sir." He turned to Andrews. "He wants to see you right away."

"I bet he does," thought Andrews. He hurried round to the C.O.'s office.

"Why didn't you tell me you had a cold, Andrews?"

"It's not much, sir. I went to sick quarters to get something to clear it, and they made me see the M.O. He says I can't fly."

"Who can we get to stand in for you?"

"Well, there are several spare navigators about." Andrews mentioned a few names.

"They're all new men. No good at all. Suppose the P.E. comes out? I can't take a new chap on a job like this."

"I'll be all right in twenty-four hours, sir."

"That may be too late. I shall have to have someone else's navigator standing by. Who can you think of?"

"There is one chap." Andrews was thinking aloud. "Al Morris."

"Who?"

"Morris. Loveitt's old navigator. He flew with Loveitt on the *Lutzow* do. Canadian. He must be just about the most experienced navigator on the squadron."

"Why don't I know about him?"

"He's finished his tour, sir. He's sitting about in the crew-room waiting for the boat back to Canada. I'm sure he'd stand in for me for a day or so."

"Good. He'll do."

"Of course, he *is* tour expired."

"Yes. Well, you'd better ask him if he'll do it. There's a chance he might have to go."

"I'll ask him right away, sir."

Andrews found Morris in the crew-room. He explained the situation. It would only be for a day or so. They'd been standing by for days and nothing had happened. Something would come off sooner or later, but there was no sign at the moment. He'd try to get the M.O. to pass him fit for flying duties tomorrow.

Morris was a shade reluctant, but he had known Andrews

for a long time. They had been on the *Lutzow* do together. The chances of his having to fly seemed remote. At length he agreed.

Later that morning, reconnaissance aircraft spotted the *Lutzow*, escorted by four destroyers and a torpedo-boat. She had left the Baltic twenty-four hours earlier and was now nearing the Skaw, on her way to Norway. And during the afternoon, a second report told of a cruiser in Trondheim Leden, preceded by two destroyers, steering south-west at speed. The *Prinz Eugen* was on her way back to Germany.

42 Squadron were held in readiness to strike at the *Lutzow*. News of the break-out of the *Prinz Eugen* did not come until late that afternoon. All day on the 16th they waited. They would not have the range to mount a strike until the *Lutzow* reached Kristiansand, which at her present rate of progress would be shortly before midnight. Meanwhile reconnaissance aircraft were keeping the *Lutzow* under observation, while others watched for signs of movement at Trondheim. Ten minutes after the *Prinz Eugen* was spotted in Trondheim Leden, the *Lutzow* was re-sighted. The reconnaissance pilot made quite sure before making his report. The *Lutzow* had put about and was steering south, back to the Baltic. The 42 Squadron strike was therefore cancelled.

But the *Lutzow* had merely doubled back on her tracks to put us off the scent. She held her southerly course until dark, then put about once again, rounded the Skaw, dodged the night patrols, and anchored in a fjord near Kristiansand shortly after daylight. It was an old trick, but it had come off. She was not seen again for nearly thirty-six hours, and although fourteen Beauforts went after her on the 18th, she escaped attack and reached Trondheim safely on 20th May.

Meanwhile, on 16th May, while 42 Squadron were being foxed by their old enemy, fourteen Beauforts of 86 Squadron took off shortly before midnight to strike at the *Prinz Eugen* off Stadtlandet, where it was computed that her rate of progress must have brought her. The reconnaissance report had been accurate and the estimate of subsequent progress unerring, and only extreme darkness prevented a sighting

149

being made. The look-out on the *Prinz Eugen* actually saw four of the Beauforts pass close astern at 01.00 hours on the 17th. Reconnaissances were flown throughout the morning, and at midday she was sighted again, accompanied by four destroyers, a few miles north of Haugesund. She had progressed south by a distance of nearly 200 miles in the last twelve hours.

Hampdens of Bomber Command had laid mines in the Haugesund area during the night and news of this had reached the German squadron. While they awaited precise information of the minefields in their path, the *Prinz Eugen* and her escort turned back on their tracks. After an hour and a half on a north-easterly course, however, and still lacking the information he needed, the German commander turned south again, taking to the open sea to avoid the minefields. No contact had been made by our reconnaissance aircraft since just after midday, but at 15.40 the German convoy was spotted outside Karmoy Island, steering south at an estimated 17 knots.

For 42 Squadron, too, the long standby was at an end. The two squadrons of Beauforts, waiting at their airfields opposite southern Norway, were given their orders to strike.

The assumption was that the enemy force would pass Lister somewhere between 19.00 and 20.00 hours that evening. The pincer-movement tactics of the *Lutzow* attack were to be attempted again. 42 Squadron were to make for a position some fifty miles south of Mandal, at the southernmost tip of Norway, and then work back in a north-westerly direction towards Lister. 86 Squadron were to make a landfall off Egero Island and sweep south-east along the coast. The timing of the take-offs of the two squadrons—17.45 and 18.00—was arranged so that the two attacks should take place in quick succession, if not simultaneously.

The A.O.C.-in-C. Coastal Command gave orders for all available aircraft to be employed on the strike. The Leuchars force comprised twelve Beauforts, led by Wing Commander Williams, with a fighter escort of four Beaufighters, together with six Blenheims, who were to spread out on either side of the Beauforts and make dummy torpedo attacks so as to confuse the anti-aircraft defences of the enemy force, and who were to attack any fighters seen in the vicinity. The Wick force consisted of fifteen Beauforts, led by Jimmy Hyde (now a flight commander on 86, at the beginning of his second tour), a fighter escort of four Beaufighters, and a high-level diversionary bombing force of twelve Hudsons. The Leuchars force set course in formation at 18.02 and the Wick Force at 18.13. It was a warm, bright, crystal-clear summer evening, and the aircraft were silhouetted against a cloudless sky.

At the final briefing at Leuchars, Williams left his men in no doubt of the determination of their leader. No one fancied his chances of getting back. If Williams went right in close, everyone else would have to do the same. Williams outlined the tactics to be employed.

"The Beauforts will be employed in two waves, each of six aircraft. I shall lead the first wave, Dinsdale the second. The two waves will be spaced 2000 yards apart. If the *Prinz Eugen* maintains her present course and speed, we shall come upon her almost dead ahead, slightly to our starboard, somewhere off Lister. I shall hold my course until I am in position to turn in and attack the *Eugen* in the stern quarter. The rest of you in the first wave will follow me in. Dinsdale in the second wave will lead his aircraft into an attack from the starboard bow. If we keep the right spacing, and time our turn in to the attack correctly, the enemy cruiser will be faced with two attacks at the same time, one aimed at her stern quarter and one at her bows.

"When I turn in to attack, my force will be committed. Dinsdale, 2000 yards astern, should be prepared to change the direction of his attack according to the manner in which the *Prinz Eugen* reacts to my turn.

"The enemy cruiser has an escort of four destroyers. She will probably be hugging the coast off Lister, and in any case will be well within range of land-based fighter protection. We can expect fierce opposition.

"For our part, our chance to complete the destruction of this already damaged ship has come at last. We shall be expected to sink it. That means going in close. After I've dropped my torpedo I shall turn towards the *Eugen* in an endeavour to draw her fire away from the aircraft following me up. As far as I'm concerned, either I'm going to get the *Eugen* or it's going to get me."

The atmosphere in the operations room was electric. The air was laden with smoke from innumerable cigarettes which were puffed at continuously. Never had men smoked like it. Morris, standing on the dais with Williams, was a man waking from a dream. Hardly had he agreed to go than the panic started. It was tempting the fates too far. He looked deeply disturbed, a man with a premonition that he wouldn't get back. But he did not flinch from his decision. The squadron needed him, and that was enough.

At Wick the atmosphere was much the same. The squadron had in Jimmy Hyde far and away the most experienced torpedo pilot on the operation. They would be well led, and they were ready to respond.

An important part of the plan for the operation was a reconnaissance Beaufighter, which was to re-locate the enemy force and report its position, course and speed. Then if the *Prinz Eugen* tried any tricks of deception, the striking force could be warned to alter course. But when the enemy force was sighted it was still steering south-east, having reached a position some fifteen miles south of Egero Island. In spite of her 'jury'-rigged stern, the *Prinz Eugen* was proceeding at high speed—very much faster than had been thought possible. The enemy commander knew that this was the critical phase.

Before she could make her report, the Beaufighter was subjected to a determined attack by Me 109s—a foretaste of what was to come. Eventually, when the attack was shaken off, a report was transmitted. A new position was then relayed to the two strike forces. 42 Squadron had already reached a point south of Mandal and turned north-west.

The work of the reconnaissance aircraft had been of such a high order that it was a tragedy that this report should contain a position error. The circumstances under which the report had been compiled made the error, if not excusable, at least understandable. To add to the confusion, a wrong time of origin was given when the message was relayed to the strike forces by the wireless control station. When the position was worked out, it showed the *Prinz Eugen* as still some way north of Egero Island. In fact, the enemy force, having travelled south-east down the Norwegian seaboard from Stavanger for some hours, had turned due east to pass through the Skagerrak just before 20.00 hours, five minutes before the strike forces received the erroneous message.

The garbled position report had no serious consequences for 42 Squadron. They had just sighted the Norwegian coast-line when the report came through. They set their faces to a longer journey along the coast before they should sight the enemy; but the true position of the *Prinz Eugen* lay only a few miles starboard of their track. As it happened, they were bound to see it.

The blue skies and sunlit waters had lasted all the way across the North Sea. But now the sun was setting and a low bank of dull-grey cloud lay over the brown hills of Norway. Visibility was perfect, the air was clear, the sky suffused with light. At 20.15 the crews in the leading wave had their first glimpse of the German ships, away to starboard, six or seven miles distant.

"What's that over there? Looks like some kind of a vessel."

"There's several of them. Three, four, five. Looks like two destroyers out in front."

"It's the *Eugen* all right."

Already Williams was turning in towards the German cruiser; but because of the angle at which they had come upon the enemy ships, Dinsdale and the second wave were better placed to make their attack at once. Dinsdale was already in position for an attack on the bow whereas Williams had to manœuvre. When Williams turned in to attack the stern quarter, Dinsdale was already approaching the bows of the target. It was out of the question to delay his attack. German reconnaissance aircraft had spotted them, and several Me 109s were bearing down on them. If he could see a clear run, he would go straight in.

Two of the escorting destroyers were about a mile ahead of the cruiser, and a third was tucked in close on the starboard side, at not more than 200 to 300 yards' distance. The fourth destroyer was a mile astern. Dinsdale decided that he would run straight in behind the first two destroyers and in front of the third, drop his torpedo some 500 yards before he came up alongside the third destroyer, and break away to star-

F*   153

board, away from the fire of the cruiser and the close destroyer, though to some extent into the fire of the leading destroyers. All he had to do was to maintain his present course.

Dindsale had Nichol on his left and Whiteside on his right. Behind him were Pett, Kerr and Dewhurst. Kerr and Dewhurst had gone in behind Dinsdale on the *Scharnhorst-Gneisenau* attack three months earlier. Pett had been on that attack and also on the first *Lutzow* attack; he was senior in squadron service to everyone except Dinsdale.

Ahead were the German ships, with just enough water between them and the shore to silhouette them. Enemy fighters weaved back and forth in front of the target. Every few moments the *Eugen*'s 8-inch guns winked a mammoth Aldous signal at them. Huge waterspouts which rose above the height of the aircraft measured the guns' accuracy. Heavy black and white puffs punctured the sky around them, ominous, deathly still. The guns of the three leading destroyers were getting their range.

Now they were stirred at the sight of the Beaufighters flashing past them, clearing the lane ahead as the swimmer cleaves the water, diving down on the leading destroyer, cannons firing, silencing the guns and thinning out those ugly puffs of smoke. Then one of the leading destroyers began laying a smoke screen. The smoke drifted down in front of them. One Beaufighter swept down on the close destroyer, right in front of the Beauforts, spattering the decks and routing the gunners. Dinsdale, with two Me 109s just above him, ran in to within 2000 yards of the *Prinz Eugen* and dropped his torpedo. Almost immediately the cruiser began to turn away to port, northwards, towards the coast. As Dinsdale broke away to starboard he looked straight up at the German fighters 500 feet above him, but they did not attack. Whiteside on his right dropped and broke away just behind him. Nichol, on Dinsdale's left, still held on, watching the *Prinz Eugen*'s turn, uncertain how it would affect the drop, determined to get as close as he could.

"Go on, drop it! Dinsdale's dropped his!" The navigator's voice was a mixture of keenness and apprehension. Nichol held his course, rushing towards the cruiser, skating over the

154

water, aiming his torpedo to pass 100 yards ahead of the close destoyer. All the cruiser's guns were firing at them point-blank. Behind the cruiser, the shore batteries were spitting wrathfully, the basso profundo of a metallic choir.

"Go on, drop it!" The navigator's voice reached a crescendo. "Go on, drop it!" And then, in petulant despair— "All right! Drop it when you bloody-well like!"

Nichol was 1000 yards from the German cruiser, and perhaps no more than 600 yards from the close destroyer. He held the aircraft steady. An Me 109 was approaching on the port bow. To take evasive action now would be to throw his torpedo away. As he dropped his torpedo at the retreating cruiser, a burst of tracer from the German fighter streaked over his head like sparks from a train.

Now he should turn away to starboard and follow Dinsdale. But he wanted to stand the aircraft on one wing and get away as quickly as possible. Sitting on the left-hand side of the Beaufort, in the pilot's cockpit, it was much easier to turn to port. You could look straight down past your wing-tip to the sea. He broke away to port, less than a quarter of a mile from the destroyer. As he did so the Me 109 passed rapidly overhead. Looking down, he saw an aircraft burning on the water.

Leading the second vic of this wave was Charlie Pett. All three aircraft were close up behind Dinsdale, but the fighters had more time to swing round into the attack. Heavy and light flak was bursting all round them, and they took evasive action until within a mile of the target. Four Me 109s attacked this formation. Kerr, on Pett's left, in the direction of the fighter attack, turned sharply to port, and the first German fighter overshot. The other three fighters split up like a fan, one attacking Pett from the port side, one from astern, and the other sweeping round and attacking from the far side. Venn, the rear gunner, the man who had dragged the two sinking pigeons out of the aircraft three months earlier and made Cliff's pigeon rescue possible, now showed himself equally alert at the guns. First he directed his attack at the fighter to port. He scored several hits and saw bits of this fighter falling away. He swung his turret at once towards the fighter astern, and as the roll of the Beaufort took his line of sight clear of the tail he fired a long burst, again scoring hits. This fighter broke away. The third fighter gave up. Now the three Beauforts hung on to the *Prinz Eugen* in her turn to port. But directly they dropped, the German cruiser turned to starboard, back on an easterly course. As the formation swung to starboard after the drop, the gunners saw three aircraft burning on the sea.

The attacks of the German fighters had been ill co-ordinated and lacking in tenacity. But they had had the effect of forcing most of the aircraft in Dinsdale's wave to drop early. Smoke was pouring now from the close-escort destroyer, but the flak was still intense, German fighters were still milling around in undisciplined fury, and although all the aircraft in this wave got away safely, none of the crews could be sure of the results of their attack.

The first wave were leaving as the second wave were dropping their torpedoes. They had had to sweep round towards the stern of the cruiser, behind the close-escort destroyer, to develop their attack. This formation was spread out in a single vic. On the extreme left was Ralph Manning, the Canadian, the man who had got lost on the day of the escape of the three ships from Brest. Next to him was Birchley, then Williams, then Archer, then McKern (another Australian), with Oughton on the extreme right. The drop was being made more difficult for them by the *Prinz Eugen's* evasive action in avoiding the torpedoes launched by Dinsdale's formation.

On sighting the enemy force, all six aircraft had turned in in tight formation, and after a minute or so running down the track of the *Eugen*, they turned to starboard again to line up for the attack, spreading out as they did so. The Beaufighters shot ahead, giving the Beaufort crews a tremendous feeling of elation as they bore down on the escorting destroyers. The crews were stirred to their depths by this impressive display of speed, strength and comradeship. It was a new exhilaration to add to the familiar one of racing along sixty feet above the water into a few packed minutes of intense danger, knowing that these minutes might be one's last and determined to savour them to the full. Surely there was not a task of such mortal danger, not a thrill of such buoyant exultation, in all the history of war.

When Williams had first sighted the *Eugen*, she had been steering due east, across the bows of the Beauforts. As the first vic in Dinsdale's formation had dropped their torpedoes, the *Eugen* had turned to port, and then to starboard to avoid the second vic, bringing her back again on an easterly course, perhaps a quarter of a mile closer to the coast. Williams, developing his attack in the stern quarter, would be attacking out of the setting sun.

The sky was a mêlée of aircraft—Beauforts, Blenheims, Beaufighters, Me 109s and Me 110s—weaving in and out of a thousand white and indigo explosions that hung in the sky like lanterns. Smoke put down by the escorting destroyers partly obscured the target. The flak was thickest in this quarter of the attack. Everything was being thrown at them, heavy-calibre shells, pom-poms, machine-gun fire, and as the range narrowed and they came nearer the coastline, they saw the flashes of the shore batteries. They were two miles from the target when the first aircraft was hit. Manning, on the extreme left, saw an Me 109 away to port bearing down on them. Manning veered towards him. Turning to face the enemy was a reflex action—he had no illusions about the comparison between his two machine-guns and the cannon of the German fighter. The German pilot pulled up right away, perhaps mistaking the Beaufort for a Beaufighter. For one triumphant moment Manning had the German fighter at his mercy, hanging in his gun-sight. He pressed the firing-button. The result was a frustrating silence, anti-climax. He'd forgotten to take the button off safe.

Manning brought his aircraft back on course. The blue and grey shape of the *Eugen* was beginning to crystallize out of the painter's palette of unrelated colour ahead. The Norwegian coast was as clear as home. He watched a fighter taking off from Lister airfield. It climbed away, its undercarriage still down. Wasn't it the damnedest sight for a torpedo pilot to be seeing?

The flak was too thick now for the fighters. They watched it racing by, could actually hear it bursting. The gunners, peering out of the waist of the aircraft, into the slipstream, or back along the fuselage from the turret, tried to get a glimpse of the target, of what was going on in front. Manning found he was approaching the starboard quarter of the German cruiser, but he seemed to be alone.

Below him on the water were three fiercely burning patches of oil. Manning's encounter with the Me 109 may have saved him. The three aircraft next to him in the formation, Birchley, Williams and Archer, had all been shot down by the *Eugen's* guns.

McKern and Oughton, on the extreme right, were going in independently. Manning was determined, having come this far, to get in as close as he could before dropping his torp. The *Eugen,* continuing its evasive action, had turned again to starboard and was steering south-east. Manning was attacking the stern on the starboard side, but the *Eugen* was moving away and the torpedo would have to overtake it. It was doubly important to get in well below 1000 yards.

Manning kept up his evasive action as long as possible, and then held the aircraft steady as the *Prinz Eugen* towered above him. His navigator gave him the range. At 800 yards Manning pressed the release button. There was an agonizing two seconds while he held the aircraft steady for the guide-wires to run out, and then, just as he was about to throw the aircraft all over the sky, there was a thud underneath him and the right rudder pedal knocked his foot back with inexorable force. The aircraft yawed violently and began to dive.

A shell from the *Prinz Eugen* had hit the fuselage just below the tailplane and had cut the rudder wire on one side, the rudder trim and the elevator trim. The effect was to make the aircraft nose-heavy and give it a heavy starboard trim. Manning's first thought was that an engine had gone. He went hastily to wind on trim, but the handle spun loosely in his hand. The only way he could control the yaw was to keep the port wing well down. This was hard to hold, but the aircraft was still flying.

It had all happened in a second or two and the Beaufort was hurtling towards the *Prinz Eugen* at fifty feet. When Manning looked up he was right alongside the *Eugen,* still on its starboard side. On his right was the close-escort destroyer, not so near as the *Eugen* but not more than 200 yards away. There was a stream of anti-aircraft fire, streaked with green, passing over and under the Beaufort in both directions. Caught between the two ships, Manning nevertheless enjoyed for a moment the realization that the cruiser and its escort were peppering each other. He daren't attempt evasive action with the aircraft scarcely maintainable in flying attitude, but he didn't pick up many more holes. A low-flying Beaufort wasn't such a sitting duck as it felt.

Miraculously the Beaufort still ploughed on, and gradually they drifted out of range of the more concentrated ack-ack fire. Occasionally plumes of water rose gracefully around them, showing that the heavier guns of the *Eugen* were still firing at them. Manning discovered by trial and error that full climbing revs on one engine, with the other engine throttled right back, pulled the aircraft along in a reasonable flying attitude.

All this time they had been travelling more or less parallel with the track of the *Eugen*, in an easterly direction, further and further away from base. But now that Manning had some degree of control, he turned south so as to get well clear of the recent action before turning west for base.

Within a few minutes they were out of sight of the German convoy. But they were still within range of the fighters. Almost as the cluster of specks that was all they could see of the German convoy merged into the sea, three Me 109s appeared astern. Manning was still holding the Beaufort down near the water, as the safest place to avoid being seen, but the aircraft was waddling along like a duck, and any attempt at evasive action was out of the question. Then the three 109s were on them.

The tactics of the fighters were to take turns in running up from astern. Here they were safe from the Beaufort's guns, which had an automatic cut-out to prevent careless or over-excited rear gunners from shooting through their own tail. The first fighter closed the range to 500 yards and then fired a burst of green tracer which fell harmlessly into the sea behind and underneath them. If all the marksmanship was like this, they might get away with it yet. But if the attack was pressed home, Manning knew there was little he could do about it.

"There's a Beaufighter coming up, chaps!" Osmond, the

gunner, called excitedly from the turret as a Beaufighter, streaking up from sea-level in rapid pursuit, fastened on to the second enemy fighter, which broke off its attack instantly. But the way was clear for the third Me 109. This pilot, thinking perhaps that the Beaufort now looked likely to escape, pressed home his attack. Manning swung the aircraft away as best he could, but the Beaufort was caught in a hail of fire. Fortunately most of it rattled against the turret armour-plating, where it did little damage except to Osmond, the gunner, who fell back out of the turret, temporarily stunned. Nimerovsky, a Lancashire Jew, left his waist gun, pulled Osmond clear, installed himself in the turret and fired a long burst just in time to break up another attack by the first Me 109. By this time Manning had turned west and they were well out to sea. The Me 109s, discouraged, gave up the chase.

Manning knew that they had been extremely lucky. There was a fighter O.T.U. at Lister, and the three German pilots must have been as green as their tracer. Any three experienced pilots would have made short work of a winged Beaufort, even with the intervention of a Beaufighter.

When Manning got to Leuchars, darkness was falling and it had begun to rain. On the way home he had decided on a wheels-up landing, but now the journey was safely completed he wondered if he couldn't perhaps get her down in one piece. The hydraulic system was leaking, but the flaps and wheels came down all right, and Manning began his descent. But the decrease in speed and the lowering of the flaps upset the precarious control he had held, and his final approach was a series of slips and bursts of engine. As a result he was two-thirds down the runway and he still hadn't touched down. Ahead of him the barbed wire on the perimeter of the airfield was looming up. Beyond it was the river. Manning lifted the undercarriage. The aircraft ploughed into the earth, grinding to a halt within forty yards.

Manning, thinking he was the last back, was unconcerned at the blocking of the runway. In any case it had been unavoidable. But on the ground at Leuchars they were still waiting for sight or sound of Williams, Birchley and Archer. Manning, having dropped his torpedo closer than anyone, flown a badly damaged aircraft back over 300 miles across the North Sea, and made a successful crash-landing at the end of it, was rewarded by a severe rocket from the station commander. What did he think he was doing? Did he think he was the only pilot on the squadron, the only one to get shot up? Conscious that it was not altogether undeserved, Manning, the quiet Canadian, accepted his rebuke without bitterness.

What of the rest of this wave? Oughton and McKern, on the extreme right, had gone in one after the other. Both estimated their dropping range as 1200 yards, and both were under attack as they dropped. Oughton kept up a fairly gentle undulation until his torpedo was safely away, and as they broke to starboard, Bladen, the waist gunner, emptied a pan of .303 at the deck of the *Prinz Eugen*. He regretted it a moment later when a voice called from the turret.

"Couple of 109s behind us. Dead astern." Bladen wrenched off the empty pan of ammunition, grabbed another and slapped it home. Now he was ready for anything.

"Look out! There's a fighter coming in dead ahead!" Bladen pushed his head out into the slipstream on the port side, saw nothing, and lurched across to starboard, grabbing the gun on that side. Red tracer was streaming by, under and over and through the starboard wing, inches from his nose. Then the fighter itself rushed by, the relative speed making sighting impossible. Bladen hosed the waist gun after him but already the fighter was far out of range.

McKern, following Oughton out, was attacked by the same fighter. The rear gunner got in a long burst of tracer, incendiary and armour-piercing, as the enemy fighter closed.

"I've got him! He's down!"

The Me 109 fell away out of control, only to recover, like a darting swallow, inches from the sea.

The gunners turned to look back at the German cruiser, hoping for some sign that she had been hit. But the *Prinz Eugen* steamed on, unmoved, indestructible, still at full speed. The gunners shook their heads in bitter disbelief. It was heartbreaking.

Now these two aircraft set course for home. But soon they overtook a Beaufighter with smoke pouring from its starboard engine. They drew up alongside. They could see the pilot clearly, giving them the thumbs down. He was going to ditch. They circled and watched him go in. The ditching was a good one, but the aircraft sank within a few seconds. No dinghy appeared. Pilot and navigator were left struggling in the North Sea, nearly three hundred miles from home.

"Get a dinghy over to them," called Oughton.

There was a small individual dinghy in the well of the Beaufort, and Bladen, on a signal from Spark, the navigator, heaved it over the side. Then a fighter Blenheim appeared on the scene. This aircraft had an interior-stowed dinghy, which the crew released so accurately that it landed within a yard or so of the two swimmers. While they were righting it and clambering aboard, Bladen was sending a wireless message giving their position. They were picked up later by a rescue launch.

And what of Williams, Birchley and Archer?

Archer and his crew were lost. Archer, gallant Australian, who had won the D.F.C. attacking the *Gneisenau*. Argue with his C.O. he might, but he followed him into action without question. Birchley, too, was shot down, but he and his crew were picked up by an escorting destroyer. And Williams? His two gunners were killed. His navigator, Al Morris, Loveitt's navigator in the *Lutzow* attack, the man who had been snatched at the last minute from the boat back to Canada and home, died from his injuries. Williams, the leader, the man who planned the strike, who was determined to succeed at all costs, alone survived; survived to taste the bitter mortification of losing his entire crew, and of being taken prisoner by the ship he had set out to destroy.

The fifteen aircraft of 86 Squadron had left Wick at 18.10, escorted by four Beaufighters, and with a high-level diversionary bombing force of twelve Hudsons. They were to make a landfall off Egero Island and then turn south to form the northern arm of the pincer movement. One of the Beauforts turned back soon after the start with engine trouble, but the remainder of the force duly made their landfall off Egero at 20.00 hours, and were about to turn south when the corrupt message was received from base giving the position of the enemy convoy to the north. The Beauforts had crossed the North Sea at 500 feet, but they came down to 50 feet as they approached the coast, and this action, prudent as it was, removed any chance they might have had of sighting the enemy convoy at a distance. Accordingly, when the message was received, Hyde led the formation northwards along the coast. The high-flying Hudsons spotted the enemy convoy clearly enough from 13,000 feet, away to the south-east, but they had no means of communicating with the Beauforts and Beaufighters. They delivered their bombing attack, losing one aircraft in the process, and returned to base. Meanwhile, Hyde and the rest of the force were speed-ing away from the target towards Stavanger.

A force of enemy fighters was stationed at Stavanger. The pilots were not so green as those at Lister. Hyde and his formation first saw three Me 110s, which kept their distance and did not attack. But as they approached Stavanger, still sweeping in vain for the enemy convoy, they became the second Beaufort squadron in one day to see German fighters taking off and forming up to attack. Sarene, Hyde's gunner, had a panoramic view of the action. The whole formation was stretched out behind him, at first in impressive sym-metry, then in increasing confusion as the Me 109s poured in amongst them. Hyde held his course for several minutes to the north, determined to press on until the *Prinz Eugen* was sighted if he could. But one by one the Beauforts, under pressure, were forced to jettison their torpedoes. The air fighting was some of the bitterest ever experienced by Beau-fort crews. The Me 109s pressed home their attacks relent-lessly, and the Beaufort gunners, answering the cannon fire of the German fighters with the twin Brownings in the turrets and the free V.G.O.s in the fuselage, put up a spirited and effective resistance. The four Beaufighters, too, harried the 109s and took their toll. Five of the 109s were seen to crash in flames into the sea. Eventually, his formation irre-trievably split, the sky a disordered jumble of aircraft, Hyde tried to rally his crews around him by turning south away from Stavanger. Those that could followed. Hyde knew that some of them had been shot down. He had seen one aircraft crash into the sea beneath him, others going down out of control. It wasn't until they got back that they could count their losses. Only ten Beauforts returned. Of the four crews shot down, three had been on their first operation.

The survivors of the raid were left bitter, frustrated and angry. They heard that 42 Squadron had delivered their attack. They heard that several hits on the *Eugen* were claimed. They were not told of the corrupt message. They had never quite got over that old inferiority complex, and they concluded that they had been used as a decoy, to draw off the fighter opposition so that 42 Squadron could go in and strike unmolested. Such an idea seems monstrous and unthinkable; but in the absence of any other explanation it was widely believed on the squadron. Such were the boomerangs of security.

After the attack the *Prinz Eugen*, undamaged apart from her stern, proceeded into the Skagerrak, rounded the Skaw, went safely through the Kattegat and the Great Belt, and arrived at Kiel at 21.15 on 18th May. Once again, when faced with fighter opposition and heavy flak, Beauforts had failed to inflict material damage on their target.

This was the last big Beaufort operation in the U.K. 22 Squadron had left for the Far East four months earlier. 217 had gone to Malta, and 86 were to follow them a few weeks later. And by the time of El Alamein, 42 were also in the Mediterranean, playing a leading part in one of the most spectacular strikes of the war.

But the attack on the *Prinz Eugen* was the turning-point in the operation of torpedo-bombers. For the first time, Beauforts had operated with diversionary bombing forces, with a close escort, and with anti-flak support. The co-ordination had been imperfect, and the results disastrous; but the hard lessons had been learnt, the experience dearly bought.

At Malta, torpedo aircraft were about to be correctly applied for the first time. And in the U.K. the attack on the *Prinz Eugen* was the germ from which grew the massive attacks by the strike wings of later years.

Chapter 8

TORPEDOES IN THE MED

THE campaigns of the Western Desert began in the winter
of 1940 when Wavell's tiny force of 20,000 men drove the
Italians back beyond Benghazi. It was first blood to us. But
we were unable to exploit our initial advantage because the
enemy's sea communications were more easily maintained
than our own. All our supplies had to come round the Cape
to Egypt and thence across the Desert, whereas the enemy
was in control of the Central Mediterranean and we could
not stop him running his supplies into Tripoli and other North
African ports. It thus became clear at an early stage that
before any notable victory could be achieved on land, the
battle for supremacy in the Mediterranean must be decided.

Only merchant shipping could carry the much-needed
supplies; and the protection of these ships presented a
problem. Even the strongest naval forces were vulnerable to
air attack in this narrow, land-locked sea, and after the
damage suffered by the Italian Fleet at Matapan, the domin-
ant factor in the command of the Mediterranean became air
power.

The British position deteriorated rapidly in the spring of
1941 with the Axis occupation of Greece and Crete, and the
retreat of the Western Desert force to the Egyptian frontier.
Previously we had been able to run convoys through from
Alexandria to Malta; but now, with the Axis air forces in
Greece, Crete, Sicily and Cyrenaica gradually developing
their strength, the passage of allied shipping to and from
Malta became more and more restricted, until finally it
ceased altogether. Our shipping routes through the Eastern
Mediterranean were severed—by enemy air power. And
worse still, the enemy, having obtained shorter and more
easily protected shipping lanes to Africa across the Central
Mediterranean, was well placed to supply and augment his
forces threatening Egypt.

165

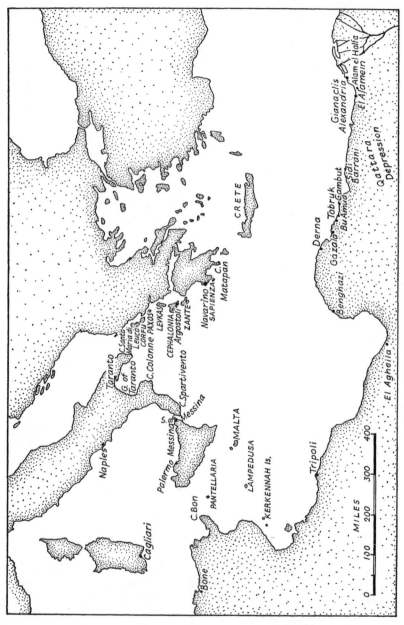

THE CENTRAL MEDITERRANEAN

Cagliari

Bone

Naples

Taranto
G. of
Taranto
C.Santa
Maria di
Leuca
CORFU
C.Colonne PAXOS
LEVKAS
CEPHALONIA
Argostoli
ZANTE

Palermo Messina
S. Messina
C.Spartivento

C.Bon

PANTELLARIA

MALTA

LAMPEDUSA

KERKENNAH Is.

Tripoli

Navarino
SAPIENZA C.
Matapan

CRETE

El Agheila

Benghazi
Derna
Gazala
Tobruk
Gambut
Bu Amud
Sidi
Barrani
El Alamein
Alam Halfa
Alexandria
Gianaclis
Qattara
Depression

MILES
0 100 200 300 400

There remained, however, one thorn in the enemy's side
—Malta. This historic island might have been dropped
thoughtfully into the Mediterranean by a God benevolent
to the British cause. All Rommel's shipping routes could be
preyed upon by a suitable medium-range aircraft based at
Malta.

In 1940 and 1941 a really suitable aircraft was not available. But from the opening of hostilities in the Mediterranean,
Malta proved its value repeatedly as a base strategically
situated astride the main Axis shipping routes to North Africa,
and within bombing range of both Tripoli and Naples.
Reconnaissance aircraft were able to maintain a watch on
the principal Italian ports, and to sight and follow the course
of enemy convoys, making a signal contribution to the success
of Malta's strike aircraft.

In addition to actual sinkings, the threat from Malta
obliged all enemy convoys sailing to Tripoli to make a wide
detour in an effort to avoid detection, almost doubling the
distance by the direct route, and at the same time exposing
them for longer periods to submarine attack. Not only was
time added to the journey—and over a period, time and
tonnage were indivisible—but the enemy shipping was forced
to consume extra fuel, of which a serious shortage already
existed. Thus the strength and striking power of the Axis
forces in North Africa were materially reduced and the
enemy's shipping resources weakened.

As a result of the combined efforts, particularly in the
summer and autumn of 1941, of Blenheim bombers by day,
Fleet Air Arm Swordfish and Albacores by night, and submarines of the Royal Navy, Rommel was seriously short of
supplies when Auchinleck began his 'Crusader' offensive in
November 1941. In January 1942 Rommel was back at El
Agheila, with practically no food, petrol or ammunition.

A very serious view of this threat from Malta was taken
by the Germans, and in December 1941 they transferred a
force of 400 aircraft to Sicily under the command of Kesselring. This force consisted mostly of units withdrawn from the
Russian front, plus some from the Western front, and it was
gradually built up to a total of some 600 aircraft. With these
aircraft, Kesselring intended to liquidate Malta as an air and

naval base by destroying all essential installations, particularly airfields, thus freeing the shipping routes from the menace of air attack.

On 5th January, a convoy of ships carrying 55 tanks and 20 armoured cars, plus anti-tank guns and supplies of all kinds, arrived safely in Tripoli. This was as good as a victory in battle to Rommel, and although he was still short of many essentials, especially fuel, he immediately began to think in terms of taking the offensive again. On 21st January, although still without the logistic backing he needed, he began a reconnaissance in strength from his position at El Agheila. It was a desperate venture. The reconnaissance force was backed by only three days' rations, and for five days the *Luftwaffe* was grounded for lack of fuel and other essentials and the Afrika Korps had to dispense with air support altogether. But the British position in the forward areas was equally difficult. Our lines of communication were extended almost to breaking-point. We had captured Benghazi, but we were unable to use its vital port facilities because of German demolitions and sunken ships. Rommel's reconnaissance in force caught us unawares, and he was able to sustain his advance for a time on captured British supplies.

By February Rommel had pushed us back to Gazala, a few miles west of Tobruk. But to maintain the position he had won, and to mount an offensive against Egypt, his supply routes must be finally safeguarded. As he advanced, the Western Desert Air Force was driven eastwards until the Axis supply routes passed out of range of Egypt-based aircraft. Rommel now threatened to be in command of the whole sweep of the Mediterranean—except for Malta, which remained an enemy within his gates. He therefore called for the final annihilation of Malta.

The policy at Malta remained the destruction of Italian shipping, but its execution became increasingly difficult as the scale of enemy attack against airfields developed, coupled with the establishment of enemy fighter patrols round the island, the installation of efficient radar facilities in Sicily, the shortage of fighters, unusually bad weather which waterlogged airfields, and an acute shortage of labour. The scale of attack became so heavy in February that Wellington and

Blenheim aircraft had to be withdrawn to the Middle East, and shipping strikes virtually ceased.

The Beauforts and Beaufort crews sent overseas towards the end of 1941 had been arriving steadily in the Middle East, in spite of losses *en route*. Here they were formed into a new Beaufort squadron, No. 39, under a newly formed Naval Co-operation Group at Alexandria. Within a few action-packed months this squadron was to outstrip all other Beaufort squadrons, even 22, in reputation and achievement.

When Rommel began his reconnaissance in strength at El Agheila on 21st January, our reconnaissance aircraft were warned to watch for signs of the large convoy which the Axis were expected to run through to Tripoli in an attempt to bolster Rommel's supply situation. The enemy did as was anticipated, and in doing so provided a worthy target for 39 Squadron's baptism in torpedo operations.

On the morning of 23rd January a large convoy was sighted, consisting of some twenty ships in all. The Italians had gone to unprecedented lengths to protect it, providing a battleship and several cruisers and destroyers as escort. The biggest of the merchant vessels was the 14,000-ton *Victoria*, described by Ciano in his diary as the 'pearl of the Italian merchant fleet'. A large striking force of Blenheims and Albacores was assembled at Benghazi, and Albacores from Malta also took part in the attack. Three Beauforts of the newly formed 39 Squadron were included in the strike force at Benghazi, and were to carry out the first Beaufort torpedo operation in the Mediterranean. The three pilots were Taylor, Grant and Jepson. In spite of an intense anti-aircraft barrage they singled out the *Victoria*, dropped their torpedoes at 1500 yards' range, and succeeded in crippling their target, which was later sunk by the Albacores, sending three hundred of the four hundred troops on board and the whole of the supply cargo to the bottom.

But the rest of the convoy got through—and so did many other convoys in the ensuing weeks. The regular unchallenged passage of enemy shipping was watched with alarm—and by none more so than a young squadron-leader recently arrived in the Middle East, kicking his heels at headquarters in Cairo. This young officer had had the temerity to extract a verbal promise from a very senior officer at the Air Ministry that he would be given command of a Beaufort squadron when he got to the Middle East. But all kinds of people arrived in overseas commands with similar tales: this officer had nothing in writing to substantiate his claim. He was given a staff job, was not even posted to 39 Squadron, where no vacancy existed. But, junior as he was, he very soon made his presence felt at headquarters, and soon they may well have felt that they would be glad to be rid of him. His name was Pat Gibbs.

The air offensive against Malta reached its peak in April 1942. The story of how the Hurricanes battled with wave after wave of fighters and bombers, of how Spitfires were flown off aircraft carriers and thrown straight into the fight, of the tireless efforts of the ground crews, is legendary. Over 1000 German aircraft were damaged or destroyed during the concentrated blitz on the island. But Malta survived.

At the height of the blitz, the enemy decided it was safe to run a large convoy through to Benghazi almost within sight of Malta. There were no strike aircraft at Malta, and the convoy would be out of range of the Beauforts in Egypt—out of range that is, for the round trip. What the Beauforts could encompass, however, was a through flight to Malta, striking at the convoy on the way.

The convoy consisted of four large merchant vessels, escorted by five destroyers and two flak-ships, the merchant vessels comprising a target for which it seemed justifiable to expose the Beauforts to a double danger—the danger not only from the convoy and its escort, but from the circus of Me 109s operating off Malta.

The aircraft and crews of 22 Squadron, on their way to the Far East, were passing through the Middle East at the time. 39 Squadron was desperately short of aircraft, and of experienced crews, and 22 Squadron found themselves shanghaied. They had already carried out several minor strikes with 39. They were held back for a few more days to take part in this strike.

Orders came through to prepare for the operation on 13th April. It was decided to send ten aircraft, one to take off early next morning to locate the convoy by radar and report its position, and three flights of three to stand by at Bu Amud, a forward airfield near Tobruk, to await news of a sighting. The pilot of the A.S.V. aircraft, Howroyd, was a member of 22 Squadron. Two other 22 Squadron crews were to take part. One of them, Belfield, like Howroyd, had been on the squadron for some nine months; the other, the Australian Johnny Lander, led the strike.

Howroyd duly took off next morning at 07.30, searched for and found the convoy, and made his report by wireless. But as he landed at Malta an Me 109 followed him in, spraying him with cannon all the way. Howroyd got the Beaufort down safely, but slumped forward as he did so, killed instantly by cannon fire. His navigator was so badly wounded that he died later in hospital. It was a foretaste of what was to come.

Howroyd's sighting report was relayed to Bu Amud, where the take-off of the strike force was timed for 12.00. The Beauforts were to have an escort of four Beaufighters, and a Maryland was to fly on ahead of them and radio the latest position of the convoy.

A few minutes before take-off, the aircraft of one of the 39 Squadron flight commanders, Beveridge, was found to have developed a turret fault. Beveridge decided to take the aircraft of one of the three crews who had been on a minor operation two days earlier. The remaining eight aircraft took off at midday in three formations of 2, 3 and 3, made up of Lander and Belfield of 22 Squadron, Beveridge, Bee and Seddon on Lander's starboard, and Leaning, Gooch and Way on his port. The four Beaufighters, much faster than the Beauforts, weaved to keep with them. The Maryland took off soon afterwards, passed the Beauforts on the way to the convoy, made contact, and continued to give position reports until it was shot down by a Ju 88 in sight of the convoy.

The Beauforts reached a position some seventy miles south-east of Malta, and then, seeing no sign of shipping, assumed rightly that they had overshot, turned south-west, and began a creeping line ahead search. As they turned back and forth in their search, some of the crews at the extremes of the formation thought they saw smoke on the horizon to the west. They had no means of communicating with the leader. They tried to attract his attention, but failed. Two Ju 88s from the convoy spotted the Beauforts, and came and had a look at them, but they did not attack. The Beaufighters peeled off and shot down both Ju 88s. But by this time the Beaufighters were running out of petrol. They flew across the front of the formation and then set course for Malta. Lander decided to press on.

By this time, as the creeping line ahead search took them further to the south-west, there was no mistaking the presence of a large convoy ahead of them. Lander turned towards it, and the rest of the Beauforts followed. The convoy was still well within range of fighter protection from Sicily, and as the Beauforts approached the crews counted fifteen to twenty Me 109s, six Me 110s and several Ju 88s. Most of the Beauforts were under attack as they went in to drop.

The merchant vessels were in a box of four, steaming away from them, and Lander led the Beauforts in close to make up for the fact that the torpedoes would have to chase their targets. Lander and Belfield attacked the rear left-hand ship from the starboard quarter. Leaning led his formation round to the port side of the same ship. Beveridge led his formation against the rear right-hand ship. Nearly all the Beauforts were still under fighter attack, the flak from the ships was thick and accurate, and the crews had little chance to observe the run of their torpedoes. Three explosions were seen on the two vessels attacked, and the left-hand ship was enveloped in smoke, but definite assessment of results was impossible.

Immediately after he dropped, Way lost contact with Leaning and Gooch, crossed behind the ship he had attacked, and joined up with Lander and Belfield. He was relentlessly pursued by an Me 109, and as he came up alongside Lander he was shot down into the sea.

There now developed a desperate race to get to Malta before the Me 109s could inflict further damage. All the Beauforts took violent evasive action, weaving and jinking incessantly and at the same time keeping as close together as possible. The gunners fired their pea-shooting Vickers guns desperately. But Malta was half an hour's flying away, and the sky was littered with fighters. The radar plot at Malta was showing a hundred-plus.

Some of the heaviest attacks were directed against the formation led by Beveridge. Beveridge himself was the first of this vic to be shot down. But all the time the surviving Beauforts were getting nearer Malta, and at long last the island was in sight. Seddon's Beaufort was the next to go. It was literally shot out of the sky, yet Seddon managed to bring it down on to the water some six miles from the island. The dinghy was badly holed and it would not inflate. Two of the crew were wounded. One of them, McGregor, a brawny Canadian, set out to swim the six miles to Malta. He was followed by Miller, one of the gunners. The two men left behind, Seddon and the injured Keegan, stood on the wing of the sinking Beaufort and watched them go.

Meanwhile, Bee had fought his way through to Malta, and at one point his aircraft was seen flying low over the island. But as he tried to manœuvre to line up on the runway, he was fastened on by Me 109s and shot down into the sea. All three of Beveridge's vic had now been shot down.

The Me 109s reserved their most determined efforts for the leading Beauforts, piloted by Lander and Belfield. Lander's aircraft was hit just above the tail wheel, rupturing the hydraulic system, and a moment later it was hit again as yet another fighter bored in. This time most of the tail unit was completely shot away, leaving only the framework. Still Lander managed to keep the aircraft on an even keel near the deck. One after the other the Me 109s came in, bursts of cannon shell went through both wings, and the windscreen was splintered and smashed. Oil from the punctured hydraulic system leaked all over the aircraft, covering everything with black grease. Suddenly Lander, banking steeply to avoid yet another attack, turned too near the water and put the starboard wing-tip in. There was a ghastly thump, like the smack of a flat oar, and the Beaufort shook to its roots; but it stayed airborne. Looking out, Lander saw the wing-tip twisted up towards the sky. Straight ahead of him was Malta. He held the Beaufort down until the white cliffs rushed towards him, hoping to shake off his pursuers. But the Me 109s stuck to him, and chunks of chalk disappeared out of the cliffs in front of his eyes, shot out by the fighters' cannon. He pulled up over the cliff edge, and at last succeeded in shaking

173

the fighters off. He found the airfield and crash-landed on the edge of the runway, jumped out, and ran for shelter.

There was no sign of Belfield. He had stuck to Lander as long as he could, but some distance from the island his aircraft had been shot down into the sea.

Leaning and Gooch, having lost Way coming out of the attack, somehow managed to stick together, Gooch holding on desperately in spite of his leader's continual and violent evasive action. At one point Leaning, in a rate 4 turn right on the deck to shake off a Ju 88, was astounded, delighted and charmed to hear from a laconic, well-disciplined gunner that "Mr Gooch was still there".

Gooch's aircraft was badly holed in the petrol tanks, and the hydraulics, too, were severed. Nevertheless both aircraft landed safely at Malta.

Nothing more was seen of Beveridge or Bee and their crews. Beveridge's body was recovered later. Way and his crew had been seen to go straight in over the convoy. Belfield and his crew were picked up next day in their dinghy. There remained one crew unaccounted for—Seddon's, the man who had ditched some six miles off Malta.

When McGregor set out to swim for Malta, he left Seddon and Keegan in good spirits, standing on the wing of the Beaufort, wearing their Mae Wests, wishing him luck. Miller followed McGregor, but the two men soon lost sight of each other.

McGregor was a powerful man and a strong swimmer, but his back was dotted with shrapnel, and he had never attempted a swim of this length before. Quite soon after he left the sinking Beaufort, he began to feel that the effort would be beyond him. He was wearing only a pair of khaki shorts and a bush-shirt, but after an hour's swimming they began to trouble him, and he slipped them off. But before he did so, he remembered he had an Egyptian pound note in the hip pocket of his shorts. He was not a Scotch-Canadian for nothing. He struggled out of the shorts and removed the pound note from the pocket before he thrust the shorts away from him. The pound note he kept clutched in his hand.

He swam for two hours, three hours, four hours, and still Malta remained tantalizingly out of reach. His left arm was numb, and yet he could feel the metal strap of his wrist watch cutting into it like an iron band. He took the watch off and held it in his other hand. Presently his grip on it loosened, and he was forced to let it go. He still had the Egyptian pound note.

Only will-power kept him going over the last hour. It took him five hours in all to reach the island, and when he got there he found himself faced by a rocky cliff. He managed to scramble up the cliff-face on to a ledge. Fortunately, a Maltese farmer had seen him swimming in, and the air-sea rescue launch found him next day. It had been a cold April night, and the wounded, exhausted McGregor had spent it naked on the ledge. But he soon recovered in hospital. And he still had the pound note.

Miller, who had set out after McGregor, was never seen again. Neither were Seddon and Keegan. Of the thirty-six men who set out in the Beauforts, seventeen were lost. When McGregor was fully fit again, he was posted to a safe job on Sunderlands. He was killed soon afterwards in an accident on take-off. Johnny Lander, who led the strike and miraculously survived, later became C.O. of 22 Squadron in Burma. One night in February 1945, driving his jeep back to his airfield from a party, he crashed through a small bridge, the jeep turned over, and Lander was pinned under the steering-wheel and drowned in six inches of water.

Leaning was the only pilot able to fly his Beaufort back to Egypt next day. His aircraft had sustained no damage whatsoever. The crew searched in vain for something to show that they had been in a scrap; but there wasn't even a single stray bullet-hole.

With their heavy losses, and the departure of 22 Squadron for India, 39 Squadron were badly depleted; and the loss of Beveridge left a vacancy for a flight commander. There was a certain grand inevitability in the posting-in some ten days later of Pat Gibbs.

Chapter 9

THE JUNE MALTA CONVOY

THE air offensive against Malta slackened considerably during the first fortnight in May. What was wanted, from the German point of view, was the invasion and occupation of Malta. It had originally been intended that a combined Axis paratroop and airborne force should take Malta immediately after the April blitz, before Rommel began the final offensive that was to sweep the British out of Africa. Such an operation, successfully completed, could have been decisive. But the heroic defence of Crete in May 1941 now bore fruit. The Germans had not forgotten the terrible losses they had suffered there. How much more costly might such an operation be against Malta! There could be little doubt that had such an invasion been seriously attempted, Malta would ultimately have fallen. But for once the Germans were afraid. They lacked confidence in themselves, and distrusted their allies.

They compromised by trying to neutralize Malta; but this was begging the military question. However damaging a campaign against Malta might be, unless it could achieve final dominance over the airfields the island could soon recover and build up its strength again. So long as Malta remained physically unconquered, some 600 aircraft must be retained in Sicily to keep the island pinned down. But Rommel had now consolidated his position and was ready to assume the offensive. He needed these aircraft for air support in the Desert.

Rommel knew that the British, too, were building up their strength in Egypt. He was impatient to begin the final assault that would take him to Cairo. He shrugged his shoulders and left Malta to do its worst in his rear.

The British, too, had their problems where Malta was concerned. The island had been successfully defended against air attack, but now it had to be re-armed and re-victualled if it was to return to its role of offensive base. Since the German

176

conquest of Greece and Crete, the risks of running a convoy through from the east had increased tenfold. A convoy from the west was fraught with just as many perils. The opposition likely to be encountered was so great that only an operation planned on a big scale could hope to succeed. It was therefore decided to run two convoys concurrently to Malta in mid-June, one from the United Kingdom via Gibraltar, and one from Alexandria. The two convoys were timed to berth within twenty-four hours of each other, with the object of splitting and reducing possible interception by the enemy.

Strategic bombing in support of the proposed operation was carried out by Malta-based aircraft against Sicilian airfields and against the harbours of Naples, Messina, Cagliari and Taranto, beginning on 24th May. Bombers based in Egypt were to attack enemy airfields in Crete and Cyrenaica just before and during the operation. Everything was done to blunt the enemy's striking power. But over the whole operation lay the ponderous, leviathan threat of a naval action—the threat of the Italian Fleet. Two squadrons of torpedo Beauforts and six torpedo Wellingtons were to be held in readiness in case the Italian Fleet attempted to intervene. Only a handful of Wellingtons had been converted for torpedo action, and so far they had not been used operationally. They were too slow and vulnerable for daylight work, but were developing a technique of night attack, either in the moon path or with the aid of flares. They carried two torpedoes. Of the Beaufort squadrons, 217 were to fly out from England just before the operation, and were to operate from Malta. 39 Squadron were to be prepared to strike from Bu Amud.

The eastbound convoy, which was proceeding from the United Kingdom via Gibraltar, consisted of four merchant vessels escorted by naval units. This force passed Gibraltar on the morning of 13th June. During the day, an enemy force from Cagliari in Sardinia, consisting of two cruisers and three destroyers, was seen by one of our submarines off the north-west coast of Sicily. A strike of four Wellingtons was despatched that night from Malta, but due to difficulties in illuminating the target they were forced to return without dropping their torpedoes. Reconnaissance aircraft searched all next day between Sicily and Sardinia and between Sicily and Pantellaria for the enemy force, without making a sighting, and it was not until last light that a P.R.U. Spitfire found them, now consisting of an additional destroyer, leaving Palermo. But meanwhile the westbound convoy, consisting of seven merchant vessels with a naval escort, which had sailed from Alexandria on 12th June, and which had come through a series of sustained air attacks in bomb alley, south of Crete, with the loss of only one merchant vessel, was nearing a position at which it might expect to be intercepted by a sortie from the main units of the Italian Fleet at Taranto. Reconnaissance effort was therefore diverted from the two cruisers and four destroyers already sighted, to the area south of Taranto. Here, on the evening of the 14th, seventy miles south of Taranto, the main units of the Italian Fleet were seen. They included two *Littorio*-class battleships, four 6-inch cruisers, and eight destroyers, steering south.

The urgency of the situation, coupled with the short hours of darkness, influenced Malta to despatch a strike of four torpedo Wellingtons, led by a radar Wellington, without waiting for a further sighting report. The enemy force was successfully located some 250 miles south of Taranto, but it threw out such an effective smoke screen that it was impossible for all except one Wellington to get in and strike. This Wellington fired two torpedoes at a large vessel seen amid the smoke. A glow on the water followed, but it was impossible to observe results. The other three returned with their loads.

Meanwhile, a strike by the Beauforts of 217 Squadron at Malta was planned for first light. It was a very different squadron from the one which had flown north in April to take part in operations off the Norwegian coast with 42 and 86; and of the men who had attacked the *Scharnhorst* and *Gneisenau* in the Channel, only Aldridge remained. Besides Aldridge, the only man on the squadron who had ever dropped a torpedo in anger was a Canadian named Stevens, formerly of 22 Squadron; and he had only dropped one. Wing Commander Davies, the C.O., was like Williams, Cliff and Gibbs in that he had flown Swordfish at Gosport for some years and dropped many torpedoes there; but he had no operational experience of torpedo work. When they arrived in the Mediterranean on 10th June, specially despatched

from the U.K. to fill the role of the main strike force threatening the Italian Fleet from Malta, 217 was nothing more than
a scratch squadron of amateurs. And their torpedo equipment, which had been removed to make room for the fitting
of auxiliary tanks for the trip out, was in a state of confusion,
so that it was only after strenuous efforts at Malta that eleven
aircraft were passed as serviceable a few hours before the
Italian Fleet came out.

Nine Beauforts, led by Wing Commander Davies, took off
from Luqa at 04.15 that morning, 15th June. The crews had
very little night-flying experience, but all but four of them
managed to form up at an agreed rendezvous off the island,
from where they set course due east for the known position of
the Italian Fleet, some 200 miles distant. The four crews who
missed the rendezvous proceeded independently. Strangely
enough, Aldridge and Stevens were among them. It was a
very dark night, and Aldridge decided to waste no time in
searching for the rest of the squadron, but to set course
straight away. Stevens, who was supposed to be leading the
last vic of three, hung about for some time before he realized
that the rest of his vic must have missed him, and he eventually set course alone some minutes after the others.

Aldridge completed over 200 miles on a course exactly due
east of Malta without seeing a sign of other aircraft or of the
shipping he had set out to attack. He had no idea whether he
was early or late; but in fact he was some minutes ahead of the
others. Dawn was breaking ahead of him as he reached a point
right in the centre of the Mediterranean, roughly equidistant
from Malta, Italy, southern Greece, Crete and Cyrenaica.
This was where the Italian Fleet was supposed to be. Many
miles ahead of him must be Greece and Crete. To his right
would be the bulge of Cyrenaica between Benghazi and
Tobruk. Away to his left was Taranto, the heel of Italy. That
was where the Fleet had come from, but whether it had
already passed this point or not he could only guess. It was
no longer intensely dark, and if he were anywhere near shipping he ought to see it.

He went on flying straight at the dawn, but the knowledge
that Taranto lay over to port, almost behind him now, held
his imagination. He was looking back to port and the pall

behind him was lifting. Suddenly he saw the ships, first one then another and then another, evanescent as stars. He had flown straight past them, not more than a mile or two from them, right across their bows.

He held his course for a moment uncertainly. If he turned back and attacked them from the port bow, he would be making his run silhouetted against the dawn. He must be almost silhouetted against it already. But so far he judged that he had not been seen. Why not make use of the way in which he had crept up on the target out of the darkness a few minutes ago, unwittingly then, but now deliberately?

He turned south, away from the Fleet, then west, back towards Malta, until he reached a point west of the target area. Then he turned back on to his original course. It was like seeing the picture round again.

So far he had seen everything dispassionately, like a text-book problem. The effect had been to give him virtually two runs at the same target.

He saw four ships in line astern, which he took to be large cruisers. He ran in on the leading ship. It was the 10,000-ton cruiser *Trento*, steaming at the head of the Fleet. No one had seen him.

It was a grey dawn, and even in the aircraft he felt the strange silence and stillness of the hour. He was approaching at a perfect dropping angle, forty-five degrees on the starboard bow. Still the ships ploughed placidly on. He was less than 1000 yards from the leading cruiser when he dropped his torpedo. The morning was still petrified, and he held his breath.

He turned gently away to starboard as the firing started, wild and indiscriminate. His torpedo was running perfectly and he knew it would strike.

He waited impatiently until the cruiser sickened from his poisoned arrow, throwing up its stomach in a column of water that rose fifty feet high. Thick smoke poured out of her and the flames acted as a beacon to Stevens, thirty-five miles away. Aldridge watched it all with a smug satisfaction, and turned for home.

The main squadron attack developed a minute or so later. Davies led a formation of three aircraft in to attack the second ship on the port bow, while two other aircraft attacked from the opposite side. The orderly progress of the Italian Fleet now deteriorated into a stampede, a fantastic circus of wildly careering ships, all steering in different directions, their wakes criss-crossing and churning up the water. The flak was intense, and several aircraft were hit.

The whole series of attacks was watched by the commander of a British submarine at periscope depth. He stood spellbound, almost forgetful of his own danger, gazing in utter amazement. But the frantic gyrations of the Italian ships combined with the intense flak to put the crews off their aim. None of these torpedoes struck home.

Last to arrive on the scene was Stevens. The main attack had been over for some minutes, and it was broad daylight. The grouping of the ships was still completely disorganized, and some of the ships were firing heavy flak which was bursting high in the sky at least 10,000 feet above them. Stevens could see no signs of a high-level attack, and in fact none was in progress.

Stevens picked out a cruiser that seemed to be apart from the main Fleet; this was the ship already badly damaged by Aldridge. It was listing, and a destroyer was attempting to lay a smoke screen round it. But long before he could get in close enough to drop, he was spotted and the flak began to search for him. The cruiser didn't seem to be making much headway, so he laid on half a length's deflection, dropped his torpedo, and turned away as soon as he could. His torpedo went wide. Had he but known it, the *Trento* was dead in the water and if he had aimed a no-deflection shot he could not have missed it.

As it happened, the *Trento* was doomed anyway. She was finished off a few minutes later by the submarine which had witnessed the attack.

In terms of ships sunk or damaged, the 217 Squadron strike had been only moderately successful; several other crews claimed hits, but none had in fact been scored, and there was no evidence that the Italian Fleet had been deterred from proceeding on its southerly course. There is little doubt that the resolution of the Italian naval command had been

181

weakened; but soon after the attack the Fleet turned south-east, on a course which within three to four hours would bring it into head-on collision with the convoy from Alexandria.

This convoy, pending news of the result of the strike from Malta, had already turned back on its tracks during the night. As soon as the news of the 217 Squadron strike came through, however, it turned once again for Malta. But reports by reconnaissance aircraft of the enemy Fleet's reaction were delayed, and the C.-in-C. Mediterranean thus became more than ever concerned at the prospect of a collision of the two forces. The convoy was therefore ordered to swing round to the north, marking time until the situation was clarified.

During the night the Italian Fleet had come within range of the Beauforts of 39 Squadron in Egypt; and a force of American Liberators in the Canal Zone was also standing by to strike. The original plan was for the Beauforts to take off from Bu Amud; but on 26th May Rommel had reopened his offensive, backed by the supplies which had been crossing the Mediterranean with depressing regularity in the past four months, and Bu Amud had fallen. 39 Squadron were thus forced back to Sidi Barrani, from where the Beauforts had barely enough petrol to attack the Fleet and fly through to Malta.

Had they been able to operate from Bu Amud, the Beauforts could have flown out to sea so as to put a safe distance between themselves and the enemy-held Cyrenaican coast. But now they would have to fly straight to the target, passing danger-ously near the enemy's Cyrenaican airfields. And there would be no fighter escort because of the necessity for cover for the retreating ground forces. The fear of fighter attack was thus added to apprehensions about range. The snowball of defeat in the Desert was rolling.

Twelve Beauforts took off from Sidi Barrani at 06.15 in four sub-flights of three, led by Wing Commander Mason (the squadron-commander), Gibbs, Taylor and Leaning respectively. Several Mark II Beauforts with twin Wasp engines had been delivered to the squadron specially for the operation, but Mason chose to fly in an old Mark I, on the principle that the slowest aircraft should lead. Everyone would thus be able to keep station. Mason and Gibbs led the two centre vics, Gibbs on Mason's right, with Taylor on the extreme right and Leaning on the extreme left. Mason and Gibbs handled the briefing between them. "You'll see cruisers and destroyers on the way in," Gibbs told them. "Ignore them. Go for the battlewagons. Follow me." Gibbs was back in the scrap again, and his manner was gay.

Mason set course as far out to sea as he dared, but for the next two hours they flew in a fever of apprehension, knowing that aircraft from the landing-grounds just out of sight on the port side had been attacking the British convoy, and that it was too much to hope that twelve Beauforts would pass by unnoticed.

They flew at fifty feet along the coastline past Gambut, past Tobruk, past Gazala. At last they were off Derna, near the northernmost promontory of Cyrenaica. From this point they would be flying directly away from the mainland. The danger of fighters would be behind them.

It was here that they met with their first mischance. Some miles behind the formation, one of the tail gunners saw splashes in the water. He took them to be falling bombs. There was no shipping in sight, he could see no aircraft, and he was puzzled. He called his skipper.

"I can see what look like bombs falling in the water about five miles behind us. Can't see anything else."

"Keep your eyes peeled."

The splashes had not been caused by bombs. A formation of five Me 109s had been on the way from an airfield near Derna to give protection to German bombers attacking the British westbound convoy. They had been carrying long-range tanks. When they saw the Beauforts, they jettisoned their auxiliary tanks and gave chase.

The German fighters attacked from the south-east, diagonally behind the Beauforts. Many of the crews saw nothing until the Beaufort on the extreme left of the formation suddenly broke in half at the turret, the two parts crashing into the sea independently, the front half in flames. Mason rammed the throttles of his Mark I Beaufort hard forward, but several of the faster Beaufort IIs shot past him, leaving their leader behind.

All the Beauforts weaved frantically, very close together,

the tail gunners firing at the fighters whenever they came within range. Several of the guns in the new Mark II Beauforts jammed, reminiscent of the early bombing attack on the *Scharnhorst*. Nevertheless, the German pilots displayed great caution, picking out only the most rearward of the weaving Beauforts and diving down from the beam to a position astern. In this way the corresponding Beaufort on the extreme right was shot down. The pilot, formerly on Sunderlands, had asked for a posting which would give him more action. It was his first torpedo operation.

Mason found himself last but one in the shattered formation. The distinction of being last now fell to a sergeant-pilot named Daffurn. His gunner called up to tell him that three fighters were on his tail. He was a long way behind the leader. His gunners opened up at the 109s, but the guns jammed almost at once. The wireless operator fired a long burst from the side guns, and was immediately silenced himself by return fire, pieces of shrapnel piercing his hand, arms and legs. The three fighters were now attacking together, one from the port quarter, one from the starboard quarter, one from dead astern. They kept 800 to 1000 yards distant, outgunning the few Beauforts still able to fire. They changed their tactics now, pointing their noses at the target, pressing the trigger continuously, watching the fall of the tracer, and then pulling the nose gently up until the tracer could be seen falling on the target.

Daffurn's tail gunner gave him the position of the fighters and a running commentary on the fall of the tracer. All Daffurn could do was to weave continually. Suddenly his feet shot off the rudder bars as the rudder received a direct hit. The tail gunner watched the rudder jerking brokenly from side to side. Daffurn's feet were thrust back and forth and the aircraft swung from left to right, out of control. With a tremendous effort he forced his feet down on the rudder bars and at last held them steady. He found that the control wires had also been damaged, the rudder only operating when the pedals were completely depressed.

All this time, as the aircraft weaved involuntarily and even more violently, the cone of fire of the fighters had been searching for them. Bursts of fire struck them from time to time, the radio was shot clean out of its housing, tracer disappeared into the engine nacelles, and the aircraft, now a flying colander, whistled shrilly as it went along. But miraculously the engines still responded and Daffurn flew on.

The hosepipe firing of the German fighters, effective as it might be, was wasteful of ammunition; and at last they turned away. One other Beaufort pilot had been forced to turn into the coast and crashland his damaged aircraft behind the German lines, and one or two others had jettisoned their torpedoes under pressure. Daffurn, with a badly damaged aircraft, no guns, no radio, and an injured gunner, decided it was hopeless to continue and turned back for Sidi Barrani. Some of the others found their petrol consumption so increased during the running fight that they now had no hope at all of striking and reaching Malta, and they too turned back. When Mason finally took stock, he found that he had only five of his twelve aircraft left.

Such a start to an operation might have persuaded many men to turn back. All the remainder had aggravated their fuel consumption worries; and Gibbs's turret was unserviceable. But the thought of giving up did not occur to them. They closed their ranks, got into rough formation again, and pressed on.

A Maryland had gone on ahead to reconnoitre and to home the Beauforts on to the target by radar. Mason's wireless operator identified the transmissions at fifty miles' range. Their track was good. Visibility was unlimited and they were still ten miles distant when they caught their first glimpse of the battle fleet. In the same moment, the Maryland appeared and fired off a star cartridge in the direction of the target.

The calm sea now erupted into great gouts of water as the 15-inch guns of the battleships put down a splash barrage in front of them. It was their first experience of this form of defence, but they kept low down on the water. The Italian ships were almost dead ahead, slightly to port. There were four destroyers out in front, in line abreast and equidistant, like the prongs of a rake; and a mile behind the destroyers they could see the two battleships, very close together, one perhaps a quarter of a mile behind and slightly to starboard of the other.

The sparkling sea beneath them was pockmarked with splashes, and the pale clear sky filled abruptly with dark blobs of cloud. Most of the flak was bursting above them at 200 feet. The Beauforts started taking evasive action, gently at first and then increasingly as they closed the range.

Mason's original plan of attack had been to lead six aircraft himself round to the starboard side of the battleships while Gibbs took his six aircraft straight in on the port side. Mason now had two other aircraft with him, and Gibbs had one. Mason intended to stick to the same plan.

At five miles' range there was a tremendous bang underneath Gibbs's aircraft, and it floundered for a moment, but Gibbs soon brought it under control. The undercarriage had been damaged and the hydraulics punctured, but the torpedo was still there. Creswell, Gibbs's navigator, had survived an earlier crash in the desert in which his pilot had been killed at his side and in which Creswell had grabbed the controls, eased himself into the pilot's seat, and landed the plane safely behind the enemy lines, where he was eventually retaken during the 'Crusader' advance. Creswell, a fair-haired, heavy-limbed boy with enormous blue eyes, now stood next to Gibbs, prepared for the worst, protecting with a tin hat that part of his anatomy which he judged most vulnerable.

Mason had just begun to swing away to port to skirt the leading destroyers, so as to develop his attack from starboard of the battleships, and Gibbs was just turning to starboard, when the leading battleship itself began to turn. Since the battleship was bows on to them, and any turn it made must present them with a beam shot, Mason and Gibbs arrested their turns and came back on to their original course. The leading battleship was clearly turning to starboard. Soon they would be able to see the whole length of it.

Whatever the Italian plan may have been, it had evidently become confused under the threat of attack. The two battleships were less than 400 yards apart; and the second battleship, after beginning a turn to starboard, altered helm and turned sharply to port. For one incredible moment it seemed that the two great ships would collide.

Meanwhile, Mason and Gibbs were leading their formations through the combing destroyers into the attack. There was no question now of either pilot manœuvring. The leading Italian battleship had turned broad on to the Beauforts and all they had to do was to run in straight and drop.

Mason and Gibbs both took the chance offered them and went for the leading battleship. But as Gibbs lined up on the target, his aircraft and that of the aircraft formating on him, flown by Dick Marshall, an Australian, were hit by flak from the destroyers. Oil seeped all over the floor of Gibbs's aircraft, and Marshall had his rudder control shot away, his elevator-trimmer control cut and his hydraulics punctured. Both pilots were thus forced to drop their torpedoes prematurely, at some 2000 yards' distance. Mason saw the two aircraft break away across him just before he dropped.

Once again, when faced with a mammoth target, Beauforts had dropped at too great a range. Partly because of the intensity of the flak, partly because of lack of experience in judging distance against capital ships, none of the torpedoes was dropped closer than a mile. The battleships steamed on.

All five Beauforts survived the attack and reached Malta. Gibbs belly-landed his damaged Beaufort, while Marshall succeeded in firing his undercarriage down but swung as he landed and hit a damaged Beaufort of 217 on the edge of the runway. Both aircraft burst into flames and were destroyed. Marshall and his crew escaped.

Had their numbers not been reduced by more than half off Derna, no doubt 39 Squadron would have registered a hit. As it was, they claimed several; but the smoke they saw rising from the *Littorio* was the result of a direct hit from a 500-lb. bomb dropped by the Liberators just before the torpedo attack.

After debriefing, the five crews to get through to Malta went to their respective Messes. They had fought their way through a protracted fighter attack, seen their comrades shot out of the sky, and come through some of the thickest flak they would ever see. Gibbs, normally a non-smoker, accepted cigarette after cigarette from his gunners. Now the tension was over, they all talked at once in a flood of excited chatter, and the line-shooting began. Suddenly they found they were ravenously hungry; and what they needed above everything was a drink. But now the importance of the convoys whose free passage they had been trying to ensure was brought home to them with depressing force. The food they sat down to was bully beef and hard biscuits; and there wasn't a drink to be had.

There was now a gap of four hours in the shadowing of the enemy force, due to a shortage of reconnaissance aircraft, and this and the lack of information on the extent of the damage sustained by the Italian Fleet greatly hampered the C.-in-C. Mediterranean in deciding whether the westbound convoy could safely proceed. By midday the convoy was turned once again for Alexandria, passing through bomb alley, and subjected to almost incessant air attacks.

The Italian Fleet, indeed, had not sustained any really crippling blows—except to its morale. The *Trento* had been sunk, the *Littorio* slightly damaged; but just before three o'clock that afternoon, when a reconnaissance aircraft again made contact, the Fleet had given up and was steering north-west for Taranto.

The way at last was clear. Was it too late for the Alexandria convoy to put about and make for Malta? In the words of Admiral Harwood, C.-in-C. Mediterranean, this was the convoy's 'golden opportunity'. But the ships were getting short of fuel; and owing to the persistent air attacks through which they had fought their way, the escort vessels were running out of ammunition. The convoy could not face another voyage through bomb alley, let alone the rigours of the final approach to Malta, and it was forced to return to Alexandria. This was depressing news; but the west-bound convoy had served its purpose if it had diverted effort from the convoy from Gibraltar. And this it had undoubtedly done.

Malta's strike aircraft were not finished with the Italian Fleet yet. 217 Squadron took off again that afternoon, for the second time in the same day; having already struck at dawn, they were now to attempt a dusk attack. Owing to mistakes in navigation and an adverse headwind, they failed to make their interception as planned, and it was dark by the time they neared the position of the Fleet. The crews had been tensed for the operation ever since they left England, and they had been on continuous standby for nearly forty-eight hours. They were nearing the end of their reserves, moral and physical. They failed to find the target.

But still Malta was not finished. The five Wellingtons that had attacked unsuccessfully the previous night left Malta again, with the same crews, shortly before dark. The leading Wellington was the original 'guinea pig' Wimpey, the proto-type Wellington torpedo-bomber, converted some months earlier, its front turret and beam guns removed. The leader of the strike, Squadron Leader D. N. Robinson, had already completed two tours on Wellingtons, the first in night-bombing operations over Germany early in the war. Then he began a tour on 70 Squadron in the Middle East, finding to his surprise that the aircraft in which he had completed his tour in England was now allocated to him on his new squadron. He completed this tour successfully, had a rest, and was then posted to 38 Squadron. Here, to his astonishment and joy, he linked up once again with Wellington T 2831, the same old faithful on which he had flown hundreds of hours over Germany, Tobruk and Benghazi, the aircraft in which he was now leading the squadron against the Italian Fleet.

As on the previous night, all the Wimpeys homed on to the Fleet by radar easily enough, flares were dropped to illumin-ate the target, and again the Italian ships put down an effective smoke screen which enclosed them in a chrysalis of grey mist. Low cloud, too, hampered the Wellington pilots, making the attacks even more difficult. Only one pilot, Pilot Officer Hawes, succeeded in penetrating the screen. He flew straight into the murk, and suddenly found himself in a clear corridor, thick billowing smoke on either side of him, but at the bottom of the corridor, steaming straight for him, a ship. It was the 35,000-ton *Littorio*.

Hawes had no time for manœuvre. He ran in on the *Littorio*, aiming his torpedoes at her port bow, dropping them both at once, One of the torpedoes missed, but the other ran true. The *Littorio*, steaming snugly between layers of cotton-wool, was taken by surprise. The crew's first intima-tion of the attack was the earthquake shock of the explosion, in the flash of which they glimpsed the Wellington disappear-ing into their own smoke screen.

189

The *Littorio* was severely damaged, the attack putting an end to any idea the Italian commander might have had of staying at sea. The Fleet was located again next day, still steaming northwards; and on 17th June a reconnaissance aircraft discovered the whole force back in harbour—minus the *Trento*, and with the *Littorio* out of action.

But the westbound convoy had been forced to abandon the struggle. Malta must look for succour to the convoy from Gibraltar.

The eastbound convoy had come under air attack from Sardinia early on 14th June, when it lost the first of its six merchant ships. A cruiser, too, was severely damaged. Then, towards evening, the convoy came within range of air attack from Sicily. These assaults were beaten off; but approaching the narrows between Sicily and Cape Bon, the main escort turned back for Gibraltar as arranged. The defence of the convoy was now taken up by Beaufighters from Malta, together with the remaining destroyers.

Meanwhile the enemy naval force of two cruisers and two destroyers from Cagliari, which had been attacked by the Wellingtons without success on the night of the 13th-14th, and sighted again by a Spitfire on the following evening, was on its way to intercept the convoy. Early on the morning of the 15th the Italian force began to close and an engagement ensued. The merchant ships in the convoy kept out of range, but the escort suffered damage, and so did one of the Italian destroyers. During the action the merchant vessels were again subjected to air attack, and another ship was lost; and the Italian warships, although parried for the moment by the escort, were still threatening to attack. An urgent call was therefore made to Malta for a torpedo strike against these vessels.

When the call came through for this daylight attack, nine of 217's Beauforts were on the way back from attacking the main units of the Italian Fleet, and the Wellingtons of 38 Squadron had only just returned from seven hours' searching for the same target. There were thus only two Beauforts available for the strike, with two very raw crews, plus the four Albacores of the Fleet Air Arm. These six aircraft took off at 09.30 and made for Pantellaria, with a comforting escort of sixteen Spitfires for high and low cover.

The enemy aircraft were working at short range under cover of heavy fighter escorts, and herein lay the difference between the German and Italian air attacks on both convoys and the attacks by the Beauforts and Wellingtons against the main Italian Fleet. But this small attacking force of Beauforts and Albacores, operating comparatively close to Malta, was well protected from the hordes of Me 109s which rose to meet it. The German fighters jettisoned their long-range tanks and attacked the Beauforts, the spearhead of the strike. The Spitfires fell on them and dogfights ensued. As a result, the Beauforts and Albacores were given a clear run to the target.

The first Beaufort pilot, Sergeant Fenton, dropped at the leading cruiser from 800 yards' range and was convinced he had scored a hit. This was confirmed by the pilots of the Spitfires and Albacores. The second Beaufort pilot, Flying Officer Minster, had never dropped a torpedo in his life. It was an interesting first attempt. Minster had had it drilled into him before take-off that distance over water was deceptive, and that when he thought he was at 1000 yards' distance he should carry on for another ten seconds, to make absolutely sure of getting in close. He saw the cruiser looming up ahead, and he could not see how he could possibly miss it, he was so close.

That was the trouble. He was too close. He dropped his torpedo at 300 yards' range and it passed right under the cruiser. He thus achieved a distinction unique in torpedo work; no other case of dropping at this range operationally is recorded. It was a strikingly gallant effort and it deserved a better fate.

No doubt Minster's attack unnerved the men on the cruiser. As he passed over the deck, he saw the Italian sailors lying down flat beside their guns. The Albacores attacked after the Beauforts; and during the afternoon the four Albacores attacked again, losing one aircraft this time to flak but claiming more hits. What damage was done in these attacks is not clear; but the Italian force did not interfere again with the eastbound convoy.

The merchant ships were now suffering their heaviest

blows. Spitfires from Malta beat off wave after wave of bombers from Sicily, but two more merchant ships were eventually sunk, and mines took a further toll of the escort. At last, on the morning of 16th June, still fiercely protected by Malta's Spitfires, the two remaining merchantmen entered the Grand Harbour. Air Vice-Marshal Hugh P. Lloyd, A.O.C. Malta, with a hundred or more civilians, watched in silence as the ships came in. "It was one of those rare occasions," he wrote afterwards, "on which everyone, without any thought, turns to bare his head. . . ."

As a result of persistent torpedo attacks, all units of the Italian Fleet had been dissuaded from pressing home their attempts to intervene. The scars of the action were as deeply impressed on the Italian naval mind as on their ships: the Italian Fleet never put to sea again. But for the British the cost of the operation had been high, and Malta remained grievously short of supplies.

Chapter 10

TARANTO TO BENGHAZI

GIBBS was only at Malta two days, but in that time he found an opportunity to talk to Lloyd about the possibility of operating Beauforts from Malta against Rommel's shipping routes, now that the island was no longer under incessant attack. Lloyd was enthusiastic; and when Gibbs got back to the Middle East he made the same suggestion at Headquarters and was received sympathetically. It was agreed that Gibbs should command a small detachment of 39 Squadron at Malta, the detachment to be maintained there for as long as its operations proved profitable. Meanwhile, Lloyd was allowed to retain 217 Squadron at Malta for the time being, possibly until a further attempt could be made to force a supply convoy through.

On 20th June, an enemy convoy of two large merchant vessels, carrying a heavy deck cargo, including rows of closely packed motor transport, escorted by three destroyers, was sighted coming out of the Gulf of Taranto, steaming down the toe of Italy, evidently making for Messina. Malta's strike aircraft had been inactive so long that all Axis shipping was now following this route, rounding northern Sicily, and then turning south past Cape Bon and on along the North African coast to Tripoli and Benghazi. On this route they were out of range of aircraft from Egypt all the way.

Twelve Beauforts of 217 Squadron took off to attack this convoy later the same day. It was an abortive strike. One aircraft was forced to turn back with a damaged airframe, and two others, flown by Minster and Hutcheson, taking off late, were attacked by four Ju 88s soon after setting course. Hutcheson managed to beat off the two Ju 88s that attacked him, and eventually returned to Luqa, but Minster was shot down, surviving his close-range attack on the Italian cruiser off Pantellaria by only five days. The other nine Beauforts failed to make contact with the convoy and returned to Luqa.

A Spitfire relocated this convoy rounding the toe of Italy

later in the evening. But next day, an entirely different convoy was sighted off the Tunisian coast south of Cape Bon,
having already completed the passage of northern Sicily.
This convoy consisted of two large merchant vessels, with a
flak-ship as escort, together with two Ju 88s and an S.M. 79.
One of the merchant vessels was a valuable German ship, the
7600-ton *Reichenfels*. Nine Beauforts, led by Squadron Leader
Lynn, with Aldridge and Stevens leading the two sub-flights,
took off later that morning, escorted by six Beaufighters. The
convoy was virtually due west of Malta. The Beauforts
approached on the port beam, very slightly astern of the
convoy; they split up so as to attack both merchant vessels,
and got to within a mile of the convoy without opposition.
Then the flak-ship suddenly exploded at them in a paroxysm
of fire, throwing up great sheets of flak. The leading Beaufort
burst into flames immediately. Two more Beauforts were shot
down a moment later. But the rest of the Beauforts ran in
from a good position on the port quarter, and four of their
torpedoes struck home, two on either ship. As they turned
away they were attacked by the air escort, but all three enemy
aircraft were shot down by the Beaufighters. Several other
Beauforts were damaged by flak, but all got back to Malta,
one wounded pilot, weak from loss of blood, landing with the
aid of his navigator. Subsequent reconnaissance showed the
Reichenfels to have sunk.

The losses had been extremely heavy, one-third of the Beaufort force. Two other aircraft were badly damaged and a pilot
put out of action. But it had been a highly successful strike,
the significance of which was at once apparent to the enemy.
Malta was armed again.

The fate of the *Reichenfels* completely unnerved the Italians,
who decided at once to change their tactics and send all convoys via the eastern route, from Taranto to Greece, down the
Greek coast, and across the Central Mediterranean to
Benghazi. The convoy which 217 had failed to find the
previous day had now reached Palermo in north-western
Sicily; but the Italians changed their minds and decided to
bring it back through the Strait of Messina and route it via
the Greek coast, in an effort to dodge pursuit from Malta.

The two heavily laden merchant vessels, escorted by two

destroyers, left Palermo on the night of the 22nd unobserved and passed once again through the Strait of Messina. But they were sighted off the toe of Italy next morning.

Twenty-four hours earlier, Gibbs had arrived in Malta with a detachment of five aircraft and crews. The orders were for the flight across the Mediterranean from Egypt to be made at night. So keen was Gibbs to get to Malta that he took off although his radio was unserviceable, the night sky obscured by cloud, and there were no other navigational aids available. Gibbs soon learned of the two strikes, of the loss of four crews in two days, and of the destruction of the *Reichenfels*; and he followed with intense interest the story of the about-turn of the two heavily laden merchantmen. When these ships were re-sighted on the morning of the 23rd, Gibbs had his detachment ready.

Here was Gibbs's opportunity, the chance to put to the test all those tenets which he had preached for so long, and sometimes as it had seemed so vainly. The key to success, Gibbs felt, lay in the employment of large numbers of Beauforts, nine or twelve at a time (and these were large numbers for those days), spreading the defensive fire, and, by dropping in quick succession, confusing the enemy's avoiding action and ensuring that enough torpedoes were converging on the target at the same time to make tolerably certain of at least one hit. It was unrealistic to imagine that a number of Beauforts could attack a target more or less independently and each hope to score a hit. And to go along with the Beauforts, Gibbs wanted diversionary, flak-busting attacks by Beaufighters, in addition to their use for fighter protection. Only given these conditions did the Beaufort pilot have a chance of getting in close to drop his torpedo—the real secret, as Gibbs had learnt from bitter experience in the North Sea, of successful torpedo work.

Gibbs and Davies studied the report of the reconnaissance Spitfire and discussed their plan of attack. The convoy was hurrying due east from the toe of Italy, across the Ionian Sea to Greece. It had reached a point about twenty miles east of Cape Spartivento. The two merchantmen were in line abreast, with two destroyers sweeping ahead and one on either flank. The Spitfire pilot estimated that the flanking destroyers were well over a mile abeam of the merchant vessels in each case, and the sweeping destroyers over a mile ahead. This gave Gibbs an idea.

The convoy was steaming away from Malta, and the Beauforts would be chasing it. Instead of trying to overtake it so as to swing round and make an attack on the bows of the merchant vessels, from ahead or abeam, why not run straight in amongst the convoy from behind, in sub-flights on either side of the two merchant vessels, but inside the flanking destroyers? This would leave the two sweeping destroyers out on a limb, powerless to interfere. And while the two outside sub-flights might have to face heavy fire from the flanking destroyers, the two centre sub-flights could make their approach virtually unopposed.

The attack developed exactly as planned. Gibbs and Leaning led their sub-flights of three Beauforts each on either side of the left-hand merchantman, Davies and Sangster led their sub-flights against the right-hand vessel. But it was soon apparent that conditions were not quite as they had anticipated. The disposition of the convoy was fundamentally unchanged: but either the reconnaissance pilot had erred in his estimate of the distance separating the ships, or the destroyers had closed up considerably, especially the two on the flanks. They were less than a mile from the merchantmen.

Gibbs and Davies realized this too late. In any case they had been seen on their approach and it would be fatal to delay the attack. But the prospect facing them, unless they were to drop their torpedoes from astern, was to fly perilously close to the flanking destroyers as they overtook the merchant vessels and turned in to attack.

Both targets looked particularly inviting, their decks packed tight with motor transport; and the four flight leaders ran up boldly inside the flanking destroyers. The flak was especially intense to the port of the convoy, where Gibbs's and Leaning's aircraft were both hit, Gibbs having his rudder controls badly damaged and Leaning his port aileron shot away, and where two other Beauforts, piloted by Gardiner and Guy, were shot down as they turned in to attack. Gardiner and his navigator were picked up by the escorting destroyers. One of the pilots in Davies's formation was hit in the leg,

Top: Smile for the camera! From left, Dick (Moose) Marshall, Joe Brown, 'Slap' Paterson, Doug Tweedie, Don Tilley, Les Worsdell, Arthur 'Pip' Peirce, Garside.

Bottom: 217 Squadron's Mk. I AW242 with Beaufighters and Spitfires.

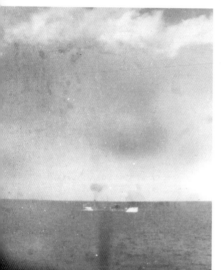

Top left and right: The real thing, Beauforts attacking with fresh and spent shell splashes in the foreground as an enemy tanker explodes in the Mediterranean.

Middle left: The *Prosperina*, 'Rommel's last tanker', is attacked.

Middle right: The men who torpedoed the *Prosperina*. Bladen, Spark and Manning. Barnes (first left) was new.

Bottom: DE108 of 47 Squadron, Wg Cdr Sprague's aircraft, damaged after the strike on 26 October 1942.

Top: 47 Squadron Beaufort IA DW880 with Mk. XII torpedo and stand and loading trolley, March 1943.

Middle: A typical 'strike-wing' mêlée in 1944 above a German convoy.

Bottom: Flack bursts from a German convoy off Den Helder.

The ship has already been set on fire as the rocket-projectile Beaufighters cross over their target.

besides having his aircraft damaged so badly that he crash-landed back at Malta. But both formations claimed hits on the merchant vessels. One of the vessels stopped, and the other slowed down.

An hour later the reconnaissance Spitfire was on the scene again. One of the merchant vessels was still stationary, down by the stern with three destroyers circling; and the fourth destroyer was escorting the other M.V. back to Taranto.

On the morning of the 25th the whole convoy was photographed back in Taranto. One of the merchant vessels, evidently severely damaged, was having its cargo transferred to another of about the same tonnage. The convoy had first sailed from Taranto five days earlier. It had been all the way to Palermo and back again; and all it had achieved was severe damage to one merchant vessel.

It was five days before the transfer of the cargo was completed; but on the 30th June a Spitfire took photographs of Taranto harbour which revealed great activity and unmistakable signs that a large convoy was about to put to sea. The enemy was presumed to be waiting for nightfall, and at dusk two bomber Wellingtons were sent into the Gulf of Taranto to locate and bomb the convoy, and to home a force of torpedo Wellingtons on to it if it had left harbour. Another Wimpey searched south of the Gulf, just in case the convoy had slipped away before dark, immediately after the harbour was photographed.

Five torpedo Wellingtons took off soon after dark, crossed the Gulf of Taranto, and orbited off Cape Santa Maria di Leuca, in the extreme heel of Italy, blocking the probable track of the convoy. They carried one torpedo and an auxiliary tank to increase their orbiting duration. The two bomber Wellingtons and three of the torpedo-carriers sighted the convoy at 01.35, hugging the coast near the exit to the Gulf. There were three merchant vessels now, with an escort of four destroyers.

Attacks on the largest merchant vessel with bombs and torpedoes developed simultaneously, although all the aircraft attacked independently. The bombers scored near misses, and one of the torpedoes failed to release. The other two Wellington pilots, Thomson and Flanagan, were fiercely engaged by light ack-ack, both aircraft were damaged, and crew-members were wounded, but both pilots dropped successfully and believed they saw their torpedoes strike the target. The convoy was thrown at once into confusion and panic, but the basic reaction was obvious: their one thought was to regain the shelter of Taranto harbour before daylight brought an attack by the Beauforts.

It was now 1st July—eleven days since the original convoy had left Taranto. The consolidation of the British forces defending the Nile delta was going on apace, while Rommel's impatience at the delay to his supply shipping in this critical period of the Desert build-up grew almost insupportable. Everything depended on his being able to sustain the momentum of his advance, and this he could not do without generous supplies. If he failed to keep up the pressure, the Eighth Army would stabilize their line and he would have to halt.

The damaged merchantman was patched up at Taranto, and forty-eight hours later the convoy sailed for the third and last time. This time the Italians tried a change of tactics, the convoy leaving port in broad daylight, early in the afternoon, soon after another visit by a reconnaissance aircraft. If it could only escape detection until nightfall, it could disappear amongst the Greek islands before daylight came again, and be lost to reconnaissance or attacks from Malta.

Malta was still desperately short of petrol, and it was impossible to keep a standing reconnaissance off the Italian ports. Even air-tests were forbidden, crews testing their aircraft as they took off on operations. Thus the convoy left Taranto unseen from the air. But it had not sailed altogether unobserved. A British submarine commander, cruising at periscope depth, saw it go.

The intelligence reached Malta that evening, and three torpedo Wellingtons, led by a radar Wellington, were sent to search the area between the heel of Italy and the Greek islands. They sighted a cruiser and a destroyer off Cape Santa Maria di Leuca soon after midnight, but there was no sign of the merchantmen. The Wellington pilots continued on course, and an hour later the radar Wellington homed them on to the convoy, three merchant vessels and two destroyers, off the island of Paxos on the Greek coast, some twenty miles south of Corfu. But due to an effective smoke screen only one aircraft was able to attack, and no results were seen.

The convoy seemed to the Wimpey crews to be spread along several miles of coastline, and they were unable to give an exact position of the major units of the enemy force. It was important that a Beaufort strike should be mounted at daybreak; so a reconnaissance Baltimore was sent out to relocate the convoy, round it up like a sheep-dog, and home the Beauforts. But the Baltimore developed engine trouble and had to return to Malta, and the question now became: should the Beauforts wait while another attempt was made to get a sighting, or should they take off without a position report, armed only with the somewhat diffuse information at present available?

The importance of good prior reconnaissance was now clearly illustrated. The convoy might have chosen any one of a number of routes round the Greek islands of Levkas, Cephalonia and Zante, or they might have taken the coastal route. The Greek coastline was near the limit of range for the Beauforts, and they could manage no more than an equilateral triangle with a very short base—Malta to Cephalonia, south for some fifty miles along the Greek coast to Zante, and then back to Malta. The Beauforts got off early enough, just before seven o'clock that morning, with a Beaufighter escort, but they failed to sight the convoy.

The Beauforts got back to Malta at midday, and during the afternoon a Spitfire, and then the original Baltimore, now serviceable again, combed the Greek islands. Soon after four o'clock the Baltimore found the three merchant vessels steaming south-west some fifteen miles south of Zante, evidently intending to cut straight across the central Mediterranean to Tripoli or Benghazi. The Italians had provided a powerful escort of no less than eight destroyers in a determined effort to get the convoy through.

The ships were only a few hours' steaming from safety. By daylight next day they would be well out of range of the Beauforts. There was no need for Lloyd to ask Gibbs if he would try again that evening. Gibbs was already planning a dusk strike.

There was only a handful of Beauforts at Malta now, with
a handful of crews. 217 had begun with nineteen crews and
they now had twelve. Gibbs still had three of his original five.
Some of the Beauforts were unserviceable, and only eight
could be got ready that evening. Gibbs led these aircraft off
from Malta at 18.30. But two of the eight developed mechanical trouble almost at once, and the strike settled down to
six Beauforts with a Beaufighter escort. Further troubles on
the outward flight narrowed the Beauforts down to four—
Gibbs himself and three 217 pilots, Stevens, Mercer and
Hutcheson. The Beaufighters also had their troubles, but as
the strike force neared the reported position of the convoy,
five Beaufighters remained.

The sun was setting directly behind them, deepening the
blue of the sky and darkening the sea. Gibbs had studied the
Baltimore's report on the disposition of the convoy and its
escort before take-off, and he had decided to steer a course
well to the rear of the convoy, turn south-west, and come up
towards the convoy from astern on the landward side. The
eight destroyers were ranged in a crescent round the convoy,
from dead ahead right round the starboard side to dead
astern. There was no chance whatever of dropping a torpedo
successfully from that side. But attacking from the direction
of the Greek coast would avoid the destroyers at least on the
approach; and there was always the chance that it might take
the convoy by surprise.

Creswell managed the navigation to a nicety and their first
sight of the convoy was the port quarter of the tail merchant
vessel. The light was fading rapidly, the phosphorescent glow
from the sun was now away to their starboard, on the far side
of the convoy, and over the Greek coast behind them dusk
was giving place to darkness. The conditions were ideal.

The biggest of the three merchantmen was the centre one,
and Gibbs went for it. Stevens followed. Behind them, Mercer
and Hutcheson lined up on the last M.V. The four Beauforts
approached unseen; they were little more than a mile away
from the convoy when the flak started. It was too late for the
destroyers to bring their heavier guns to bear, but in a few
moments the sky was a ribboned tangle of vari-coloured
tracer, an orgy of bright-hued ticker tape, resplendent in the

iridescent light. Ahead of Gibbs, the Beaufighters went in to spray the decks of the nearest destroyers with cannon and machine-gun fire. Gibbs got right in close to drop his torpedo. Stevens, just behind him, dropped his almost in the same splash. A chunk of metal disappeared out of the tail of Gibbs's aircraft as Stevens followed him out. The aircraft staggered low over the water, and for a moment Stevens thought it had gone. The two Beauforts raced between three destroyers on the starboard side and hurtled on in the direction of Malta.

Behind them, Mercer and Hutcheson were about to drop their torpedoes. The tail gunners in the two leading aircraft saw them come safely past the merchant vessels, saw the ribbons of tracer snaking around them as they came away from the convoy. These two aircraft failed to return.

The last view the gunners had of the convoy was a column of smoke from one of the merchantmen and a red glow on the water. They were certain that at least one of the ships was hit.

It was one-o'clock in the morning when Gibbs and Stevens got back to Malta. Gibbs had taken off on the first strike eighteen hours earlier, after working out the details of the reconnaissance and plan of attack for some hours before that. Once before he had attempted two strikes in one day, and on that occasion he and his crew had finished up in the Lincolnshire dyke. Gibbs alone of his present crew had any memory of that—unless one could credit with a memory the battered mascot which still sat by the pilot, the toy which had once represented a Panda.

Stevens's aircraft was undamaged and he landed safely. Gibbs reached Malta a few minutes later. His damaged Beaufort was none too easy to control, but he eventually found himself over the island. Lloyd was waiting in the control tower at Luqa, as he invariably did, for the return of the Beauforts. Also in the control tower was the duty wing commander, a charming character with a slight stammer, and Tony Leaning. Suddenly they heard aircraft engines and had a momentary glimpse of a low-flying Beaufort on the far side of the island. They switched on the chance-light and waited.

Gibbs's aircraft was badly damaged and the undercarriage was jammed. He had lost count of the times he had belly-landed a Beaufort, and regarded it with hardly less apprehension than a normal night landing. Beauforts were strong, they stayed in one piece, and they didn't burn easily. He saw the chance-light and began his approach.

The brightness of the chance-light spoiled the night vision of the men in the control tower, and they did not see the Beaufort until it was touched by the glow from the chance-light as it roared over the end of the runway. They saw at once that the undercarriage was still up.

The duty wing commander turned to the airman of the watch, who had charge of the Very pistol. He wanted to stop Gibbs landing.

"Give him a r-r-r-r-r-. . ." He wanted to say 'red', but for the moment the stammer got in the way. The airman waited patiently for the word of command. It never came.

Gibbs was now a few feet above the runway, breasting the Beaufort into the ground. There was a deafening metallic crunch, and a cloud of smoke, the men in the watch-tower felt themselves recoil, and then the Beaufort severed the chance-light cable, throwing the airfield with awful abruptness into the fierce darkness that follows intensely bright light.

"R-r-red," said the wing commander.

But Gibbs had landed safely, and he soon gave news of the attack. Two Wellingtons had a last try at the convoy during the night, but once again an effective smoke screen prevented more than one aircraft from attacking, and no results were seen. The convoy now passed out of range of Malta's strike aircraft.

By the morning of 5th July, two of the merchant vessels had reached Benghazi harbour. The third vessel, following the attack led by Gibbs, had been forced to put into a Greek port for repairs. The original convoy had set out from Taranto on 20th June. Owing to the hounding it had undergone at the hands of Malta's reconnaissance and strike aircraft the routine forty-eight-hour crossing of the central Mediterranean had taken sixteen days.

Chapter 11

BEFORE THE AUGUST CONVOY

THE enemy reacted vigorously to this renewed threat to Rommel's supply shipping. Mussolini had stipulated that if Malta was not to be invaded until the autumn it must be neutralized meanwhile, and after the interference with the convoy of 20th June Kesselring began a new attempt to bomb the island into submissiveness, if not actual submission. Since early May the attack had been maintained on a minor scale only, while Rommel's victorious advance across Libya and Egypt to the gates of Alexandria threatened to isolate Malta for good. But at the beginning of July, Rommel was finally halted at El Alamein, and the last round of the battle of supplies began.

Rommel went over to the defensive for the time being in the Desert, and Kesselring was free to have one more try at obliterating Malta. Wave after wave of aircraft, German and Italian, were flung across from Sicily in an attempt to knock out Malta's fighters. But this force, stiffened by the arrival of more Spitfire squadrons, was very different from the one which had been powerless against the circus of Me 109s three months earlier. Kesselring was able to call on nearly six hundred aircraft, against a hundred or so Spitfires, but after a fortnight of the new blitz nearly fifty of his aircraft had been destroyed, losses which persuaded him that the cost was too great. The *Luftwaffe* was desperately short of aircraft to meet its many commitments; and after the middle of July the attacks died down.

The offensive against Rommel's shipping was renewed at once, and the few Beauforts and Beaufort crews that had survived the previous month's operations were now reinforced by the arrival of the first six crews of 86 Squadron, led by Jimmy Hyde. Davies had returned to the U.K., and the whole force of Beauforts at Malta was amalgamated under Gibbs, who was promoted to Wing Commander. Gibbs was delighted at the prospect of operating once again with Jimmy Hyde.

Another old 22 Squadron man to arrive with Hyde was Hank Sharman. Sharman had been instructing at Abbotsinch when one of his pupils had landed inadvertently with his undercarriage up. Sharman had caught up with him in the crew-room and dressed him down in front of the whole course. A week later Sharman had done exactly the same thing himself. He could no longer face life at Abbotsinch, and there was only one thing left for him to do. He applied for a posting to a squadron the same day, and went to 86.

The tactics of torpedo work were now firmly delineated in Gibbs's mind. The sequence of events invariably began with the reconnaissance sighting. The standby crews sat in the open at Luqa, and if the P.R.U. aircraft had found anything, instead of breaking W/T silence the pilot waited until he reached the island and then shot up the squadron hut on the airfield. The standby crews then gathered their kit and assembled in the hut.

When the Spitfire pilot's report came through, the strike leader and his navigator decided on the most promising point of interception and the best method of attack. Normally the strike force flew to a point well ahead of the convoy and then turned up the line of the convoy's advance. Part of the strike force would attack on the starboard bow, part on the port bow, and the rest would drop their torpedoes straight down the track of the target. This way, although some of the torpedoes were inevitably wasted, the ship attacked could not possibly avoid them all. If it turned away from the attacks on the bow, it could not then comb the frontal attack. The tactics were never static, and varied with the disposition of the escort and its proximity to land. And they often had to be adjusted at the last minute to cope with the avoiding action taken by the convoy under attack.

Briefing took place in the open outside the small squadron hut, and was attended by the Beaufighter crews as well. Those escort vessels which seemed most likely to interfere with the torpedo attack were singled out for particular attention by the Beaufighters. When everyone understood exactly what the strike was trying to achieve and what was expected of him personally, the strike leader's navigator gave details of tracks, distances, turning points and so on. The strike force always set course at fifty feet, due east of Malta, away from the radar at Sicily, so that its presence was not disclosed and its destination not revealed by its course out of Malta.

The success of the attack depended on the accuracy of the interception, without which surprise was lost and the carefully chosen plan of attack could not be developed. A good interception minimized losses, enabling the Beauforts to get into position to attack before the escort vessels could deploy. The accuracy of the interception depended first on the reconnaissance report, secondly on the strike leader's navigator. The whole operation was discussed afterwards at the de-briefing, when photographs of the attack were generally available, taken by a P.R.U. Baltimore which went along with the strike force.

The first operation after the July blitz took place on 21st July. A Spitfire sighted a 7000-ton merchantman escorted by two destroyers off Cephalonia at first light, and by half past nine the Beauforts were off, nine of them, led by Pat Gibbs, with the usual Beaufighter escort. Of the other eight crews there were three of 217, Tony Leaning, and four of the newly arrived 86, including Hyde and Sharman, on their first strike from Malta. The nine aircraft attacked from dead ahead in three sub-flights of three, the evasive action of the convoy resulting in two sub-flights attacking on the starboard side and one from the port. The two destroyers were steaming ahead of the merchant vessel in line abreast, the M.V. forming the apex of a triangle behind them. The destroyers were nicely placed in the path of a bows attack, and the Beauforts on the starboard bow hit not only the merchant vessel but the destroyer as well. Both were left in difficulties.

Three days later came a strike by six Beauforts against a large merchant vessel laden with deck cargo in almost exactly the same spot, off the island of Cephalonia. It was a highly successful strike from the point of view of one sub-flight, but almost unbelievably tragic for the other.

The strike was led by Jimmy Hyde, the first one he had led from Malta. With him in the leading flight were two other 86 Squadron pilots, Furphy and Thompson. The second vic was all 217, Stevens, Hutcheson (a young Canadian pilot officer, not the Hutcheson shot down three weeks earlier) and Grey.

205

There were nine escorting Beaufighters. The convoy had been sighted leaving Taranto the previous evening and it had made good progress during the night. The escort was an unusually strong one—two destroyers and two flak-ships.

Hyde led the six Beauforts in a long beam approach at the convoy, straight from Malta. The memory of the running fight with the Me 109s off Stavanger was still strong in his mind, and in the minds of the other 86 Squadron crews, and the three aircraft tucked in very close together, so as to present their combined fire to any attacker. Hyde was unused to the smooth, glassy Mediterranean, and his approach was rather high. Two miles from the convoy he put the nose of his Beaufort down, and Furphy and Thompson followed. Behind them Stevens and his sub-flight, in loose formation, were almost scraping the water.

86 Squadron had been posted to Malta at such short notice that none of the squadron aircraft had been camouflaged for the Mediterranean theatre. Two hundred feet above the water, wing-tip to wing-tip, their European camouflage etching them cleanly against the sky, they presented a target to the defending gunners some two hundred feet across.

The first salvoes from the destroyers and flak-ships were all directed at Hyde's formation. The three aircraft were still descending for the attack, still out of torpedo range. The flak-busting Beaufighters had timed their run so as to silence the escort's guns at the moment when the Beaufort pilots had to hold their aircraft steady for the drop. They were diving down on the nearest destroyers, but they had not yet opened fire.

Hyde's aircraft was the first to be hit. It blew up instantaneously. Sarene, in the turret, felt a tremendous kick in the back, followed by a sensation of falling backwards down a lift-shaft. The next thing he knew he was at the bottom of the Mediterranean. The explosion in Hyde's aircraft threw chunks of metal and debris across the path of Furphy's aircraft on the left. This aircraft was actually brought down like a skittle by the flying debris. Thompson on the right was shot down a moment later. For the first and only time the Italian gunners had swept a whole flight of Beauforts from the sky.

But retribution, skimming the surface of the water, was speeding towards them. Stevens's formation, widely spread, was converging on the merchantman unseen. The Italians were naturally jubilant; and the Beaufighters were diving on them, peppering them with cannon, so that for the moment they had their hands full. Thus the second flight of Beauforts aimed their torpedoes unchallenged, at a target steering a steady course. It was not until the three Beauforts flashed past the bows of the destroyers that the convoy realized the attack was not over—and then it was too late.

Two of the three torpedoes struck the merchant vessel on the starboard bow, sending up billowing flames which were choked by a dense mushroom of smoke as they rose. In the afternoon the vessel was photographed in tow, stern first, down by the bows and still on fire. Later it was photographed in the port of Argostoli, on the island of Cephalonia, completely burnt out.

When Sarene found himself deep in the Mediterranean, with thousands of tons of water above him, he struggled and kicked until eventually darkness turned into opalescence and suddenly he shot to the surface. There was no sign of the crashed Beaufort, not even a trace of wreckage, but to the east the brightness of the day was blackened by the burning merchantman. He looked round for the rest of his crew, and soon saw them, all three of them, quite near. He swam across and spoke to them. Their faces were calm, they showed no sign of stress, terror or pain; but they were all dead, killed instantly when the aircraft blew up. It was a tragic end to a long road for Jimmy Hyde.

Sarene saw the dinghy some thirty to forty yards away, and he swam over to it and climbed in. Cephalonia looked about three miles distant. He was picked up by the convoy and taken to Argostoli.

Furphy, on Hyde's left, had managed to bring his aircraft down safely, and the whole crew escaped. Thompson, shot down, crashed into the sea more violently, but none of the crew was badly hurt. The tail gunner, short and fair-haired, typical of the under-sized A/G, who wore his forage-cap lodged precariously over one ear, balancing it by cultivating a pronounced tilt at the neck, whose walk was a mixture of insolence, arrogance and spirit, was trapped in the flare-chute, gripped by the legs, and the rest of the crew were unable to extricate him. He went down with the aircraft.

Furphy and his crew, and the three survivors of Thompson's crew, were also picked up by the escort. They met Sarene again at Argostoli.

The supply of petrol at Malta, as well as other essentials, was now almost exhausted, and plans for a further inbound convoy operation were being laid. Only one more strike was attempted before the arrival of this convoy; but an incident which resulted from it typified the courage, initiative and morale of the Beaufort crews.

The strike took place on 28th July. It was led by Pat Gibbs, against a large merchant vessel escorted by two destroyers and a motor torpedo-boat near Sapienza in southern Greece. A Spitfire found the convoy at dawn, flew back to Malta and shot up the airfield at Luqa, and nine Beauforts took off soon afterwards, with an escort of six Beaufighters. The attack was made by two sub-flights of Beauforts on either bow, after an approach from astern, the third sub-flight synchronizing with a shallow bombing attack, while the Beaufighters beat up the destroyers with cannon. Two hits were scored on the M.V., and it was seen in port at Navarino that evening. Leaning, on his last operation before going on rest, followed Gibbs in. After he dropped his torpedo he saw a Cant floatplane ahead of him and he was about to fire at it when he was attacked by three Macchi fighters. Two of the Beauforts were shot down, but one crew was picked up later by the Cant floatplane which Leaning had so nearly attacked. The crew were taken to Corfu. Next day, while they were being flown in another Cant to a prisoner-of-war camp in southern Italy, they over-powered the Italian crew, took control of the aircraft, and flew it to Malta, only to be shot down by Spitfires as they neared the island. But both the British and Italian crews escaped unhurt.

The chief lesson learnt from the June attempt to re-supply Malta had been that it was impossible to run a convoy through from Alexandria without the certainty of crippling losses, even without interference from the Italian Fleet. With the Libyan coastline out of our hands, adequate air protection for our ships could not be given, and the weight of enemy air attack, poised at close range, was too great to be faced. The lesser risk was to run a convoy through from Gibraltar, though even this meant heavy air and submarine attack and the certainty of severe losses. But the supply situation at Malta was desperate, and desperate measures were called for.

A convoy of fourteen merchant vessels, escorted by two battleships, four aircraft carriers, three heavy cruisers, four A.A. cruisers, and twenty-four destroyers, passed Gibraltar on the night of 9th-10th August. In preparation, Malta was reinforced early in August by some fifty Spitfires, two squadrons of Beaufighters, another eight crews of 86 Squadron, and reinforcements for the 39 Squadron detachment, which by this time consisted of Pat Gibbs alone.

The story of the August convoy is legendary. The enemy began to attack the convoy on 11th August, and the first victim was the aircraft carrier *Eagle*, sunk by a U-boat. In the next two and a half days, nine of the fourteen merchant vessels and three more warships were sunk, either by German bombers or by U-boats or E-boats, or were so badly damaged that they had to be finished off by our own gunfire. At 18.30 hours on 13th August, three of the remaining merchant vessels entered the Grand Harbour. The fourth, damaged and stopped for a time off the Tunisian coast, limped in on the afternoon of the 14th. There was one more merchant vessel afloat—the tanker *Ohio*. This was the ship for which the Beauforts were waiting. For a further twenty-four hours she was subjected to almost incessant air attack, and when she was finally towed in by destroyers early on the 15th, her decks were awash. But her fuel was safe.

Fifteen Beauforts under Gibbs with fifteen Beaufighters as escort had been waiting impatiently for the Italian Fleet to sail against the convoy. But the very existence of the Beauforts, a strike force in being, was enough to keep the Italian capital ships—even at this crisis in the fortunes of the Mediterranean campaign—in port. The Beauforts were thus denied the chance of taking part in one of the most glorious operations of the war.

But Rommel's last attempt to force his way through to the Nile valley was about to begin; and the Beauforts were ready to strike.

Chapter 12

TEN DAYS TO ALAM EL HALFA

R OMMEL'S supply position had never been better than
when he began his victorious campaign on 26th May;
but in the ensuing weeks the fighting was bitter and his losses
heavy, and by the time he had succeeded in taking Tobruk
he had dissipated most of his strength. A vast quantity of
booty, however, fell to him with Tobruk, including ammunition, petrol, food, and war material of all kinds, so that he
was able to pursue the retreating British forces with renewed
vigour. But by the time he was finally halted at El Alamein,
his reserves of material, including all the immediately usable
booty, had virtually disappeared.

In the first three weeks of June, when the British had been
preoccupied with the attempt to provision Malta, the Axis
had had a golden opportunity to amass stocks of war materials
in Italian ports and ferry them across the Mediterranean unmolested. But with an almost myopic lack of foresight the
supply authorities had sent only 3000 tons to Africa in this
period; and when they attempted to run convoys through
later in the month, Malta had been ready for them.

Throughout July and the first half of August the work of
the Italian supply staffs remained muddled and irresolute,
and the lack of striking power at Malta in the period immediately preceding the arrival of the *Ohio* was not turned to
account. Rommel's lines of communication were stretched to
breaking-point; but his chief concern was that he should be
in a position to attempt the final leap to his goal before the
balance of power tipped too heavily against him. He knew
that the British were building up their forces inexorably; and
he had the greatest respect for the industrial potential of
America, the products of which he knew were flowing into
position in front of him. He had received information that a
large British convoy of well over 100,000 tons, low in the
water with its cargo of new weapons and materials for the
Eighth Army, was expected in Suez at the beginning of

September. The final, knock-out blow must therefore be delivered before the end of August.

Rommel thereupon began to exert the fiercest pressure on the Italians to provide him with the necessary supplies for his final push to Cairo, and eventually he extracted the promise that a steady flow of tankers would be despatched in time for his offensive. Furthermore, if these tankers were sunk, the Italians undertook to replace them at once by others; and if necessary, submarines, warships and aircraft would be used to ferry across the most urgent materials.

Rommel's aim was to avoid a static battle at all costs. In static warfare, between evenly matched forces, he knew that the tenacity of the British soldier was likely to turn the scale. The decisive battle must be fought behind the British front, where the commanders and troops of the Afrika Korps would have the chance of proving their greater tactical skill and aptitude for mobile warfare.

Rommel's plan was to move his two panzer divisions to the south under the strictest secrecy. He would then make a feint attack in the north, a holding attack in the centre, and stage his main effort in the south, where he believed the British were weakest. The Panzer Army was to penetrate the British defences above the Qattara Depression, and then swing round northwards to the sea. By this means he would turn the whole El Alamein position, and the entire Eighth Army would be encircled and its communications severed. The decisive battle, in Rommel's view, would be fought at Alam el Halfa. The British would be left with the option of fighting it out to the end or breaking out and falling back to the east, thus relinquishing their hold on Egypt.

But first, the petrol.

Immediately after the August convoy operation was concluded, 217 Squadron were released from Malta, their ultimate destination being the Far East. Of the nineteen crews that had flown through to Malta two months earlier, only eight remained. The gap was filled by 86 Squadron, who now numbered twelve crews, plus the reinforced detachment of 39 Squadron, which grew in the next few days to ten crews. The two squadrons were now amalgamated and re-formed as 39 Squadron under Pat Gibbs. There were twenty Mark I Beauforts on the island, but no Mark IIs, since there were no ground crews at Malta capable of servicing the Wasp engine, which was a feature of this Mark. Gibbs was campaigning for the general introduction of the Mark II, in which the crews had much greater confidence. But the vital strikes of the next few days were fought with the old Mark I.

Among the crews in the detachment from Egypt were Ken Grant, who had taken part in the first Beaufort torpedo attack in the Mediterranean against the *Victoria* seven months earlier, and Dick Marshall, the Australian who had flown with Gibbs against the Italian Fleet. Grant, a shortish, fair-skinned, almost insignificant Englishman, was one of the leading torpedo pilots until he was shot down off Tobruk in the following November. He and two of his crew scrambled into their dinghy, and finished up in a P.O.W. camp. Marshall was one of the great characters of torpedo work, perhaps the best-loved of all the men of the Beauforts. He looked, and was, as solid as a rock.

Marshall was well over six feet in height. He had thick, short, light-brown hair which grew low over his forehead, and a tremendously elongated skull terminating in a powerfully abutting jaw. There wasn't an ounce of fat on him, but he was well made, and the hooked, prominent nose and abutting jaw gave an instant impression of strength. He had done his pilot training in Canada, at a station called Moose-jaw, and this name was quickly applied to him. Surprisingly, when shortened to 'Moose', it stuck. He was 'Moose' Marshall ever afterwards.

Moose was accustomed to a spartan life back in Australia, and he was equally at home in the Desert and in the hectic, austere life of Malta. But, like most Australians, he was without inhibitions; he had a tremendous capacity for enjoying himself, for enjoying the good things and the so-called bad things of life. He was not difficult to irritate—no man could look or sound more irritated. He even had a partiality for the word itself. "Now isn't that irritating," he would say, when something put him out. But a moment later his face would relax into a huge grin—he could not be out of temper for long. He liked to think of himself as a games player, and was a useful rugger forward, but he was not generally adept at ball games. When a game of cricket was suggested he was the first to assent, and he would wait patiently for his knock; but when he got out first or second ball, as he invariably did, he would throw the bat down in genuine chagrin, with a "That's what I hate about cricket". He was quite capable of going off in a huff. Afterwards he would laugh disarmingly and not be in the least abashed or ashamed.

Later he was joined in the crew by an Australian navigator, Paterson, so slap-happy that he soon earned the nickname of 'Slap'. Slap was pale-faced, with protruding grey-blue eyes, and a full-lipped, half-open, almost adenoidal mouth. No pair of eyes could shine with excitement like Slap's.

Moose and Slap's buoyant, independent spirits got them into no end of scrapes and scraps, but they were incapable of malice. As N.C.O.s they were fatally attracted by an 'Officers Only' sign, weighing in and often disarming rebuff with their rugged good humour. But the M.P.s would get them when they left. On one of these occasions, in Alexandria, they fought for over an hour with a squad of M.P.s who were out to get their man. Their man was Moose Marshall. They beat him very nearly to a pulp, bludgeoned him until that great head was swollen to the size of a pumpkin and the man himself was unconscious for minutes at a time and incapable of speech. But each time he recovered, and the M.P.s gave it up in the end. Eight months later, when he was killed, he was a squadron leader, D.F.C.

No one who knew Moose and Slap could ever quite believe that they had gone. Men who were inured to the daily recital of the names of men who had been killed, walked away when they heard the news, and stood for a moment alone. No two men of the Beauforts were loved like these.

There were other men, too, who arrived at Malta at this time and were to make their mark in the Beaufort world. Colin Milson, another Australian, Don Tilley, a South African, Leslie Worsdell, a fair-haired Englishman with a traditional R.A.F. moustache, and Sanderson, a black-haired Cornishman, also with a moustache to match. They were all extremely young. Gibbs at twenty-five was one of the oldest in years, and much the oldest in experience, but he remained youthful in appearance and mind. The games he had played with Leaning during the July blitz were the kind of games that boys might play—last out of bed during an air raid, or, in the daytime, last down into the underground operations room, waiting long enough to see the bomb-doors of the attacking aircraft open, watching the bombs fall lazily for several thousand feet before diving for shelter. Leaning was a ready contestant in this adolescent bravado; but Gibbs generally won.

These, then, were some of the men on whom, in the next fortnight, the severing of Rommel's supply line would depend.

Rommel's persistent nagging and entreaties had at last borne fruit, and a schedule of supply shipping was mustered in Italian ports of such aggregate tonnage that if its combined cargo could be delivered, the delicate balance of strength in the Desert might swing irrevocably against the Eighth Army. The first of some ten ships, the 8300-ton *Rosalina Pilo*, carrying 3500 tons of mixed cargo, including 1200 tons of ammunition and 400 tons of petrol, left Naples on 16th August. Malta's strike aircraft had been grounded for lack of fuel since 28th July, and the Italians decided to run the convoy via the shorter western route, round northern Sicily and south past Cape Bon. The *Rosalina Pilo*, escorted by two destroyers, four Ju 88s and two Me 109s, escaped detection until it had passed Pantellaria. But here it was sighted by a reconnaissance Spitfire.

Six Beauforts, led by Hank Sharman, took off from Malta to strike at the convoy off the island of Lampedusa. The action of the convoy in taking the route nearer Malta meant that the Beauforts enjoyed the luxury of a Spitfire escort, as well as the usual one of Beaufighters, six of which were briefed for flak suppression and three for dive-bombing. There were eight Spitfires—twenty-three aircraft in all.

The convoy was due south of Pantellaria, some thirty-five miles west of Lampedusa, steaming down the Tunisian coast, the two destroyers disposed to seaward of the merchant vessel. Sharman decided to come up astern of the convoy, swing round to its starboard side, make the attack from landward, and run straight for home.

Sharman got his Beauforts into position, and then fired a Very cartridge as the agreed signal for the Beaufighters to silence the flak. But as he led his two sub-flights of three Beauforts into the attack there was an explosion in the nose of his aircraft, the navigator fell back wounded, and the front of the aircraft forward of the cockpit burst into flames. In spite of his wounds, the navigator went forward and succeeded in extinguishing the fire. Sharman, choked for the moment by the acrid smoke from the explosion, nevertheless kept his gaze fixed firmly on the target. He was leading, and if he faltered the whole attack might fail.

He watched the Beaufighters climb to 1000 feet and then begin their dive down at the escorting destroyers. The Spitfires were engaging the Ju 88s and the Me 109s. Suddenly he saw bombs bursting around the merchant vessel, and then a bomb from the last Beaufighter scored a direct hit on the stern. The cannon and bomb attacks confused and cowed the convoy, and the ships took their evasive action uncertainly. The six Beauforts were nearly all in a good position to drop. After they dropped they flew right over the convoy, machine-gunning all the way, and as they cleared the target area and looked back towards the land, they saw two immense explosions as their torpedoes went home.

Later the *Rosalina Pilo* was seen abandoned, and subsequently she was found to have sunk. A Ju 88 and an Me 109 had been shot down, and all the British aircraft had got through safely. It was a highly satisfactory start.

39 Squadron were now allotted a permanent Beaufighter squadron to work with them exclusively on shipping strikes. This was a move for which Gibbs had long campaigned. When men lived, worked and drank together, they began to feel the same way about things, to jell into a composite fighting force. Each quickly formed a profound respect for the other's role; and incidents like failing to meet at a rendezvous, which had happened so often in the U.K. and in the early days in North Africa, became unthinkable. The loss of a Beaufort became a personal affront to the men of the Beaufighters, and often a personal grief.

The sinking of the *Rosalina Pilo*, like that of the *Reichenfels* two months earlier, convinced the Italians that they must abandon the western route via the Tunisian coastline. The next convoy had already reached Palermo; but history repeated itself and it was brought back through the Strait of Messina on 19th August, and sighted off the toe of Italy next day. This was the 7800-ton *Pozarica*, one of the biggest tankers in the Mediterranean, powerfully escorted by five destroyers and a flak-ship, with an air umbrella of six Macchis and a Cant floatplane. Gibbs organized a strike of twelve Beauforts, and led them himself. Of the men who had taken part in the strike three days earlier there were two Canadians, Roper and Watlington, and Allsopp and Gillies. Of the new men from Egypt there were Grant, Marshall, Worsdell and Gordon Head, a young powerfully built N.C.O. They took off at 08.45 that morning, escorted by ten Beaufighters, six with bombs and four for flak suppression.

The formation set course due east of Malta, and then turned north, aiming for Punta di Stilo, on the ball of the foot of Italy, just over two hours' flying. As usual the convoy was coast crawling, with the destroyer escort fanned out on its starboard side, relying on the shallow water to port to protect it from torpedo attack from the landward. The Italian seamen never seemed to learn the lesson that while the shallows protected them from submarine attack, there was generally sufficient depth of water for the run of a torpedo. For the Beauforts, attacking from landward had everything to recommend it—surprise, keeping the escort on the far side of the ship to be attacked, and setting the aircraft on an approximate course for home.

The convoy was steaming north-east, and the four flights of Beauforts, led by Gibbs, Roper, Allsopp and Grant respectively, approached from astern, skirted the rear of the convoy, overtook it, and turned in to attack while actually over land. All twelve Beauforts dropped in quick succession on the port bow.

The *Pozarica* had been assumed to be fully laden, and the torpedoes were set to run at a depth of twenty-two feet. But evidently she had a much smaller draft than had been thought. Most of the torpedoes were seen to run well, and the tanker was almost stationary, but there was no sign of a single hit. Later the photographs taken by the Baltimore pilot showed several torpedoes passing directly under the tanker.

The Beaufighters bombed the destroyers and sprayed them with cannon, and all aircraft carried out machine-gun attacks on the escort, the navigators stretched out face down in the nose, head tucked behind a propped-up parachute, hosing the front guns almost without looking. But the combined fire of the five destroyers and the flak-ship took their toll. Pete Roper and an Australian named Condon, on his first trip, were shot down, and a Beaufighter was also lost. Roper and Condon and their crews were picked up by the escort. They were glad enough to be pulled out of the drink; but they had a nasty feeling that Gibbs and the others would be back.

When they got back to Malta, Keith Park, who had replaced Lloyd as A.O.C. in the previous month, showed them a signal from Tedder, who, aware of Rommel's preparations for a final push, spoke of the supreme importance he attached to the destruction of all south-bound enemy convoys in the next ten days. It was a depressing moment for such a message to arrive, and the crews gazed at the Baltimore's photographs dejectedly. As far as they knew, they had lost ten good friends, eight in the Beauforts and two in the Beaufighter, and had exposed themselves to mortal danger in an operation which had been doomed to failure from the start. And Tedder's telegram told them just how expensive failure was likely to prove.

But the *Pozarica* still had a long way to go before it passed out of Beaufort range, and Gibbs decided to await a further sighting report before attempting another strike.

During the night the convoy crossed the Gulf of Taranto, passed the heel of Italy, and hit the Greek coast north of Corfu, where it was sighted by reconnaissance next day. Gibbs decided to send nine Beauforts, and to stiffen the Beaufighter escort in view of the very strong opposition encountered the previous day. The sighting report gave the convoy escort as still the same—five destroyers and a flak-ship. There were eight Beaufighters for escort and flak suppression, and five carrying bombs.

Gibbs led the strike himself, taking Sharman to lead the second sub-flight and Grant to lead the third. At the briefing

H* 217

he reminded the crews of Tedder's signal, and added his own personal exhortation to the pilots to get in really close for the drop. "I'm sure that when you see what I've got for you," he said, "I shall be able to rely on your response." He then, with the utmost seriousness, handed each pilot a bar of chocolate.

Yesterday's losses were still fresh in the minds of the crews, and they knew they were after a strongly protected ship. But this flash of dry humour did more to bolster morale than any pep talk. There was a gasp of appreciation, not only for the way Gibbs had fooled them, but for the chocolate, which was a rare luxury at Malta and would be shared round the crew meticulously. But there wasn't any actual laughter. The ceremony had an air of pagan communion about it. In some subtle, obscure way, Gibbs was sharing his strength.

Creswell, as usual, managed the navigation perfectly and the formation turned north some thirty miles ahead of the convoy, which was tucked in between Corfu and the mainland, with an air umbrella of at least a dozen fighters. Gibbs made his attack from the Corfu side of the channel, the three sub-flights going in one behind the other on the tanker's starboard bow. The Beaufighters hurried on ahead at a signal from Gibbs, the bombers scoring near misses on the tanker and a direct hit on the destroyer, and the fighters shooting down an assorted bag of six Axis aircraft—two Piaggio 32s, two BR 20s, a Ju 88 and, of all things, a Ju 52, besides raking the escort's decks with cannon fire. Gibbs ran in close and made no mistake with his torpedo; and one and possibly two more hits were scored by the last sub-flight, who had time to adjust themselves to the tanker's evasive action. Wolfe, a South African in the last sub-flight, and on his first trip, was shot down. But the Mediterranean was a gentle sea to ditch in. He and his crew joined Roper and Condon on one of the destroyers.

Photographs taken immediately after the attack showed the *Pozarica* stationary with oil flowing from both sides; and later reconnaissance discovered her beached and abandoned in three fathoms of water off Corfu.

Three days later, on the 24th, the reconnaissance squadron found yet another target, this time a small but important tanker, the 1500-ton *Dielpi*. The tanker was seen early that morning emerging from the Gulf of Taranto escorted by two destroyers, with the usual air escort of Macchis and Ju 88s, and Gibbs decided to delay his attack so as to strike at the convoy at dusk. The ships were kept under observation, and early that evening they had reached a point a few miles south of Corfu.

Gibbs sent nine Beauforts escorted by nine Beaufighters, six for fighter protection and flak suppression and three carrying bombs. The strike was led by Allsopp, with Worsdell and Marshall leading the other two sub-flights.

The formation took off at 16.45, flew for fifteen minutes due east as usual, and then turned north-east for Corfu. The last reconnaissance report showed that the two destroyers were steaming out in front, and the plan was to attack from astern.

One of the pilots in Worsdell's formation, Gordon Head, found that no guns had been fitted to his turret. He reported the aircraft as unserviceable, and taxied back to the dispersal pen. This was a mile from the airfield, and it was some minutes before he got there. As he cut the engines, he saw someone racing across on a bicycle. It was Gibbs.

"What's the matter?"

Gibbs sat astride the bicycle, his feet planted firmly on the tarmac. He looked hot from the ride, and angry, and he was waiting for his answer. Head looked down at him from his side window. He had been in Malta for only four days. He was a sergeant-pilot, and Gibbs was God.

"I'm sorry, sir. The armourers forgot to fit the guns. I couldn't go."

"Couldn't go? What do you mean, couldn't go? You've got a fighter escort, haven't you? Why, I've taken off on ops on one engine!"

Head recognized this as a palpable exaggeration, but he could hardly join issue with his C.O. on a point like that. Besides, he knew well enough what Gibbs meant.

"I'm sorry, sir. If I'd known you wanted me to go, I'd have gone."

Gibbs ignored this. "Do you realize what this sort of thing means to the others? The stronger the force, the more chance you have of coming through. Every kite that gives up means less chance of a hit, more chance of the others getting shot down. Do you understand that?"

"Yes, sir."

Head had been brought up to treat the absence of guns in a turret as a perfectly good reason for putting an aircraft u/s. But he sensed that, in his predicament, Gibbs would have gone. No one had ever heard of Gibbs putting a kite u/s on a strike, and it couldn't have been all luck with his aircraft. Head was not slow in the uptake, and he was beginning to catch on. He hadn't quite adjusted himself to the tempo of life at Malta.

Gibbs was watching him, dissecting his reactions, sizing him up, judging his keenness, determination, valour. Malta was a hard school, and Gibbs had been ruthless in sending away crews who didn't measure up to his exacting standards, branding them as lacking in moral fibre. On one occasion he overheard two officers questioning the value of the strikes and doubting the need for exposing the squadron to further heavy losses. He had them off the island within twenty-four hours. This sort of thing might sometimes be distasteful; but the fate of an army depended on these strikes. And the result of his methods was that in 39 Squadron he had built up a *corps d'élite*.

"Well, are you going?"

Head was completely taken aback at the question. The others had taken off fifteen minutes ago. He would never catch them now. He had accepted the tearing off of the strip, but he hadn't realized it was leading up to this.

If he went now, there was probably not much future for him, a lone aircraft, twenty minutes or more late in attacking an alerted target. And if he didn't go, perhaps not much future either.

Yet Gibbs wasn't giving him any orders. He was leaving it to him.

He would never forget the sight of Gibbs's outthrust chin, the appraising eyes. "Well, what stuff are you made of?" they said.

To a proud young man like Head there was only one answer. He restarted his engines, taxied out, and set off after the others.

Head got a course from his navigator which would take him to Corfu direct, cutting straight across the two legs taken by the formation. This way there was an outside chance that he might catch them up. He had to watch his petrol consumption, but he flew rather faster than economical cruising speed. He found he was making good time, and as the southern tip of the island of Corfu came in sight he felt that with luck he might just converge on the rest of the formation in time.

He saw an aircraft away to starboard, and looked quickly for others. But this one was alone, and it was chasing him. It was a Ju 88.

Head's calculations, however, were not far wrong. Suddenly the men in the formation, Beauforts and Beaufighters, had the tension of the last moments before a sighting broken for them by the spectacle of a lone Beaufort appearing apparently from nowhere, hotly pursued by an enemy fighter. Who could it possibly be? The men inside the protection of the Beaufighter escort pointed it out to each other with a fascinated horror and settled down to watch the fun.

Fortunately, one of the Beaufighter pilots had a proper sense of comradeship. Amidst intense excitement in the formation he peeled off, chased the Ju 88, caught up with it, and shot it down into the sea.

Head joined up now with the formation, just in time to see the wake of the tanker spreading out ahead, far down the Greek coast, perhaps ten miles away.

At five miles' range, McGarry, Allsopp's navigator, fired a yellow-yellow cartridge as the signal for the Beaufighters to pull up and press on ahead to silence the escort. At the strike leader's signal a Ju 88, flying over the convoy and carrying depth charges in case of submarine attack, fired a signal of its own to warn the convoy, jettisoned its depth charges to be ready for the affray, and was promptly shot down by the destroyer escort.

The Beaufighters went ahead and bombed the tanker, and then carried on and strafed the decks of the two destroyers. One Beaufighter was shot down. To the Beaufort crews it seemed that the bombs had overshot. The torpedo attack was carried out as planned, the Beauforts overtaking the tanker on either side before turning in to make their attack on the bow. Allsopp came up with the tanker on the starboard side, the second sub-flight on the port, and the last three Beauforts, led by Moose Marshall, watched for the tanker's evasive action and eventually made their attack on the starboard beam. This formation encountered the worst of the flak, and Dewhurst, an old 42 Squadron man who had followed Dinsdale in the attack on the *Scharnhorst* and *Gneisenau* and again against the *Prinz Eugen*, and who was on his first strike from Malta, was shot down.

An explosion was seen on the starboard side of the tanker, but the attack was made at twilight, and it was impossible to be sure whether the tanker had in fact sustained a hit. The explosion might have been the crashing Beaufort. No smoke or fire was seen, and no claims were made.

Darkness was falling as the strike aircraft left the convoy, and the crews flew back to Malta independently. Head knew that his petrol consumption had been high, and he kept his engines throttled right back to 1500 revs a minute on the return journey. It was just as well he did. His navigator missed Malta, and they ploughed on towards Tunisia, unaware that they had overshot base. But eventually they recognized Pantellaria, got their pinpoint, and turned southeast for Malta. The low reading of the petrol gauges gave them no chance at all of making it. The wireless operator sent an S O S but Head coaxed the Beaufort along the whole way back, and they landed at Luqa with their tanks dry.

Head didn't have to prove himself to Gibbs again, and he settled down to being one of the squadron's most cheerful and reliable men. But there were many hazards at Malta, and the fine, strong, enviable body of Gordon Head fell a victim to one of them. The crews were living and fighting on a diet that was very little above starvation level. Men who were wounded on operations had to be sent home, since their wounds would not heal on the diet available to them at Malta. The most minor skin ailments took weeks to cure, or remained to torment the sufferer. Men avoided going sick if they could: Gibbs had no time for hypochondriacs. But in December 1942, when the worst of the island's troubles were over, reaction set in in the form of an outbreak of polio. Many people died, and Head was desperately ill for many weeks. The kind of courage he had shown with 39 Squadron came to his aid, and he fought his way through a terrible illness and survived. But it left him completely disabled for life.

Although the tanker *Dielpi* had survived the Beaufort attack of 24th August, it suffered minor damage and was delayed in Greece, so that Rommel, who had planned to begin his final push about 26th August, found himself on that date still awaiting the promised deliveries of petrol. So far, not a drop had been received. He therefore arranged a special meeting between himself, Kesselring and Cavallero, the Italian Comando Supremo. The conference took place on 27th August, and Rommel extracted a promise from Cavallero that 5000 tons of petrol would be despatched to arrive in Benghazi within seven days. Two tankers, said Cavallero, were already on the way. One, the 5400-ton *Istria*, had slipped away from an Italian port unobserved, followed a tortuous route along the Greek coast and inside the Greek islands to avoid attacks from Malta, and was about to begin the last lap across the open sea to Benghazi. The other, the *Dielpi*, had suffered superficial damage in the torpedo attack, but was now safely hidden among the Greek islands, waiting a chance to cross the central Mediterranean. Rommel therefore postponed his planned offensive for a further two to three days.

Reconnaissance of southern Greece was not only carried out from Malta; aircraft from Egypt, too, combed the area thoroughly, particularly south of Sapienza, off Cape Matapan and Crete, which was outside the range of Malta's strike and reconnaissance aircraft. The Wellington torpedo squadron, No. 38, was now stationed in Egypt, specially to attack shipping found between this area and North African ports, shipping which had somehow escaped the depredations of 39 Squadron. Since the attack on the Italian battle fleet, the squadron had had little success; and in any case only a few of the crews were torpedo trained, and much of the squadron's time was taken up in training schedules. But the squadron became fully operational in time to play its part in the vital ten-day period before the battle of Alam el Halfa.

Early on the morning of 27th August, a reconnaissance aircraft from Egypt spotted the *Dielpi* south-east of Cape

Matapan, amongst the islands off north-west Crete. It was assumed that the convoy was about to make a break for it across to Benghazi, and a Baltimore took off from Malta to search up the convoy's probable track. The pilot found the convoy at midday some hundred miles north of Derna, and flew back to Malta with his report. Nine Beauforts, led by Ken Grant, took off at four o'clock that afternoon, accompanied by nine Beaufighters, five of which carried bombs, four Beaufighters for flak suppression being considered enough against a single destroyer escort.

Once again the Beauforts attacked at sunset, but their arrival was no surprise to the Italians, who had been dreading interception all day. Many of the tanker's crew were standing about on deck, watching the sky anxiously, praying for night to fall. Another few minutes and they would be safe at least from the Beauforts. Only the Wellingtons and the Swordfish were known to attack at night. But then, low out of the sea from the direction of the hated island of Malta, the Beauforts and the Beaufighters swept towards them. They saw the Beaufighters climb to 2000 feet some three miles away, and then begin a long shallow dive towards them. The tanker crew took what shelter they could, but refused to leave the deck. The scream of bombs reached a crescendo, the decks were raked by cannon and machine-gun fire, the water round them rose in great gouts from the near misses of the bombs, and one bomb hit the tanker fair and square in the stern.

The Beaufighters passed over the tanker and continued firing into the decks of the destroyer. The crew of the tanker turned and watched them go. But looking again to the north-west, they saw the Beauforts on their starboard beam, racing across the water at sixty feet, pointing those long, glistening fingers of destruction straight at them. The morale of the Italians was broken. The Beaufort crews could see them diving off the sides of the tanker even before the torpedoes were dropped.

Grant and Worsdell scored direct hits on the tanker, and one other torpedo hit was claimed. As the Beaufort crews looked back at their handiwork, there was a violent explosion on the *Dielpi*, and when the smoke cleared they could see the clear outline of the tanker ablaze and sinking, its decks awash and its back broken.

Three Ju 88s attempted to attack the Beauforts as they broke away, but were driven off by the Beaufighters, and not a single aircraft was lost. The science of torpedo-dropping had come a long way from the lone Rover attacks of 1940-41, and from the early attacks in the Mediterranean by single vics of three Beauforts. Against this modest convoy of one tanker and one destroyer, eighteen aircraft had been employed, resulting in the complete destruction of the target without loss to the attacking force. There was never anything easy about torpedo work, especially when targets were provided with powerful escorts, and to the end of the war it remained as dangerous and highly skilled a job as any. But once the fundamentals of the art were understood, and applied by men of the calibre of Pat Gibbs, the torpedo-bombers at last came into their own.

The second convoy already *en route* for Benghazi, the 5400-ton *Istria* with destroyer escort, waited for darkness before it attempted to cross the Mediterranean, thus cheating the Beauforts. But a radar Wellington went out to search for it, and twelve torpedo Wellingtons followed, listening out for a sighting report. The A.S.V. aircraft found the *Istria* after five hours' searching, and several of the torpedo aircraft picked up the sighting report. Flying Officer Foulis, one of the original pilots to attack the Italian Fleet the previous June, was first on the scene. He attacked the *Istria* into the moon path, releasing both his torpedoes on one run, the first at 700 yards and the second from very close in. The second torpedo, the one dropped from close in, reached the target first, striking the *Istria* square amidships. The first torpedo had further to travel, but the drop had been beautifully accurate, and as the orange flash and the column of water that rose from the second torpedo began to suck back into the ship, the first torpedo struck the stern, with identical results.

Foulis circled the convoy, watching the smoke spread until it completely enveloped the stricken vessel. Some of the other Wellington crews, arriving on the scene ten minutes after the attack, watched the smoke slowly disperse until, when they flew directly over the spot, nothing remained but a few thin wisps of smoke through which the moon shone palely, and a large patch of oil on the water.

On 30th August, none of the ammunition and petrol promised by Cavallero had yet arrived in North Africa. This was Rommel's deadline. The full moon, indispensable to his planned offensive, was already on the wane. Facing him, the British were proceeding apace with the consolidation of their position, and would soon be building up their strength. Any further delay meant giving up all idea of ever resuming the offensive.

Rommel therefore made a last desperate appeal to the Italian Supreme Command for supplies, and above all for petrol. And in spite of the calamitous sinkings of the last ten days, totalling nearly 23,000 tons of merchant shipping, Cavallero felt himself able to promise that the necessary tankers would embark within a few hours, and that the first deliveries would begin at the very latest next day.

For the fulfilment of the first part of his promise, Cavallero pinned his faith on the safe delivery of the 5000-ton tanker *San Andrea*. This was the only ship which was ready to leave at once. There was only one destroyer available for escort, but somehow the tanker must be got through. This would enable Rommel to maintain his offensive. Several more ships, with powerful escorts, would be ready to follow up the *San Andrea* within a few days.

Trusting to the fulfilment of these and other promises, and above all in the certainty that if he did not act now, in this full moon, his last chance of mounting an offensive would be gone for ever, Rommel gave the order for the attack to open on the night of 30th–31st August.

He was thus committed to a major action on the strength of a blank cheque that might not be honoured; he was hanging himself on the expectation of plenty. If the *San Andrea* could be destroyed, Rommel's last desperate bid for supremacy in the Desert would be stillborn.

The day after the sinking of the *Dielpi*, Gibbs was told that he was to return to the U.K. early in September. Gibbs was at this time a man living entirely on his nerves. The standards he demanded from others were exceeded only by the standards he set for himself. He refused to admit weakness in himself, would not tolerate weakness in others. From the outbreak of war he had been fighting, first against the circumstances which tied him to a training job, then against the enemy, then against severe injuries, then the enemy again, emerging from his first tour of operations as one of the few of his time to survive. Then came the struggle to infect his seniors with his own dearly won faith in the potentialities of the aerial torpedo. Eventually, despairing of a hearing in the U.K., and foreseeing the part a small but highly trained force might play in the Mediterranean, he engineered a posting to the Middle East, to find once again that he was alone in his fanatical belief in the torpedo, and that in spite of the fact that he was the most experienced torpedo pilot living, he was too junior to demand a hearing. Then at last he had been given his chance, the opportunity to fulfil his destiny. In the fulfilment, glorious as it was, he had driven himself to the brink of human endurance, and perhaps beyond.

Gibbs believed that a commanding officer must lead; and in this he was subjected to no restraint at Malta, as Braithwaite had been in the U.K. Other leaders had to be trained, and Gibbs stood down from operations often enough to give the right experience to selected men; but he knew the value of a personal following, and he led the squadron into action as often as he could. By the end of his tour at Malta, men followed him blindly on his reputation, shutting their eyes to the truth that he was becoming a nervous wreck. But in action Gibbs remained supreme, the same man who had inspired the doubters in past months. The knowledge of his presence in the leading Beaufort gave those who followed an unreasoning sense of security. They knew that Gibbs had the priceless gift of thinking clearly through all adversity; they felt that somehow he would get them through.

Life at Malta was of a kind to fray tempers that were often naturally quick, to make taut nerves brittle, even when operations were few. Although the weight of air attack from Sicily lessened in August, there was still an average of two air raids a day. The Beauforts had to be housed in dispersal pens in daylight, but they were kept parked on the edge of the runway during the night, ready for an early take-off if a sighting report came through. In order to move the aircraft back to dispersal before daylight, the Beaufort crews on standby had to be on the airfield at least an hour before first light. Standby came round not less than once in two days. Shove-halfpenny games in the Mess during the early hours often developed into little less than brawls, reasonable men arguing bitterly over a fraction of an inch. Gibbs went through all this, and in addition he had the tremendous moral and spiritual burden of administration and leadership.

When, on the morning of 30th August, a reconnaissance aircraft spotted the *San Andrea* emerging from the Gulf of Taranto, Gibbs knew that this would be his last operation from Malta. It was the end, too, of the ten-day period to which Tedder had attached such vital importance.

In an attempt to cheat the Beauforts, the *San Andrea* was hugging the coastline, less than a mile from the shore, off Santa Maria di Leuca, in the extreme heel of Italy. There were sandbanks between the tanker and the coast—surely no torpedoes dropped from that side could possibly run. To starboard, directly in the path of a bows attack, was the destroyer. The tanker would be able to comb attacks from any other direction.

The convoy had an unusually strong air umbrella, including seven Macchi fighters, a Ju 88, and a Cant floatplane. The way the tanker was tucked in to the coast, the Beauforts would have difficulty in finding a good run in. They would be limited to an attack from astern on the starboard side, and here the Macchis would be waiting for them.

Gibbs studied the reconnaissance report, and eventually decided that no ship dare steer too far into the shallows for fear of running aground. In spite of the obvious difficulties, he would lead the Beauforts in from the landward side. They would drop closer than ever before, and some at least of the torpedoes would run. He took nine Beauforts, the other two sub-flights being led by Sharman and Worsdell, and nine Beaufighters, four with bombs. They took off at 11.45.

They flew north-north-east to the heel of Italy, skirted the stern of the convoy, climbed so as to clear the 300-foot coastal hills, and then turned and began their torpedo run from two miles inland, letting down gently all the way. The scorched, yellow surface of the Italian mainland rushed past beneath them. Ahead was the lip of the coastline, then a lace fringe of surf, then a narrow channel of green-blue water, and then, incredibly near the coast, the *San Andrea*. Seawards of the *San Andrea*, and about two lengths ahead, was the destroyer and beyond lay the broad sweep of the Mediterranean. As they crossed the coast they could see the hard rippled sand beneath the pellucid water. Two men in a rowing-boat, rowing frantically to get clear of the line of fire, saw that they were too late and jumped from their rowing-boat into the water.

The Beaufighters had gone on ahead, tearing into the Macchi fighters as they came in to attack the Beauforts, scattering them, and then bombing the tanker and raking the destroyer with cannon and machine-gun fire. One Beaufighter was shot down, but the sky began to clear of flak bursts. Even so, three of the Beauforts were hit as they settled down to drop.

Gibbs held on until he could make out every detail of the tanker. Flying at mast height, with the exhilarating sense of speed that accompanies low flying, he was staring point-blank into the tanker's hull.

He dropped at 500 yards' range. If the torpedo ran, he could not miss. The men in the second vic saw him drop, saw his aircraft flying straight at the tanker, saw it miss the tanker's mast by inches, saw it emerge safely on the far side. Now Gibbs carried out for the last time his favourite anti-flak manœuvre, pulling up steeply beyond the tanker and then dropping off the top of his climb straight down at the escorting destroyer, firing all the way. He pulled out as the deck of the destroyer began to fill his windscreen, inertia making his Beaufort stagger and squat low over the water before it climbed away.

Only Sharman of the second vic of three had dropped when the whole world in front of the other Beauforts erupted like a vast volcano, flames spurted out as if belched from the sea-bed, and a cottage-loaf of intense black billowing smoke rolled first upwards and then outwards, as though the weight of smoke above it forced it to seek a fresh outlet. Some of the men following Gibbs tried to turn away, but they could not avoid the spreading thunder-cloud ahead, and even as they pulled up to pass over the top, new jets of smoke enveloped them and pieces of debris fell from above them.

Beyond the tanker the Mediterranean remained intensely blue, peaceful and still, nothing in sight but the Cant float-plane, which flew ponderously on, ignoring the Beauforts, each of which shattered the illusion of peace on this side of the convoy by peppering the Cant with machine-gun fire. The Cant pilot took no evasive action, holding his unswerving course, even when one of his floats was shot clean off and fell away into the sea, bemused, perhaps, by the awful conflagration below.

It was one of those rare occasions when five or six crews had been able to follow the track of three torpedoes from the moment of launching right through their run in the water to the moment of impact. Clearly and unmistakably, Pat Gibbs and the leading vic had wrought the destruction of the *San Andrea*.

Rommel's absolute dependence upon the petrol carried by this ship made its destruction the plum of the whole Mediterranean campaign, the kind of crowning triumph which Gibbs's career so well deserved.

Without the promised petrol, Rommel was compelled on the morning of 1st September to give up any further attempt at a major action, and the following day he called off his attack and ordered the Panzer Army to retire. Contrary to his reconnaissance reports, the British positions in the south had been constructed in great strength; and they were stubbornly defended. The R.A.F. had complete command of the air. And, most important of all, he was still without petrol, the first essential to the fulfilment of his plans. The night before he finally called off the attack, the Panzer Army had only enough petrol to travel sixty miles over good going; and of the 5000 tons of petrol promised by Cavallero, none had arrived.

Gibbs was now awarded the D.S.O. and posted to the U.K. His navigator, John Creswell, was awarded the D.F.M., commissioned, and on commissioning awarded the D.F.C. Grant, Worsdell, Marshall, Watlington and Sanderson were awarded the D.F.C. for their work in the last ten days of August, and Tester, one of the gunners, was awarded the D.F.M.

The day before Gibbs left Malta, Hank Sharman led the squadron against a big and heavily defended convoy of four merchant vessels and no less than eleven destroyers off Greece. Cavallero had at last mustered a convoy of real consequence, but it was too late for the battle of Alam el Halfa. What might have been achieved, however, was shown by the damage suffered by the Beauforts. Sharman's aircraft was hit some miles from the convoy, and one engine caught fire. But as on a previous occasion, he held his course, determined to keep his formation together. As his Beaufort neared the convoy, it flickered into a streamer of fire and plunged into the sea. One other aircraft failed to return, and nearly every aircraft was badly shot up. Only one of the merchant vessels was seriously damaged.

Sharman was one of the last remaining links with the early days of 22 Squadron. He had flown as second-pilot/navigator with Dick Beauman on the first Beaufort torpedo attack of the war. His work at Malta had been marked by great leadership and courage, and he lost his life pressing home an attack when he might have saved himself by turning away. He died undecorated.

All Gibbs's tenets on torpedo work had been vindicated, and everywhere people were pronouncing them as their own. A great future lay before him in the U.K., where Joubert was now forming strike wings to bring a crushing weight to bear against the German North Sea shipping routes. But the last two years had exhausted the young idealist who had once seemed so inexhaustible, so unquenchable. Gibbs suffered a nervous collapse in England, from which recovery was a long and slow process, and complete recovery, perhaps, out of reach even of his unmatched spirit. He was invalided out of the Service in 1944.

The foundations he had laid, however, were sure. 39 Squadron was taken over by Larry Gaine, as different a man from Gibbs as could be imagined, but a man steeped in torpedo lore. He carried out his attacks just as he had at Abbotsinch, in copybook style, taking no evasive action, ignoring the flak,

231

to which he seemed oblivious. No one thought he could last. But he led the squadron to the end of its Beaufort days, and survived. His partnership with McGarry, his navigator, was as successful as that between Gibbs and Creswell which had preceded it.

In early October, 39 Squadron were withdrawn from Malta for a short rest, and while they were still in Egypt the battle of El Alamein began. Rommel now had his back to the wall.

Chapter 13

ROMMEL'S LAST TANKER

MONTGOMERY's strategy at El Alamein was to persuade Rommel that the main blow would fall in the south, and then to deliver it in the north. Rommel was undeceived, but he could not altogether ignore the threat to his southern flank. While he rightly guessed where the main attack would fall, he dare not leave the south unprotected.

Montgomery duly made his show of strength in the south and then developed his main attack at El Alamein. What Rommel would have liked to do was to assemble all his motorized units in the north in order to hurl the British back to their main defence line in a planned and concentrated counter-attack. But he did not have the petrol to do it. There wasn't even enough petrol to keep supply traffic going between Tripoli and the front for more than two or three days.

Under these circumstances a decision to move forces from the southern front would be hazardous in the extreme. The fuel situation would not have allowed Rommel to keep a mobile battle going for more than a day or two in any case; and he could never have switched his armour back to the south if Montgomery had attacked there.

Nevertheless, once Rommel felt that Montgomery was committed to a major attack at El Alamein, he decided to bring the whole of the 21st Panzer Division up north and about half the Army artillery, fully realizing that whatever happened it could not return. This was on 25th October. At the same time he signalled a warning to Hitler that the battle would be lost unless there was an immediate improvement in the supply position.

Meanwhile, it had at last dawned on Hitler and Mussolini that the Afrika Korps faced annihilation unless its mobile formations could be supplied at once with fuel. Additional shipping space, even submarines, warships and civilian aircraft, were pressed into service. But to Rommel's annoyance the ships, some of them heavily armed and escorted, were

233

being sent to Benghazi in order to keep them out of range of British torpedo-carrying aircraft. It would take days longer to bring the precious supplies up from Benghazi, and additional fuel would be expended in the process. Rommel therefore insisted that the 5000-ton tanker *Proserpina*, which was on its way with three and a half thousand tons of fuel, together with the *Tergestea*, a 6000-ton merchant vessel carrying food, vehicles and ammunition, and a small 900-ton freighter, should be sent straight into Tobruk. The *Proserpina* represented the most important delivery of fuel for many months.

By the afternoon of 26th October the *Proserpina*, in company with the two merchant ships, and with an escort of four destroyers, had successfully completed the crossing of the Mediterranean and was in sight of Tobruk. High-ranking German officers were assembled on the cliffs above Tobruk, waiting for the tanker to come in.

Rommel, conscious that the British were re-grouping before launching their big attack (Montgomery was not ready until the night of 1st November), anxiously awaited news of the safe arrival of the tanker. The British were being extraordinarily cautious and hesitant. It might still be possible to assemble his armour for a concentrated attack.

Altogether there were now three Beaufort squadrons in Egypt—39, temporarily withdrawn from Malta; 42, on their way to the Far East; and 47, a squadron that had been forming for some time, operational at last. 42 Squadron, however, had given up all their aircraft to 39 and 47; their crews were to operate for the moment jointly with 47 Squadron. In addition to the Beauforts, there were the night Wellingtons.

The composite Beaufort squadron, 42/47, was based at Shandur in the Canal Zone, with an advanced landing-ground at Gianaclis, five miles south-east of Alexandria. Everyone in Egypt knew that the big build-up was on and that an offensive designed to clear the Afrika Korps out of Egypt and Cyrenaica was imminent, and 42/47 had only about six weeks in which to work up to an operational state. They spent most of the time in planning and carrying out various modifications to their aircraft.

One of the problems of the Beaufort squadrons was that

Tobruk, well out of range of Malta, was only barely within range of squadrons based in Egypt, even from the advanced landing-grounds in the Alexandria area. So far, most of the enemy shipping had made for Benghazi, where nothing but the heavy bombers could reach it. But there was always the possibility that, if the need were great enough, the Germans might attempt to run their supply shipping straight into Tobruk. If that happened, 42/47 wanted to be ready for them.

In the U.K. the Beaufort, with its engines set for normal cruising, moved along comfortably at 140 to 150 knots; but in the Middle East, with the same power settings, they wallowed along in a tail-down attitude at 120 knots. This was partly due to the atmosphere and partly due to a number of modifications carried out in the U.K. to make them suitable for Middle East conditions.

The chief causes of additional drag were the sand-filters, which protruded above the wings because it had been found impossible to fit them inside the air intakes. At Shandur, tin fairings were improvised on a guinea-pig aircraft to stream-line these filters, and a noticeable improvement in speed resulted.

The second modification was a simple one. The standard ladder-type A.S.V. aerial was removed from the guinea-pig aircraft and a home-made aerial installed which consisted simply of an iron rod with two very small cross-pieces, anchored to the main spar and sticking straight out from the leading edge of the wing. There were doubts that anything as elementary and straight-forward would work efficiently; but it proved as good as its predecessor and added further to the speed of the aircraft.

The third modification was to remove the high cupola from the turret and substitute a tin fairing round the open edges of the forward part of the turret. It made things draughty for the gunner—but it reduced drag still further and added yet a few more knots to the economical cruising speed.

All this was done to the guinea-pig aircraft and a full series of trials carried out. But no one had asked for authority to do it, and none had been given. It was out of the question to modify the aircraft of an entire squadron without permission.

But to go through the usual channels might take weeks. And the decisive battle could not be far off. It was decided to produce the modified aircraft at the advanced landing-ground at Gianaclis, like a rabbit out of a hat, for inspection by the A.O.C. of the naval co-operation group, now Air Vice-Marshal Sir Hugh P. Lloyd.

Lloyd could not fail to be impressed—not only by the 10 to 15 knots that had been added to the cruising speed of his aircraft, increasing their range by 50 to 100 miles, but by the enterprise and ingenuity of his men. The squadron commander went back to Shandur with *carte blanche* to modify a striking force of eight aircraft.

The task was completed two days before El Alamein. The Middle East now had a Beaufort squadron capable of striking at Tobruk, not right at the limit of range, but with the utmost confidence.

Three days later, on 24th October, six crews left Shandur for the advanced landing-ground at Gianaclis. They were Wing Commander Sprague, the new commanding officer, an amiable, courageous man, but without much experience of torpedo work; 'Aunty' Gee, veteran of the attack on the *Scharnhorst*, *Gneisenau* and *Prinz Eugen* of the previous February; Ralph Manning, the quiet, unassuming Canadian, now commissioned, who had lost his way on the day of the escape of the battle-cruisers but had attacked the *Prinz Eugen* on 17th May; McKern, who had also attacked the *Prinz Eugen*; McLaren; and Davidson, another Canadian, anxious to get over his first operation. Next day, four aircraft were called for to locate and attack a small 800-ton freighter reported north of Tobruk. Sprague led the formation and took with him the three most experienced crews—Gee, Manning, and McKern. To keep them company they had four Bisleys (Blenheim Vs) armed with bombs and six Beaufighters for flak suppression and fighter protection.

Nearing Tobruk the formation passed close to a small single-funnelled vessel, apparently carrying troops, travelling eastwards. Some of the men on deck waved to them. Spark, Manning's navigator, took some photographs. Manning judged the vessel to be 100-150 feet long, probably an 'F'-boat. These were primarily tank-landing craft, but they were also used to carry M.T., troops and cargo. He'd had a look at one the day before in an Intelligence digest. Then the Tobruk flak began to get their range and the formation started a wide sweep to starboard through 360 degrees. Manning kept a close look-out for other aircraft and took violent evasive action to avoid the flak.

It seemed to Manning that they were exposing themselves to the flak and to the risk of fighter interception unnecessarily. The freighter must be further west. Then he saw Sprague turning away to port and heading out to sea, not in a westerly direction, but in the direction of home. Manning followed, disappointed to have come so far without seeing the target and dropping his torpedo, but relieved enough to get out of range of the flak from Tobruk. The formation returned to Gianaclis.

When Manning taxied to dispersal the ground crew gave him that knowing look which they reserved for a crew which they thought hadn't, perhaps, tried too hard. There was no subtlety about it, and nothing was more demoralizing to air-crew, not even a rocket from the C.O. The Wingco might give you the benefit of the doubt—but never the ground crew.

"Why didn't you drop your torp?"

Manning had hardly cut the engines before the question was fired at him.

"We didn't find the target."

The ground crew exchanged looks among themselves. "Funny. All the others dropped theirs."

Manning was flabbergasted. They'd sighted nothing except the launch, or 'F'-boat, or whatever it was. He hadn't seen anyone make an attack. Surely the others couldn't have dropped at the 'F'-boat.

When Manning got to the briefing room, Sprague and Gee were being de-briefed and were in the act of describing their attack on what they thought was the freighter to the A.O.C., who had rushed down to hear the first news of the success. Manning got hold of McKern, the Australian who had piloted the fourth Beaufort.

"Did you drop, Mac?"

"Yes. I saw the C.O. drop, so I dropped too."

"But it was only an 'F'-boat."

The Australian looked pained. "Hell's teeth, Ralph, it was a tiddler, I'll grant you that, but it wasn't as small as that."

By this time Sprague had seen Manning.

"What did you think of it, Manning?"

"I didn't drop, sir. I thought it was a launch."

Manning blurted out his answer without thinking, and he knew at once that it had been too blunt altogether. Sprague gave him a tortured look and turned away. The A.O.C. turned to stone. The others stood about untidily, feeling in the way. Manning thought of his only defence—the photographs his navigator had taken. But already Spark, hearing that the identity of the vessel was in question, had hurried off to develop and print the negatives. Manning went after him.

Three of the four Bisley pilots had brought their bombs back because they had seen nothing worth dropping them at. But Sprague, Gee and McKern stuck to their story, though they did not claim any hits. Had Manning stayed, he would have heard them relate how the vessel had been of such shallow draught that the torpedoes, launched shorewards from out to sea, at right angles to the vessel as it steamed along parallel with the coast, had passed underneath the stern and finished up on the beach, where they had glinted wetly in the sunshine, like basking seals.

At eight o'clock that night one of the photographs was ready. It showed clearly that the vessel was small, had no superstructure, and was certainly not a freighter. Manning showed it to Gee and McKern, but he didn't show it to any-one else. He wasn't exactly the C.O.'s favourite Canadian as it was. There were times when it could be so wrong to be right.

In its first action the squadron had failed—and somehow put itself out of temper into the bargain. And during that afternoon, while they had been attacking the disputed freighter, news of a far bigger strike had been on its way. A reconnaissance Baltimore from Malta had spotted two merchant vessels and a tanker, north-east of Benghazi, apparently making for Tobruk. The tanker was the *Proserpina*.

As yet this convoy, vital to Rommel's hopes of holding his ground, was out of range of the Beauforts. It would not come within range until it was almost in sight of Tobruk. But the

Wellingtons could attack it at once. Three torpedo and four bomber Wellingtons attacked it singly during the night, but no definite results were seen. On the morning of the 26th, a Baltimore and a Maryland went out on early reconnaissance, and the Baltimore re-located the convoy, with two Ju 88s as escort, nine miles north-west of Derna. The ships had come through the night attacks unscathed and were making good progress.

Although the convoy was now within range of single-engine fighter protection from the shore, the Baltimore kept it under observation. Soon it would come within range of the day striking force.

During the morning, two more Beauforts arrived at Gianaclis from Shandur—the last two to be modified under the mandate given by Lloyd. The pilot of one of these aircraft was the veteran Hearn-Phillips, now a member of 42 Squadron, about to undertake the first operation of his second tour. His wireless operator was 'Ginger' Coulson, Gibbs's original gunner, a survivor of the crash at North Coates in 1941 that had put Gibbs out of action for five months. The other pilot was Garriock, of 47 Squadron, about to fly on his first operation.

All available aircraft of 201 Group were to be employed on the strike, with the exception of 39 Squadron, who were to attack independently later, and the Wellingtons, who were to wait for dusk before making a further attempt. When briefing began at Gianaclis later that morning, the men being briefed consisted of the eight Beaufort crews of 42/47, six Bisley crews of No. 15 Squadron of the South African Air Force, led by their C.O., Major D. W. Pidsley, and six Beaufighter crews; twenty aircraft in all.

Sprague, like Braithwaite before him, was big enough to realize that there might be men in the squadron with more recent experience, or in better practice, than him. He had learned a lot the previous day—enough to realize that leading a strike of this nature called for a background in torpedo work that he did not possess. He therefore appointed 'Aunty' Gee to lead the strike, and went along himself as just another member of the 42/47 formation. It was a courageous decision and altogether typical of the man.

The group captain who handled the briefing made sure that the crews had a clear picture of what they were trying to do. "The Germans have decided to run the gauntlet of our strike forces and try to get a good-sized and vitally important convoy into Tobruk," he told them. "It consists of a 6000-ton merchant vessel, a small 900-ton freighter, and a 6000-ton tanker loaded with petrol. This tanker is the primary target. Rommel is desperately short of fuel for his tanks, the Eighth Army is attempting a break-through, and the battle is approaching a critical stage. Rommel must get this tanker through to stand a chance. In making the attempt he's presented us with an opportunity of playing a decisive part in the Desert battle that's now being waged. We've got to get this tanker at all costs.

"Here's the plan of attack. The South African Bisleys will go in first, thirty seconds ahead of the Beauforts, and create a diversion by attacking the small freighter. The Beauforts will go for the tanker. Top cover will be provided by the Beaufighters. The Bisleys will formate on the Beauforts, three on either side.

"At the moment the convoy is in a position some twenty miles north-west of Tobruk. There's an escort of three destroyers and two Ju 88s, and by the time you get there the convoy will be well within cover of shore-based flak and fighters.

"When you've sunk the tanker you can have a go at the larger merchant vessel, rather than bring any torpedoes back. But the tanker's the primary target. Good luck."

The aircraft took off at 12.30, formed up over Gianaclis, and set course. One of the Bisleys was left behind through refuelling difficulties. The crews had been half-roasted sitting in the metal aircraft on the ground, but now the draught from the slipstream struck deliciously cool on their sweaty backs. It was a beautiful, clear day and there wasn't a cloud to be seen. Flying was the only escape from the heat on a day like this.

They flew out to sea, as they had done the day before, and turned west, right down on the deck, flying parallel to the coast about thirty miles out. After nearly two hours Gee turned in to make a landfall short of Tobruk, so as to be quite sure of their position, and the formation followed. A few minutes later they saw the coastline. They turned west again about five miles out to sea, keeping the coastline comfortably in sight. They would pinpoint themselves off Tobruk and then make for the convoy.

Almost at once they saw ahead of them a cluster of about twelve vessels, well in to the shore. Gee turned towards them and again the formation followed. The vessels seemed to be nothing more than power-driven barges, but they put up plenty of light flak. Gee swung the formation out to sea again and then back on course. Soon away on the port side they recognized the sandy crevice of Tobruk harbour. There was no shipping in sight.

Gee looked up and noted the Beaufighters, some at 500 feet and the others at about 2000. Hearn-Phillips was on his right, Manning on his left. The rest of the Beauforts were spread out in a loose but tidy line. They must come across the convoy soon.

At fifty feet visibility was limited, but Gee thought he could see something on the water ahead and slightly to port. It might just be spots on the windscreen. But the Beaufighters above him were waggling their wings. Half a minute passed, and they could see the ships clearly now. Somewhere amongst them must be the ship they had come to attack. For a time the outlines were blurred, and then they came into focus with a sudden clarity. First was the small freighter, then a destroyer, then the larger merchant vessel, then two more destroyers, steaming obliquely across the bows of the formation. There was no sign of the tanker.

Gee called Francis, his navigator. "Where's the tanker?"

"I can't see it."

"What about the smaller vessel out in front? Could that be the tanker?"

"It might be."

"It's the nearest thing to a tanker there, anyway. I'm going in."

Gee swung the formation to port and began his attack on the leading vessel. The three Bisleys on the port side of the formation, led by Lieutenant Lithgow, opened up to get ahead of the Beauforts and drop their bombs. They, too, aimed for the leading vessel. Sprague, Davidson, Garriock, McKern and McLaren followed Gee. Manning and Hearn-Phillips, and the two Bisley pilots on the starboard side, hesitated.

Manning, quiet and unassuming as he was, was very much a young man with a mind of his own. The incident of the day before had made him more than ever prepared to trust his own judgment. He was convinced that there was no tanker there.

"Looks like Aunty Gee's going in after one of those," called Manning. "I can't see the tanker there. What do you think, blokes?"

Spark and Bladen, the wireless operator, had a look.

"We're not sure. It doesn't look like a tanker, but it might be. That one out in front. I wouldn't like to swear to it."

"I reckon the tanker must be further down the coast," said Manning. "What do you say we take a look?"

The rest of the crew considered the proposition. It meant leaving the comparative security of the formation and forging ahead on their own, without fighter protection. Already they had seen an Italian seaplane. The 109s and Macchis would soon be whistled up. The last thing they wanted to do was to stick their necks out. But you didn't let on about things like that.

"It's up to you, Ralph. You're the skipper. Do what you want. Press on, if you like."

Manning pulled up over the formation and continued on ahead. Either the tanker was along here somewhere or it had already made the harbour. If they couldn't find it, they would have the unattractive task of making a lone attack on the ships they were about to pass.

"We're on our own, chaps. Keep your eyes open."

The shore batteries had opened up and the destroyers were putting down a curtain of fire. But Manning was not alone. The two Bisleys on the right of the formation had now drawn level with him, their crews having made the same deductions. Manning had never seen a more comforting sight. And half a mile behind, unknown to Manning, the shrewd H-P had made up his mind to follow up behind Manning and keep a look out for the tanker.

Meanwhile Gee, Sprague, Davidson, McKern and Garriock were running in on the smaller merchant vessel—the 900-ton freighter. H-P watched them go in. First the three Blenheims made their bombing run. All three seemed to squat right down on the deck of the freighter to drop their bombs. But the flak was fierce, and the second Bisley, piloted by Lieutenant Groch, was hit as it dropped its bombs. One shell exploded in the nose, killing the navigator outright, and half stunning Groch. Another shell burst in the port engine. Groch pulled the Bisley up over the freighter but the port wing dropped and struck the mast. Groch struggled to regain control, but the Bisley crashed into the sea beyond the freighter. Groch's gunner pulled him from the wreck, inflated the dinghy, and dragged him into it. Groch lost consciousness but recovered soon afterwards. All that remained of his Bisley was the tailplane, broken off from the fuselage and burning on the water.

Then the Beauforts went in. H-P could see that their torpedoes were right on the mark. So was the flak. He saw Sprague's aircraft stagger as half its rudder was shot away, but the pilot somehow recovered control and pulled up safely. Davidson, the Canadian, on his first operation, was not so lucky. Immediately after dropping his torpedo he pulled up shakily, flicked over on his back and crashed in a pall of smoke.

To H-P it was all too horribly familiar. Fine things to be seeing on the first trip of his second tour.

Meanwhile, Manning and the two Bisley pilots, Pidsley and Dustow, had seen a plume of smoke ahead of them, which soon resolved itself into the missing tanker and the fourth destroyer. The tanker, too, was slightly to port. No doubt the Germans had let the faster merchant vessels go on ahead, hoping that they would absorb whatever effort was directed against the convoy, leaving the tanker unmolested. Manning waited until he was abreast of the tanker and then turned in to attack. The tanker immediately turned towards him. Manning could see that he would be dropping from an impossible angle, and he resolved to hold off and fly right round the tanker, keeping it guessing as to the direction of attack for as long as possible, and then make his attack from shorewards out to sea. The flak from the escorting destroyer was thick and accurate, and he noticed the two Bisleys turn off to shoot it up.

While Manning was skirting the tanker in his 180-degree turn, H-P had come safely through the first convoy and had sighted the tanker. He knew that 'Ginger' Coulson, his wireless operator, was keen to take a few pictures, and as there were no fighters about he called him forward. A few moments later, as they flew past the destroyer escorting the tanker, a huge piece of flak burst through the fuselage on the port side by the wireless seat and passed out on the starboard side through the electrical panel. If Coulson had stayed in his seat he would have been decapitated.

"You've dropped your torp!" called the gunner.

H-P did a steep turn to follow Manning round the tanker, but he knew what had happened. The flak had broken all the electrical circuits and the torpedo had released itself. All he could do now was sit back and watch Manning.

Manning, in fact, had a large and apprehensive audience. The men who had dropped against the merchant vessels had seen the tanker after pulling out, had realized that Manning and H-P and the two Bisleys were after it, and had come along to lend what support they could. The Beaufighters were there too. They made straight for the destroyer, shooting it up with their cannon, diverting attention from Manning as he manoeuvred to attack the tanker.

When Manning had completed his turn and was about to make his approach from the coast, he saw that the tanker had attempted to reverse its turn but that in doing so it had lost way and was almost dead in the water. It was an easy target. The guns of the destroyer were mostly silenced but the shore batteries had their range now and great black puffs of smoke hung in the air around them with a deceptive gentleness. Spark could hear the crumps of the explosions above the noise of the engines. Manning held his course, maintaining a smooth, undulating evasive action until the tanker was only half a mile distant. Now he held the Beaufort steady, ran in to what he judged was about 600 yards, and launched his torpedo. As he did so he was thrilled to see the two Bisleys streak across in front of him on their bombing run. Again they seemed to squat on the ship to drop their bombs, bomb doors open, in some monstrous bowel evacuation, pulling up over the tanker at the last minute. As they dropped, Spark clicked his camera. Dustow, in the first Bisley, pulled up a fraction too late, and one wing struck the mast of the tanker. The aircraft staggered on giddily for a second or two, and then dived into the sea. This time there were no survivors. The second Bisley pulled out just in time. Both aircraft had dropped sticks of 250-pound bombs with delays of a few seconds. Out of the corner of his eye Manning could see two other Beauforts converging on the tanker, evidently making dummy runs to create a further diversion. The sky was a confusion of British aircraft, the crews waiting breathlessly for the result of the torpedo run. A Beaufighter came from nowhere and opened up at the destroyer, and the bridge disappeared in a cloud of smoke. So much was happening that Manning almost forgot that crossing the tanker was a dangerous business. He pulled up sharply but still got a nasty jolt from the delayed-action bombs as they exploded. In addition to the concussion, the aircraft was struck by a piece of wreckage from the tanker which flew up and made a dent in the starboard wing, inboard of the engine, leaving the nacelle daubed with sticky red paint.

Nothing more could be done now to the tanker. The success of the whole strike depended on Manning's torpedo. The remaining aircraft circled hungrily, like birds of prey, waiting for the animal to die. On the cliffs above Tobruk, German staff officers watched anxiously for signs that the tanker had escaped.

H-P had the best view of the run of Manning's torpedo. He saw that it was dropped accurately. But he saw, too, that the tanker was not dead yet. Although scarcely under way, it was turning towards the track of the torpedo in an endeavour to 'comb' it.

Gee, the formation leader, was circling above the tanker. Suddenly Francis, his navigator, pointed to the track of the torpedo. The way the tanker was manœuvring, the torpedo would strike it at an angle on the port bow.

Gee and Francis stared down hypnotized as they saw the torpedo strike the tanker a glancing blow and fail to explode. The torpedo ran harmlessly along the side of the hull. But as it reached the stern, there was a tremendous explosion below the water against the underside of the tanker, which disappeared in a column of water and smoke.

"Take a picture! Take a picture!" shouted H-P. Coulson was dazed at the sight of the explosion and almost forgot what he was trying to do, but he clicked the camera just in time.

Manning had crossed over the tanker twenty seconds earlier and he didn't see the explosion. He was still seeing in his mind the convulsed pool beyond the tanker where the Bisley had gone in. When he finally looked back at the tanker it was enveloped in smoke. But already he knew of the hit from the shouting, yelling, cheering and *clapping* that came from his gunners. All the men who had watched the attack were jubilant. It was a long time later before they thought of the men who must have been on board. And anyway they had their own losses to think of, as well as their own skins. They were still off Tobruk, a long way from home; and now the fighters were coming.

They were Macchi 202s. They came in repeatedly in long shallow dives, firing as they reached about 800 yards' range, and then pulling up and throttling back before they came within range of the Beauforts' tail guns. When they had dropped back to 1500 yards, in they came again in another long shallow dive. Bullets spattered the sea all round the Beauforts.

They had been briefed to form up after the attack fifteen miles north of Tobruk. Now they hurried to the rendezvous, chased by the Macchis. H-P's gunner gave him evasive action, and was surprised at the calmness with which it was received. The Macchi attacking H-P's aircraft, finding no answering fire, pressed his attack closer. The gunner's instructions for evasive action became more urgent. H-P retained his aplomb. He had forgotten that the tail guns were fired electrically and that this circuit, like all the others, had been cut when the electrical panel was hit. But the Macchi pilot still respected those two Brownings sticking out from the turret. The Beaufort gunner might be holding his fire; the Macchi pilot did not come in for the kill. When H-P got back, with characteristic thoroughness he had his aircraft modified so that the guns would fire manually in the event of electrical failure. No pilot could command the odds against him, but some of them, H-P among them, certainly deserved to survive.

As the aircraft were making their way out to sea, the gunners counted 25 Messerschmidts racing from the north-west across the surface of the sea like flying fish. But the Beauforts and the Bisleys were even lower. They stayed right down on the deck and escaped being seen. They formed up safely about ten miles north-east of Tobruk and set course for home. Now the Beaufighters went on ahead, their task of protection done.

Surviving the attack were seven of the eight Beauforts and three of the five Bisleys. But now a tragic accident added two more to their losses. H-P had just tried to call the leader on the R/T to ask how much petrol they had for the return trip, as his own gauges had all collapsed when the electrical panel was hit; he had found that his R/T, too, was out of action. Then he saw two of the Bisleys weaving dangerously. One of them passed directly underneath him, not more than thirty feet below. Either the pilot's vision was obscured or there was something wrong with his aircraft.

The Bisley seemed to steady for a moment, but it was still floating across the line of flight of the formation. The Beauforts were not flying in tight formation, but Garriock, on H-P's right, was perhaps 200 feet distant, and the Bisley was crabbing across towards him, still some thirty feet below, close enough to Garriock now to be dangerous. If Garriock hadn't seen the Bisley already, he probably wouldn't see it as it drifted beneath him.

H-P could see that if the Bisley pulled up a few feet as it crossed under the Beaufort the two aircraft would collide. He was the only man with a clear view of the Bisley, the only one in the whole formation to have seen the strange course it was taking. It would have been a simple matter to call Garriock on the R/T. But of all the aircraft in the formation his was the only one whose R/T was not working.

He was thus the mute witness of a ghastly accident that he was powerless to prevent. The Bisley pulled up right under-neath the Beaufort. Immediately after the collision, one of the men in the Beaufort was catapulted through the perspex nose straight ahead until he splashed into the sea. The two aircraft flew on, locked together but still getting the necessary lift to keep airborne, for fully fifteen seconds. Then they dipped suddenly and crashed together into the Mediterranean.

It was a sad ending to one of the outstanding successes of the war. To the men who got back, the skyline of Alexandria looked poignantly beautiful, the white stucco glinting in the late afternoon sunshine, the evenly topped array of buildings on the seashore rising gracefully out of the blue Mediterranean. After the terrible destruction of the tanker, and the known loss of many good friends, it was a sight that could hardly be borne.

The 6ooo-ton merchant vessel was badly hit in a dusk attack by three Wellingtons, and when six more Wellingtons went out at midnight, the vessel had disappeared and was presumed to have sunk. Further along the coast was the tanker, on fire from stem to stern, still burning fiercely, its hull red hot. Not one of the three ships had escaped.

On the morning of 2nd November Gee, as the leader of the Beaufort strike, was awarded the D.F.C.; he left Egypt with other 42 Squadron crews for the Far East that afternoon. Pidsley, leader of the South African Bisleys, one of the two pilots to bomb the tanker, Yudelman, his navigator, and Lithgow, leader of the other Bisley formation, were also awarded the D.F.C. Manning, inexplicably, received no award at the time; but several months later, following a successful ditching in the Indian Ocean in which he gave great help and encouragement to his crew, he too was awarded the D.F.C. The citation mentioned his good work in the attack on the *Prinz Eugen* in May 1942, and in the attack on the tanker.

It had been a devastating blow for Rommel. The last chance of a substantial delivery of fuel and ammunition before Montgomery struck had gone.

Chapter 14

THE STRIKE WINGS IN THE U.K.

T HE *Proserpina* represented the last delivery of fuel which
could possibly have helped Rommel in the Battle of El
Alamein. It was not, of course, strictly his last tanker by any
means, and for many more months our aircraft continued to
sink and harry his shipping. Three days after the sinking of
the *Proserpina*, the Wellingtons sank its replacement, the
Louisiana, and on 2nd November the Beauforts, led by Larry
Gaine, sank yet another tanker outside Tobruk. This was the
strike on which Ken Grant was shot down. But Rommel was
now in full retreat before the victorious Eighth Army, and
it was only a question of time before he would be driven from
Africa for good.

On 8th November came the Allied landings in French
North Africa, and the Axis supply routes across the Mediter-
ranean gradually shrank until, on 13th May 1943, the two
Allied armies met in Tunisia, and the last German and
Italian soldier was either captured or driven from African
soil.

The Beaufort squadrons then converted to Beaufighters,
and carried on the offensive against enemy shipping, switch-
ing their attacks as the Mediterranean campaigns developed
to the supply routes round Sicily and Italy, Sardinia, Corsica,
the Adriatic and the Aegean. This period bred its own heroes
and aces, had its own peaks of heavy losses.

By far the outstanding torpedo pilot in the Mediterranean
in the year 1943 was Stan Muller-Rowland. Very young,
and of slight build, almost insignificant, he had qualities
which no one would have guessed to look at him. Like Gibbs,
he was obsessed with tactics; operational flying was his life.
No one of his time compared with him, and some who knew
both men put him on a par even with Gibbs. He had to be
ordered off operations by his A.O.C., and when he eventually
returned to the U.K. he had dropped eighteen torpedoes,

more than any other man alive except Gibbs, whose record he had deliberately set out to eclipse. When he was shot down into the Aegean by an enemy fighter during the operations against Cos and Leros, he escaped through Turkey, and, arriving back in the Middle East, applied at once for an air-to-air firing course, determined that his anti-shipping career should not be interrupted again. When he got back to the U.K., he joined one of the strike wings, and was shot down by flak in October 1944.

Stan Muller-Rowland was one of three brothers, all of whom were decorated and two of whom were killed during the war. The third brother was killed testing the D.H. 108 experimental tail-less aircraft in February 1950.

The anti-shipping war in the Mediterranean developed into a war of attrition, a protracted battle against sea communications. Europe could now withdraw into herself, and the sinking of one or two ships, or even half a dozen or a dozen, important though it might be, could never again have the same shattering impact on a land battle. The same was true in the U.K.; but here the war against communications could at least be brought right home to the Germans themselves.

With the transfer of the Beaufort squadrons overseas in the course of 1942, the anti-shipping offensive in the North Sea was taken up by the Hudson squadrons, outstanding among which was the Canadian squadron, No. 407, the one that had shared the airfield at North Coates with 86. 407 stayed at North Coates and continued to concentrate on shipping between the estuary of the Elbe and the Hook of Holland, as 22 Squadron had done before them. Their low-level bombing attacks brought some of the most successful anti-shipping results of the war—until the Germans applied the obvious remedy of providing four or five escort vessels for each merchant ship. The Hudson losses, already considerable, rose alarmingly. In a three-month period 407 Squadron lost twelve crews; nearly fifty Canadians missing or dead, half the squadron. The other Hudson squadrons, which included three Dutch squadrons, suffered losses at very nearly the same rate, losses which no force could bear for long. At such a rate, no crew could hope to get even half way through an operational tour.

The Hudsons were having the same experience as the Beauforts and Blenheims before them. The meagre resources of Coastal Command were already strained to the uttermost, and Joubert, the C.-in-C., was forced to make a comparable decision to that taken by Bomber Command when the Blenheims of No. 2 Group were called off the anti-shipping offensive in 1941. In July he ordered the Hudson crews to abandon low-level attacks and to bomb from a comparatively safe height. This greatly reduced the losses; but it reduced the sinkings even more sharply.

To help fill the gap left by the transfer overseas of the Beauforts, four Hampden squadrons were converted for use as torpedo-bombers. But these aircraft were too slow to be operated against the more strongly protected convoys, and they were employed mostly against enemy shipping off Norway, on Rover operations similar to those formerly undertaken on the same coastline by 42 Squadron. Their tactics were mostly hit-and-run raids under conditions of low cloud by one or two aircraft at a time, and they achieved a fair measure of success in this role.

The enemy's convoys were divided roughly into two types —traffic from the Baltic ports to Rotterdam and other Dutch ports, carrying Swedish iron-ore and other essential war supplies destined for the German heavy industries in the Ruhr; and supply shipping for the German garrison in Norway. The war against enemy communications was conducted against railways and marshalling yards by Bomber Command, and against shipping by Coastal Command. The value of the one depended to some extent on the success of the other. Joubert knew that with his existing resources he could not hope to close the German shipping routes, and he therefore pressed for a more modern type of torpedo aircraft. Experiments had shown that torpedoes could be launched successfully from the Beaufighter, an aircraft far superior in speed and manœuvrability to the Beaufort or Hampden, which were both regarded now as obsolescent.

Joubert wanted to form a number of wings of Beaufighters, two or three squadrons to a wing, some aircraft to operate as torpedo droppers and some to accompany them for flak suppression. Each wing, comprising an integrated force of torpedo and anti-flak aircraft trained and operated together as one unit, would achieve a drill and cohesion which had never before been possible, not even between the Beauforts and Beaufighters at Malta.

Joubert's proposals were eventually agreed to, and the first of the new 'strike wings' began to form at North Coates about the time of El Alamein.

The wing was formed specifically to deal with the enemy's convoys off the Dutch coast, which were always well covered by escort vessels and flak-ships and well within reach of fighter protection. The principle of the wing was to saturate flak defences by the concentration of a large number of aircraft carrying cannon and bombs, so as to give the torpedo aircraft the maximum chance of dropping their torpedoes successfully at close range without serious interference from flak. This was in line with the naval precept that the gun was the weapon for crippling, stopping or disabling ships, and the torpedo, fired at a range from which it could not miss, the weapon for sinking them. It was assumed that three anti-flak aircraft were needed to neutralize each escort vessel and that six torpedoes must be dropped to sink a single ship.

Fighter escorts were to accompany the Beaufighters whenever range allowed, to prevent interception by enemy single-seater fighters, which held the advantage in speed and manoeuvrability even over the Beaufighters. The task of the escort was to establish local air superiority over the convoy for the short time it took to carry out a strike.

The new wing carried out its first operation on 20th November 1942. It was a costly failure. The target was a large and heavily escorted convoy off the Frisian Islands, steering south-west towards Rotterdam, consisting of fifteen ships altogether. Two squadrons of Beaufighters were sent, No. 236 to deal with the flak and No. 254, known now as the 'Torbeaus', to follow them up and launch torpedoes at the merchant vessels. An escort of twelve Spitfires was provided. The Spitfires missed the rendezvous in bad weather, and some of the Beaufighters, too, lost the formation. The attack was pressed home with great determination and the largest merchant vessel was hit, but the convoy was protected by a fierce flak barrage and by a number of FW 190s, so that three of the Beaufighters were lost and four more badly damaged. It was plain that the new strike wing, like the Beauforts that had operated in these waters before them, was under-trained.

The strike showed that fast modern aircraft, saturation of defences, and gallantry, were not enough unless allied to experience, leadership and a flair for anti-shipping work. Joubert decided at once to withdraw the new wing from the line of battle for a long period of intense training, leaving the Hudsons and the Hampdens to carry on as best they could for the moment.

It was not until the following April that the wing was judged ready to resume operations; but when it took the offensive again the difference was at once apparent. In the first strike twenty-one Beaufighters attacked a large convoy off Texel, damaging three of the escort vessels and destroying the largest M.V., the main target vessel. All the Beaufighters returned safely, landing back at their base within the space of fifteen minutes.

The story was repeated many times in the course of the year, and once again our successes forced the Germans to provide stronger and stronger escorts. Meticulous planning and timing remained obligatory, and anti-flak support had to be stepped up.

In spite of the many successful sorties, the intrinsic dangers of this type of operation remained right to the end. Low flying in daylight into the teeth of the most violent opposition, to deliver precision attacks against selected targets where the defenders knew that if their fire failed to arrest the attacker they were personally doomed, called for a determination unequalled in air fighting, and inevitably took its toll of the most gallant crews. So, often, it was the best men who went.

The build-up of the strike wings to the strength envisaged by Slessor, the new Coastal Command C.-in-C., was frustrated to some extent by the demands of other types of operation and other theatres, so that the most destructive days of the strike wings were not reached until 1944. Meanwhile, the few anti-shipping squadrons in existence made life as unpleasant as possible for the enemy, so much so that the port of Rotterdam, which for three years had been the terminal for the iron-ore trade with Sweden, was virtually closed. The Germans were forced to unload those ships which managed to escape destruction at Emden, where the port facilities did not compare with those at Rotterdam. This was the first major strategic victory for the anti-shipping offensive.

In June 1943 a new weapon of unparalleled virulence for its size was introduced into the anti-shipping war. This was the rocket projectile. Previously, the firing of heavy-calibre guns from aircraft had been limited by the capacity of the structure of the aircraft to withstand the recoil; but this problem disappeared with the rocket projectile, because the recoil was taken up by the high velocity gases ejected by the rocket itself. These gases blew beneath the wing surfaces, where they did not affect the aircraft so long as no part of its structure lay in their path. During the firing of its 20-millimetre cannon the Beaufighter shuddered violently; but it flew steadily on its course during the firing of the R.P., which was released at a low velocity but gained speed after release through the recoil action of its gases.

The Beaufighters' 20-millimetre cannon, when pressed well home by three aircraft against an escort vessel, was devastating in its effect on gun crews, amongst whom it caused terrible casualties. But a well-aimed R.P. salvo could do more than kill the escort's gun crew and quell the flak; it could completely destroy the escort vessel. The tactical sequence therefore became the cannon attack on the escort, the R.P. attack, and finally the torpedo attack on the main target.

Various improvements had been made to the torpedo over the years, so that it could be dropped at a slightly increased speed and from a greater height; but its destructive power was little altered, and fundamentally it was the same weapon that Beauman and Francis had dropped in the first Beaufort torpedo attack of the war in September 1940. The torpedo had stood almost still while the bomb had multiplied its weight and destructive power many times over; yet, because of its power to strike below water, it remained the most lethal anti-shipping weapon.

For smaller ships not warranting the use of a torpedo, however, rocket projectiles, preceded by cannon attack, began to be used alone. The writing was on the wall for the aerial torpedo.

Along both the Dutch and Norwegian coasts there were many stretches of shallow water, and since enemy shipping usually sailed close inshore, and stretches of open deep water were few, torpedo attacks had always been to some extent restricted. This was especially true of the Norwegian coast north of Stavanger, where coastal shipping made its tortuous way through the Leads. The rocket projectile, however, was not baulked by these conditions. It was not affected by depth of water, or by a rough sea, which sometimes spoiled the run of a torpedo; and being launched in a dive, from a greater height, it gave the aircraft more freedom of manœuvre.

Before the end of 1944, many daring R.P. attacks had been carried out in the extremely confined spaces of the Norwegian fjords, where mountains on either side were precipitous and there was barely room for an aircraft to dive down at the target, pull out, and climb away. In the open sea, however, the torpedo still remained supreme, and the combined endeavours of all other aircraft of the strike wings were employed so that the Torbeaus could get a clear run and drop from close range at the main target. The elements of success then were exactly the same as they had been at Malta under Gibbs; good prior reconnaissance, careful briefing, inspired leadership, the saturation of defences, and a close range of drop.

The enemy's respect for the strike wings grew, so that even the employment of a whole wing, plus a large fighter escort, was insufficient to quieten the flak defences of some of the convoys. Under these circumstances, losses could quickly have become prohibitive again. But if there was one thing better than a strike wing, it was two strike wings. On 15th June 1944, nine days after D-Day, two wings were employed together, as a single strike force, for the first time.

Some days earlier, a report had filtered through from the Dutch underground that a large convoy was preparing to leave Rotterdam for the Baltic, consisting of two new vessels which had just been completed and would be on their maiden voyage, the 8000-ton merchant vessel *Amerskerke* and a 4000-ton naval auxiliary, escorted by no less than eighteen smaller vessels. The disruption and chaos wrought amongst German rail and road communications prior to D-Day had forced the Germans to rely more than ever on their sea routes, so that the destruction of these two new vessels, almost as soon as they were launched, would represent an important contribution to the breaking down of the enemy's power to resist and to the shortening of the war.

The advance information given by the Dutch resistance gave us the chance to plan a large-scale operation, the biggest of its kind so far. A new wing had been formed at Langham in Norfolk to deal with enemy shipping that might attempt to interfere with our invasion convoys, and it was decided to send two squadrons of this wing together with two of the North Coates wing, the whole to be escorted by ten Mustangs of Fighter Command.

Of the four squadrons, three were to dive on the convoy and smother the defences with cannon and rockets, and the fourth was to come in at low level and aim torpedoes at the two new ships.

The two squadrons of the Langham wing, 455 (Australian) and 489 [New Zealand), had done most of their earlier operations off the Norwegian coast, too far from base to allow escort by single-seater fighters. They operated in the same way as Gibbs and his formations had operated at Malta—the whole formation flew out low on the deck, and when the target was sighted, the anti-flak aircraft went on ahead, climbed to 2000 feet, and then dived down on the convoy. The North Coates wing, however, operating mostly off the Dutch coast, could generally rely on the luxury of a strong single-seater fighter escort, and they were not so worried about fighter interception. They therefore approached their targets at the height required for the actual attack—the anti-flak and R.P. aircraft at 2000 feet, the torpedo aircraft on the deck. The fusion of the two wings thus threatened a collision over tactics. Fortunately, thanks to the warning given by the Dutch, there was plenty of time to thrash out the squadrons' differences and arrive at a conclusion. The two North Coates squadrons, 236 (anti-flak and R.P.) and 254

(Torbeaus), flew down to Langham on 14th June, and the arguments began.

The strike was to be led by Tony Gadd, formerly a flight commander with Gibbs on 22 Squadron, now wing commander flying of the North Coates wing. The leadership was given to North Coates because of their greater experience of operating off the Dutch coast. Gadd was a tall, slim, rather typical R.A.F. figure, of fair complexion, equable temperament and supreme self-confidence. Uniform sat easily on him. He had been an instructor at Gosport, and had dropped over a thousand torpedoes in practice, besides completing his tour on 22 Squadron. He was not over imaginative, but was quick to grasp essentials and discard irrelevencies. Life for him was never complicated. He had the unshakable practicality of the man who is adept at making things with his hands.

Gadd was quite unmoved by the pressure put on him by the men of the Langham wing to revert to their tactical approach. There was no stubbornness about it; he was absolutely sure of his ground and did not for one moment consider giving an inch. Eventually the men of the Langham wing, aware that, since Gadd was to lead, the success of the strike must be resigned to his leadership, acquiesced.

When the reconnaissance report came through on the night of 14th-15th June, Gadd disposed his forces. Leading the convoy were six R-boats,[1] proceeding two by two. Behind them were four minesweepers. Then came the naval auxiliary, followed by the merchant vessel. Four more minesweepers were spread round the port side of the big ships (the seaward side) and two more were stationed to starboard. Bringing up the rear of the convoy were another minesweeper and an R-boat. The whole convoy was proceeding almost due east a few miles off the Frisian Islands opposite Emden, at a speed of ten knots. The draught of the main ships, however, had forced the convoy to take to deep open water. The torpedo could therefore be applied as the primary weapon.

Gadd decided to send cannon-firing aircraft against all the escort vessels, one squadron on his left to attack the leading vessels and a squadron on his right to take the close screen to

---

[1] R-boats were small general-purpose boats, used mostly for local patrol duties and occasionally for minesweeping.

seaward and in rear of the main targets. He himself, in the centre of the formation at 2000 feet, would carry eight rockets, with three other aircraft similarly armed. The rocket attack would be made on the big vessels in the centre of the convoy, sixteen rockets being fired at each.

The whole anti-flak formation would sweep into the breadth of the convoy in line abreast on the port side, synchronizing their attacks. At the moment of the dive down from 2000 feet, when cannon and rockets were tearing into the port beam along the whole length of the convoy, the torpedo aircraft would reach dropping position. Six of the torpedo aircraft were to attack the *Amerskerke* and four the naval auxiliary.

The anti-flak aircraft were not briefed to attack any particular ship, since the exact disposition of the convoy might change. But the two target vessels would be certain to be in the centre of the convoy, so that the squadrons on either side of the four R.P. aircraft would fall naturally on to the front and rear vessels respectively. Experience taught a pilot to choose his target on the run in. Diving down from 2000 feet to 300, at over 300 miles an hour, there was no time to change one's aim.

Gadd made the briefing as straight-forward as possible. He warned the crews that nearly every ship was flying a balloon, but he did not stress the many dangers inherent in an attack on so large a convoy. They were known and feared well enough.

Many of these dangers would be heightened by the employment of so large a striking force. There would be over fifty aircraft converging on the convoy at high speed, and the smallest error in timing or flying discipline could be disastrous. They ought to be able to silence the flak, yes; but the last few moments of that 300-mile-an-hour dive, and the pull out afterwards, were another matter. With so many aircraft concentrated in time and space, collision was an ever-present threat. Many crews had been lost in this way. The Beaufighter was extremely stable at high speed, but the controls were leaden, and pulling out from that powered dive could so easily be too late. There were the masts of the ship to miss, and then the balloon cables. And the rest of the formation was coming in right behind you, aiming their fire as best they

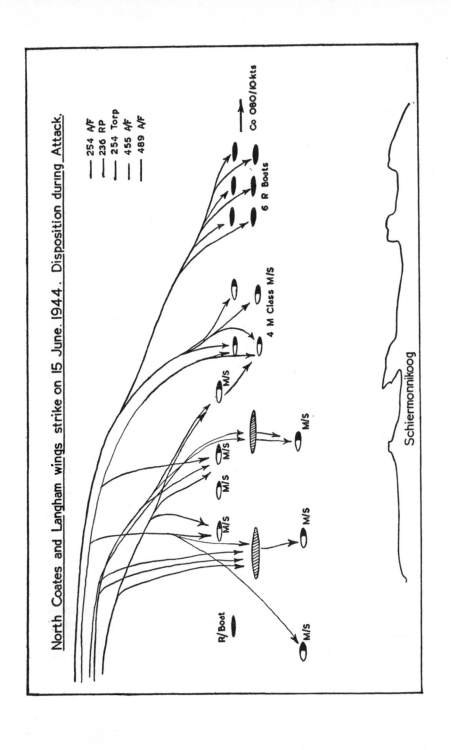

North Coates and Langham wings strike on 15 June. 1944. Disposition during Attack.

—— 254 A/F
—— 236 RP
—— 254 Torp
—— 455 A/F
—— 489 A/F

Co 080/10 kts

6 R Boats

4 M Class M/S

M/S

M/S   M/S

M/S

M/S

M/S

R/Boot

M/S

M/S

Schiermonnikoog

could, but not too discriminately. It was easy enough to get hit by the chap behind. Gadd himself had had a rocket clean through his port wing on his last operation, and right through the outer petrol tank at that, severing the aileron control and spreading petrol all over the wing. Miraculously it had not caught fire or broken up.

All these were occupational hazards, quite apart from the flak and the fighters. Every man's mind would dwell for a moment on each of them. There was no need to remind them.

The crews drove from the operations room out to their aircraft in darkness. An airfield was a chill, cheerless place at night, even in midsummer. This was the time when one took two or three deep breaths, to steady the nerves.

The crews climbed into their aircraft, allowing themselves the momentary luxury of wondering about their personal fate. Then the engines roared into life, their bridges were burned, and their nerves were gone.

The Beaufighters took off and formed up at first light, picked up their fighter escort a few minutes later over Coltishall, and set course at 05.00. They expected to intercept the convoy within forty-five minutes. The German ships, however, had made better progress than had been anticipated. The strike force made their landfall on the Dutch islands some way short of the progress of the convoy.

This was the first setback. The only feasible direction of attack was abeam of the convoy, to smother all the escort ships simultaneously. But they would now come up on the convoy from astern. They would have to execute a complicated manœuvre to get into position. No one had ever flown on a shipping strike before in such a large formation, and there was no telling what would happen.

There was another factor, too. So large a force patrolling off the Dutch islands would not go unobserved. They had proof of this a moment later when the shore batteries began to fire at them.

And the weather conditions had deteriorated. There was a lot of sea fog about, and at 2000 feet there was six-tenths' cloud, so that the anti-flak squadrons had only an intermittent view of the sea below them and a restricted view ahead. Gadd could not see the Torbeaus at all.

But difficulties of communication, which had been the downfall of 86 Squadron in the attack on the *Prinz Eugen* two years earlier, and which had often hampered 39 Squadron in the Mediterranean in 1942, had been solved by the fitting of V.H.F. wireless equipment in all strike aircraft. Gadd was able to talk to the whole formation, telling them what he planned to do.

At 05.50, off Schiermonnikoog, near Borkum, they had their first glimpse of the escort vessels astern of the convoy, only four miles ahead. Then they sighted the two major vessels, standing out from the minesweepers and R-boats like a brace of swans with their cygnets.

Now, thought Gadd, for that complicated manœuvre. But at least it was only in one dimension. How much more complicated it would have been if the anti-flak aircraft had not already been at the attacking height.

He called the formation. "I'm going to make an 'S' turn, to bring us up abeam of the convoy.

"First I shall turn to port, out to sea, come up level with the convoy, and then turn back to starboard, delivering the attack at an angle of ninety degrees as planned. Aircraft on the left of the formation will have to open up as they've got further to travel. Aircraft on the right will throttle back and give the others a chance to get into position.

"Turning to port now."

The whole formation swung away to port, kept on until it was almost abreast of the convoy, and then turned in towards land. The crews could never quite stifle the thought, in the still moment after the thrill of the sighting and before the clamour of the attack, that they might not come through.

The final turn in was made like an enfilade of guardsmen, the aircraft on the inside of the turn standing on their props, almost marking time, while the aircraft on the outside swept forward like a wave.

Included in the strike force were many aces of the strike wing period, with a leavening of the men of the Beauforts, now on their second tour. Colin Milson, the Australian who had distinguished himself at Malta with 39 Squadron, was in the anti-flak formation. Ewan Gillies, a contemporary of

Milson's on 39, one of the men to go to Malta with 86, was with the Torbeaus. Roy Cannell, a contemporary of Ray Loveitt's on 42 Squadron, was with 489 on the left. Tony Gadd was leading. The anti-shipping torch had been jealously passed on. And of the newer men, Wing Commander Paddy Burns led the Torbeaus, cursing the manœuvring of the aircraft above him over the intercom in his Irish brogue; and Squadron Leader Billy Tacon, a short, slight, wiry New Zealander, perhaps the greatest of all exponents of the rocket projectile, was No. 2 to Tony Gadd in the centre.

Most pilots, wisely enough, used their 20-millimetre cannon purely to silence the flak. But not Tacon. His faith in the rocket was reminiscent of Gibbs and the torpedo. He believed in it as a primary weapon, *the* primary weapon. And he used his cannon as a sighter for his rockets. What he did was to go into the dive, wait until he was at about 1000 yards' range, hold his sight on the target, press the tit of his cannon without allowing for bullet drop, watch the cannon shells tearing up the water short of the target, lift the nose gently until the trail of cannon fire crept along the water into the ship, and then fire his rockets. This way, he reckoned he could not miss. It meant accepting all the fire that the ship could hurl at him meanwhile, but he thought it was worth it. His percentage of hits fully supported his view.

The whole formation was now in position abeam of the convoy, going through those moments of fear and frustration when they were within range of the convoy's guns but still out of range with their own. For twenty seconds the flak rose at them, first an isolated burst, then a steady barrage, then a curtain of fire.

"Attack! Attack! Attack!"

Immediately on the signal, the thirty-two anti-flak Beaufighters, in line abreast, tore down from 2000 feet into the convoy, each pilot selecting his own target. Half way down in the dive, with the world beneath them tilted at a steep angle, the pilots began firing their cannon. And as each man fired, the whole aircraft juddered, the cockpit filled with acrid smoke which blew back from the barrels of the guns, and the pilot screwed up his eyes and squinted down through the flak at his target, still firing, immensely comforted by the thunderous racket of the ammunition feed behind him and the guns in front.

And then to pull out, just in time, swerving to miss the masts, swinging away to avoid the balloons, flying across the fire of the rest of the formation. None of them knew for certain, in the smell and the noise and the juddering, whether his aircraft had been hit.

On the left 489 attacked the leading R-boats and minesweepers with such devastating effect that the flak from the van of the convoy was silenced completely. 455 attacked the close screen of minesweepers and the R-boat astern. 236, in the centre, went for the major vessels. As the four R.P. aircraft fired their rockets, thirty-two bright arrows of flame raced on ahead of them, two by two, their quiet sibilance heard only by the men on the ships under attack. There were ten rocket hits on the naval auxiliary and eight on the merchant vessel. The flak, which had filled the sky as the Beaufighters began their dive, was silenced.

Paddy Burns, in the leading torpedo aircraft, had watched the Beaufighters manœuvring above him like a flock of migrating birds, and had held his own formation in check so as to time the torpedo run exactly. Now the Torbeaus of 254 Squadron launched their torpedoes. One of the pilots lost position and was squeezed out on the final run in, but the other nine dropped unopposed from a perfect position. Two hits were scored on the *Amerskerke* and two on the naval auxiliary.

As the R.P. formation crossed to the far side of the convoy they silenced the flak on that side with their cannon, so that the Torbeaus flew straight through without having a shot fired at them.

Five of the anti-flak Beaufighters had suffered superficial damage as they dived down through the barrage at the beginning of the attack. But in a complex strike employing an air fleet of forty-two Beaufighters against one of the biggest convoys ever attacked, not a single aircraft had been lost.

As they turned short of the islands, climbed to 1500 feet, and formed up for the return flight, the crews looked back through the mist and smoke and cloud at the stricken convoy. The 8000-ton *Amerskerke* and the 4000-ton naval auxiliary were both down by the stern, listing badly, and sinking. One of the minesweepers blew up as they came away, and five others were on fire.

Stretched out behind the ship-busters was an awful scene of carnage to contrast with the peaceful progress of twenty ships a few minutes earlier.

At long last the anti-shipping squadrons, Cinderellas of the air forces for so long, possessed the strength and equipment necessary to guarantee the concentration of fire-power which every strike pilot knew was the first essential to success against well-protected convoys in daylight. The most formidable defences were parried and then swept aside, stunned by a barrage of minor blows, leaving the way clear for the torpedo or rocket to deliver the knock-out punch.

The attack of 15th June was the pattern for many more combined strike wing attacks in the ensuing months. The offensive was maintained in the North Sea; and at the same time the rapid overrunning of western France by our armies increased the importance of operations in the Bay of Biscay.

Two new landmarks in the anti-shipping war were reached in August 1944. First, the Swedish Government announced that, due to the repeated hammering which their ships had taken, they would no longer insure them for trading with German or German-occupied ports. This was a body blow to Hitler's hopes of fighting on. And secondly, a strike of profound significance took place on the 24th of the month, when a German destroyer and a motor torpedo-boat were sunk in the Gironde estuary by rocket attack alone. Billy Tacon, who fired the rockets that sank the destroyer, was thus confirmed in his view that the rocket was potentially a primary weapon, and that the Torbeaus could now be dispensed with, except perhaps against capital ships.

By September all enemy shipping had been driven from the Dutch coast by day, and few targets could be found even at night. And on the Norwegian coast, shipping now skulked by day in landlocked fjords and in small defended anchorages. But even here the strike wings sought them out, flying boldly, if not fearlessly, into precipitous retreats where there was hardly room to turn, knowing that German fighters were now concentrated in Norway, facing as many as forty fighters on occasion. They had the protection of the Mustangs, and they still wrought havoc amongst enemy shipping; but casualties were often severe.

The climax did not come until the last week of the war. Then, as the defeated German forces fled for Norway and the northern Danish ports in every kind of craft, all the strike wings were thrown in against them.

Amongst the Germans, the lucky ones were those left behind. Terrible damage was inflicted on every type of ship, nearly all of them crowded with troops, in the final débâcle of the German armed forces.

EPILOGUE

In November 1944 the last of the big German capital ships, the *Tirpitz*, was bombed and sunk by No. 617 Squadron —the Dam-Busters. The wheel had come full circle, from bombing, through torpedo-bombing, back to bombing.

The bomb-load of aircraft, the weight and effectiveness of bombs and the accuracy of bomb-aiming devices had overtaken the simple advantage that the torpedo had in striking at the target below the water-line. A bomb had been developed capable of blasting the *Tirpitz* out of the water.

In his book, *The Dam-Busters*, Paul Brickhill relates how, on returning to a strange airfield near Lossiemouth following the *Tirpitz* raid, Wing Commander Tait, who led the squadron, was asked by the flying control officer if he had 'just got back from an exercise'. There is a link here with the torpedo-bomber men.

There was a Coastal Command strike wing airfield— Dallachy—only a few miles from Lossiemouth, and the airfield control officer there had known for some time that a squadron of Lancasters was undergoing operational training at Lossiemouth. News of navigation exercises carried out by 617 Squadron in the North Sea was continually coming through, but there were four squadrons of Beaufighters operating from Dallachy, and the controller had other things on his mind than the Bomber Command training programme.

One dismal, drizzly day in November, when all flying by the strike wing had been cancelled, the flying control officer was sitting in the control tower relaxing, battledress unfastened, reading a Peter Cheyney. During the afternoon he received a report that a Lancaster was in the circuit. It must be one of the Bomber Command boys looking for Lossiemouth. There was no point in trying to raise the pilot on the R/T, as the Lancasters were not calibrated to the Coastal Command speech wavelength. But it certainly seemed as though the Lanc was coming in. He called out the crash and fire tenders, and, keeping a weather eye open, went back to his Peter Cheyney.

The Lancaster emerged from the murk beyond the air-field boundary at 300 feet, landed safely, and taxied round to the control tower. A minute or so later the crew stepped down from their aircraft and walked across to the control office. They were wearing aircrew pullovers, coloured scarves, flying-jackets and flying-boots—the full-dress uniform of operational flight. No badges of rank were in evidence.

The flying control officer looked up from his Peter Cheyney. These Bomber Command boys were becoming a nuisance. He would have to fill in arrival forms and all the usual bumff, even though they would probably take off again in a few minutes and press on to Lossiemouth. He began to go through the usual questions.

"What happened? Lost your way?"

The strange loyalties of the Service put up a barrier between them. They belonged to different Commands.

"We saw the airfield and decided to come in."

"Pilot's name?"

"Tait."

Still the penny didn't drop. He spelt out the name.

"T-a-t-e?"

"T-a-i-t."

It didn't sound any different said like that from any other Tait.

"Rank?"

"Wing Commander."

The controller dropped his pencil and rocketed to his feet, fumbling with his battledress buttons embarrassedly. The pencil clattered to the floor.

"I'm sorry, sir."

"Perfectly all right."

"Been on an exercise, sir?"

The wing commander shook his head. "No." He seemed to consider a moment before he spoke again. "As a matter of fact we've just sunk the *Tirpitz*."

He was looking hard at the controller's battledress, but not at the buttons this time. Under the pilot's wings was sewn the purple-and-white striped medal ribbon of the D.F.M., awarded three and a half years earlier for putting a torpedo into the *Lutzow*.

267

INDEX

268